D0153776

reading science fiction

Also by the editors

James Gunn, THE ROAD TO SCIENCE FICTION, Volumes 1–4

James Gunn, THE SCIENCE OF SCIENCE FICTION WRITING

James Gunn and Matthew Candelaria, SPECULATIONS ON SPECULATION: Theories of Science Fiction

Marleen S. Barr, FEMINIST FABULATION: Space/Postmodern Fiction

Marleen S. Barr, ALIEN TO FEMININITY: Speculative Fiction and Feminist Theory

Marleen S. Barr, LOST IN SPACE: Probing Feminist Science Fiction and Beyond

reading science fiction

edited by
james gunn, marleen s. barr,
and
matthew candelaria

palgrave
macmillan

Introduction, selection and editorial matter © James Gunn, Marleen S. Barr and Matthew Candelaria 2009.

Individual chapters (in order) © Eric S. Rabkin; H. Bruce Franklin; Brian Stableford; Sherryl Vint and Mark Bould; George Zebrowski; Michael Cassutt; Brooks Landon; Orson Scott Card; Jane Donawerth; Carl Freedman; Matthew Candelaria; Roberto de Sousa Causo; James Gunn; Jeanne Cortiel; Doug Davis and Lisa Yaszek; Joseph D. Miller; Gregory Benford; Pamela Sargent; James Gunn; Bruce Sterling; Marleen S. Barr

All rights reserved. No reproduction, copy or transmission of this publication may be made without written permission.

No portion of this publication may be reproduced, copied or transmitted save with written permission or in accordance with the provisions of the Copyright, Designs and Patents Act 1988, or under the terms of any licence permitting limited copying issued by the Copyright Licensing Agency, Saffron House, 6-10 Kirby Street, London EC1N 8TS.

Any person who does any unauthorized act in relation to this publication may be liable to criminal prosecution and civil claims for damages.

The authors have asserted their rights to be identified as the authors of this work in accordance with the Copyright, Designs and Patents Act 1988.

First published 2009 by
PALGRAVE MACMILLAN

Palgrave Macmillan in the UK is an imprint of Macmillan Publishers Limited, registered in England, company number 785998, of Houndmills, Basingstoke, Hampshire RG21 6XS.

Palgrave Macmillan in the US is a division of St Martin's Press LLC, 175 Fifth Avenue, New York, NY 10010.

Palgrave Macmillan is the global academic imprint of the above companies and has companies and representatives throughout the world.

Palgrave® and Macmillan® are registered trademarks in the United States, the United Kingdom, Europe and other countries.

ISBN-13: 978–0–230–52717–1 hardback
ISBN-10: 0–230–52717–5 hardback
ISBN-13: 978–0–230–52718–8 paperback
ISBN-10: 0–230–52718–3 paperback

This book is printed on paper suitable for recycling and made from fully managed and sustained forest sources. Logging, pulping and manufacturing processes are expected to conform to the environmental regulations of the country of origin.

A catalogue record for this book is available from the British Library.

A catalog record for this book is available from the Library of Congress.

10 9 8 7 6 5 4 3 2 1
18 17 16 15 14 13 12 11 10 09

Printed and bound in China

contents

notes on contributors

the editors

James Gunn, Emeritus Professor of English at the University of Kansas, has published more than a dozen novels and half a dozen collections of stories, and has edited more than a dozen and a half books. His best-known novels are *The Immortals, The Dreamers, The Listeners, Kampus,* and *The Joy Makers. The Immortals* was filmed as *The Immortal* and became a TV series. His academic publications include *Alternate Worlds: The Illustrated History of Science Fiction, The New Encyclopedia of Science Fiction,* the six-volume anthology *The Road to Science Fiction, The Science of Science-Fiction Writing, Speculations on Speculation: Theories of Science Fiction,* and *Inside Science Fiction.*

Marleen S. Barr, who is known for her pioneering work in feminist science fiction scholarship, teaches in the Department of Communication and Media Studies at Fordham University. She has won the Science Fiction Research Association Pilgrim Award for lifetime achievement in science fiction criticism. Barr is the author of *Alien to Femininity: Speculative Fiction and Feminist Theory, Lost In Space: Probing Feminist Science Fiction and Beyond, Feminist Fabulation: Space/Postmodern Fiction, Genre Fission: A New Discourse Practice for Cultural Studies,* and *Oy Pioneer!: A Novel.* Barr has edited many anthologies and co-edited the special science fiction issue of *PMLA.*

Matthew Candelaria, who recently received his Ph.D. from the University of Kansas, has published articles on science fiction and is recipient of the 2003 Golden Quill Award from the L. Ron Hubbard's Writers of the Future Contest. Candelaria is the co-editor of *Speculations on Speculation: Theories of Science Fiction.*

the contributors

Gregory Benford has published over twenty books, mostly novels. Nearly all remain in print, some after a quarter of a century. His fiction has won many awards, including the Nebula Award for his novel *Timescape*. A winner of the United Nations Medal for Literature, he is a Professor of Physics at the University of California, Irvine. He is a Woodrow Wilson Fellow, was Visiting Fellow at Cambridge University, and in 1995 received the Lord Prize for contributions to science. His 1999 analysis of what endures, *Deep Time: How Humanity Communicates Across Millennia*, has been widely read. A fellow of the American Physical Society and a member of the World Academy of Arts and Sciences, he continues his research in both astrophysics and plasma physics.

Mark Bould is a senior lecturer in film studies at the University of the West of England. He is the author of Film Noir: *From Berlin to Sin City* and the co-editor of *Parietal Games: Critical Writings By and On M. John Harrison*. Bould serves as a consultant editor of *Science Fiction Studies*, an advisory editor of *The Horror Journal: The International Journal of Horror Studies*, and an editorial board member of Liverpool University Press's 'Science Fiction Texts and Studies' book series.

Orson Scott Card is the author of the novels *Ender's Game, Ender's Shadow*, and *Speaker for the Dead*, which are widely read by adults and younger readers, and are increasingly used in schools. Besides these and other science fiction novels, Card writes contemporary fantasy (*Magic Street, Enchantment, Lost Boys*), biblical novels (*Stone Tables, Rachel and Leah*), the American frontier fantasy series *The Tales of Alvin Maker* (beginning with *Seventh Son*), poetry (*An Open Book*), and many plays and scripts.

Michael Cassutt has been writing and producing award-winning television since 1985. He was co-executive producer of the Showtime revival of *The Outer Limits*, which won the CableACE for best drama series in 1995. Among his other credits: staff writer for *The Twilight Zone* (CBS, 1986), story editor for the acclaimed *Max Headroom* series (ABC, 1987, more recently re-run on the Sci-Fi channel), and producer for the CBS series *TV-101* (1988-89), for which Cassutt won the Nancy Susan Reynolds Award of the Center for Population Options for a three-part episode called 'First Love.' His novels include *Red Moon, We Have Capture, Missing Man, Dragon Season*, and *Tango Midnight*.

Roberto de Sousa Causo is the author of *Ficção Científica, Fantasia e Horror no Brasil: 1875 a 1950* (*Science Fiction, Fantasy, and Horror in Brazil: 1875-1950*, 2003). His first book of stories appeared in Portugal in 1999. Causo is the Brazilian correspondent for *Locus—The Magazine of the Science Fiction and Fantasy Field*. In Brazil, he published a story collection, a prize-winning novella in book form, and a novel. He has contributed to newspapers and literary magazines, edited fiction professionally, organized SF events, and is the SF/F columnist of a professional electronic internet-based magazine in Brazil, *Terra Magazine*. With Bruce Sterling he founded in 1997 the Rede Global Paraliterária ('Global Paraliterary Network') for the discussion and promotion of global SF.

Jeanne Cortiel is an Assistant Professor in the English and American Studies Department at the University of Dortmund. She specializes in Science Fiction/Fantasy, American religious discourse, Antebellum American Literature, and Gender, Race and Ethnicity. Cortiel is the author of *Passion für das Unmögliche: Befreiung als Narrativ in der amerikanischen feministischen Theologie* and *Demand My Writing: Joanna Russ/ Feminism/ Science Fiction*. In this major study of the work of Joanna Russ, Jeanne Cortiel gives a clear introduction to the major feminist issues relevant to Russ's work and assesses its development. Although Cortiel deals principally with Russ's novels, she also examines her short stories, and the focus on critically neglected texts is a particularly valuable feature of the study.

R. Doug Davis is an Assistant Professor of English at Gordon College. Davis synthesizes ideas from literary theory and science studies to analyze how works of literature give readers real knowledge about the world. He is particularly interested in the literary history of American war storytelling, and how war stories told during the cold war impacted the course of both American literary history and international relations. He is currently finishing a scholarly monograph on this topic entitled *Strategic Fictions: American War Stories in the World of Nuclear Defense*.

Jane Donawerth is Professor of English at the University of Maryland at College Park, where she teaches Renaissance literature, history of rhetorical theory, and science fiction and utopias by women. Her authored books: *Shakespeare and the Sixteenth-Century Study of Language* and *Frankenstein's Daughters: Women Writing Science Fiction*. Her edited books: *Utopian and Science Fiction by Women: Worlds of Difference, Women, Writing, and the Reproduction of Culture in Tudor and Stuart*

Britain, Crossing Boundaries: Attending to Early Modern Women, and *Rhetorical Theory by Women before 1900*.

Carl Freedman is Professor of English at Louisiana State University, author of many articles and of *George Orwell: A Study in Ideology and Literary Form* (1988), and recipient of the Science Fiction Research Association's 1999 Pioneer Award. His *Critical Theory and Science Fiction* was selected by *Choice* as an Outstanding Academic Book of the Year. In *Critical Theory and Science Fiction* Freedman traces the fundamental and mostly unexamined relationships between the discourses of science fiction and critical theory, arguing that science fiction is (or ought to be) a privileged genre for critical theory. He asserts that it is no accident that the upsurge of academic interest in science fiction since the 1970s coincides with the heyday of literary theory, and that likewise science fiction is one of the most theoretically informed areas of the literary profession. Extended readings of novels by five of the most important modern science fiction authors illustrate the affinity between science fiction and critical theory, in each case concentrating on one major novel that resonates with concerns proper to critical theory.

H. Bruce Franklin, one of America's leading cultural historians, is the author or editor of eighteen books and more than 200 articles on culture and history published in more than a hundred major magazines and newspapers, academic journals, and reference works. He has given over five hundred addresses on college campuses, on radio and TV shows, and at academic conferences, museums, and libraries, and he has participated in making four films. He has taught at Stanford University, Johns Hopkins, Wesleyan, and Yale and currently is the John Cotton Dana Professor of English and American Studies at Rutgers University in Newark.

Brooks Landon, who teaches in the English Department at the University of Iowa, specializes in 20th-century American fiction, contemporary fiction, science fiction literature and film, postmodernism, electronic media/hypertext theory, and nonfiction writing. He describes himself in this way: 'The ways in which people interact with science and technology seem to be at the heart of my scholarship, my teaching, and my service to the Department and the University. My last two books have explored constructions, representations, and implications of science and technology in science fiction film and in science fiction literature. Most of my classes either focus on various literary responses to technology or ways in which American culture has made technology, usually constructed as progress, one of its central concerns. Most of my classes also employ learning technologies, study electronic textuality, and require multimedia writing. And I've been deeply committed to helping the Iowa English Department figure out how technology will revolutionize the way we do business in the twenty-first century. In short, I'm fascinated by what comes next.'

Joseph D. Miller is Associate Professor in the Department of Cell and Neurobiology at the University of Southern California Keck School of Medicine. He states: 'My research utilizes behavioral, cellular and molecular approaches to the study of sleep and circadian rhythms. I do behavioral, electrophysiological and neuropharmacological studies of neurons in the anatomical locus of the biological clock in mammals, the suprachiasmatic nucleus (SCN) of the hypothalamus. I examine the effects of such agents as serotonin, nicotine and dioxin on circadian behavioral rhythms in vivo and circadian neuronal rhythms in vitro. I am also involved in a joint research project which seeks to understand the role of dopamine in the sleep disorder known as narcolepsy. Finally, I am reanalyzing data from the Viking Mars mission from a circadian perspective under the hypothesis that circadian rhythmicity in life detection experiments is an adequate biosignature.' Miller is the author of many science fiction criticism articles.

Eric S. Rabkin is Professor of English Language and Literature at the University of Michigan in Ann Arbor. He has lectured in Europe, Australia, and throughout the U.S. on fantasy, science fiction, fairy tales, humor, American literature, literary theory, culture studies, pedagogy, composition, and administration. He has over one-hundred-ten publications, including twenty-six books written, co-written, edited, or co-edited, including *Narrative Suspense* (1973); *The Fantastic in Literature* (1976); *Science Fiction: History, Science, Vision* (with Robert Scholes, 1977); *Teaching Writing That Works: A Group Approach to Practical English* (with Macklin Smith, 1990); *It's A Gas: A Study of Flatulence* (with Eugene M. Silverman, 1991); *Stories: An Anthology and an Introduction* (1995); *and Effective Writing* (videotape series, 1995). An innovative teacher, Rabkin has received the University Teaching Award and held a chair as an Arthur F. Thurnau Professor. His other honors include awards from the American Council of Learned Societies and the American Philosophical Association.

Pamela Sargent's novel *Venus of Dreams* (1986) was selected by The Easton Press for its 'Masterpieces of Science Fiction' series. *Venus* *of Shadows* (1988) is the sequel. *The Shore of Women* (1986) is one of Sargent's best-known books. Sargent is also the author of *Earthseed* (1983), chosen as a Best Book for Young Adults by the American Library Association, and two collections of short fiction, *Starshadows* (1977) and *The Best of Pamela Sargent* (1987). Her novels *Watchstar* (1980), *Eye of the Comet* (1984), and *Homesmind* (1984) comprise a trilogy. She has won the Nebula Award, the Locus Award, and has been a finalist for the Hugo Award. Her work has been translated into French, German, Dutch, Spanish, Portuguese, Italian, Swedish, Japanese, Polish, Chinese, Russian, and Serbo-Croatian.

Brian Stableford is one of Britain's most prolific and respected science fiction authors. He began writing at the age of 9, made his first professional sale in 1965 at the age of 16, and has written and edited over 70 books. . . . A trained biologist and sociologist, Stableford often produces visions of the future that are at odds with the current popular hysteria about biotechnology. However, his speculations are always thoughtful, and always centered on achieving a future that is beneficial to mankind' (Cheryl Morgan, 'Interview: Brian Stableford,' March 12, 2001). His novels include *Kiss the Goat, Asgard's Secret, The Carnival of Destruction, The Omega Expedition, The Angel of Pain*, and *The Third Millennium*.

Bruce Sterling is an Austin based science fiction writer and Net critic, internationally recognized as cyberspace theorist. His novels *Involution Ocean; The Artificial Kid, Schismatrix; Islands in the Net, Heavy Weather* influenced the cyberpunk literary movement. He co-authored with William Gibson the novel *The Difference Machine*, and is one of the founders of the Electronic Frontier Foundation. Editor of *Mirrorshades*, and co-editor of *The Cyberpunk Anthology*. Other books: *Zeitgeist; Distraction; Holy Fire; The Hacker Crackdown. Tomorrow is Now.*

Sherryl Vint is an Asistant Professor in the Department of English at St. Francis Xavier University. In *Bodies of Tomorrow*, Vint argues for a new model of an ethical and embodied posthuman subject through close readings of the works of Gwyneth Jones, Octavia Butler, Iain M. Banks, William Gibson, and other science fiction authors. Vint's perspective is firmly contextualized by discussions of contemporary technoscience, specifically genetics and information technology, and the implications of this technology for the way we consider human subjectivity.

Lisa Yaszek is Associate Professor in the School of Literature, Communication and Culture at the Georgia Institute of Technology.

She is the author of *The Self Wired: Technology and Subjectivity in Contemporary Narrative*, a critical examination of the use of the mixing of body and technology (such as cyborgs, androids, and cyberpunks) in SF and other genres. Her *Galactic Suburbia: Gender, Technology, and the Rise of Women's Science Fiction* explores how women authors shaped contemporary representations of gender and technoculture in the decades immediately following World War II. Yaszek contends that women turned to science fiction writing in increasing numbers throughout the 1940s, 1950s, and 1960s because the genre provided them with allegorical narrative spaces in which to critically assess the new scientific and social relations that emerged at the dawn of the contemporary era. More specifically, authors including Judith Merril, Marion Zimmer Bradley, Anne McCaffrey, and a host of less-known writers staked claims for women in the American future imaginary by making the gender issues that preoccupied postwar Americans—such as marriage, motherhood, and domesticity—central to the narrative.

George Zebrowski's nearly forty books include novels, short fiction collections, anthologies, and a book of essays. Zebrowski has published more than seventy works of short fiction and more than a hundred and forty articles and essays, and has written about science for *Omni Magazine*. His short fiction and essays have appeared in *Amazing Stories, The Magazine of Fantasy & Science Fiction, Science Fiction Age, Nature*, the *Bertrand Russell Society News*, and many other publications. His best known novel is *Macrolife*, which Arthur C. Clarke described as 'a worthy successor to Olaf Stapledon's *Star Maker*.' It was also highly praised by Arthur C. Clarke.

introduction

discovering the future in my grandmother's back closet

james gunn

The science fiction magazine was born three years after I was, but I didn't discover it until I was eleven. My first encounter with fantastic literature was in the second grade when I read my way through Andrew Lang's books of fairy tales—red, blue, and gold. Then I graduated to Hugh Lofting's Dr. Doolittle novels, with some Altsheller juvenile historical novels thrown in for seasoning. In 1933 my father brought home the second issue of *Doc Savage*, and I got hooked on the hero pulps, including *The Shadow, Operator #5, The Spider,* and (that historical element again) *G-8 and His Battle Aces.*

The next year I discovered a used-magazine store in downtown Kansas City, and in the back, dusty stacks of magazines with names like *Amazing Stories, Wonder Stories,* and *Astounding Stories of Super Science.* Eight years after the creation of *Amazing Stories,* I came across these adventure stories that had the added quality of sense-of-wonder ideas. I liked these best of all, and traded two of my hero pulp magazines for one of these marvelous magazines while the old man in the green eyeshade at the front of the store, surrounded by all that fabulous reading material, grumbled that he couldn't live on old paper.

Five years later *Famous Fantastic Mysteries* began reprinting the old Munsey pulp scientific romances and fantasies, and my imprinting was complete. I recorded all that in *Alternate Worlds: The Illustrated History of Science Fiction,* which was not so much a history as a record of my love affair with science fiction. I have always felt that the truest critical approach to a literature was the analysis of one's responses to it. Interviewers ask me why I started writing science fiction, and the

1

answer seems so obvious that I feel like answering: "What else could I have written?"

My approach to the study of science fiction (SF) was not as predestined. Clearly I thought I should share my own love of SF with the world. I wrote under a pseudonym (Edwin James) for my first ten stories because I wanted to save my full name for critical writing, and I wrote an article about SF for the *Kansas City Star* in 1948. The editorial page editor said I was "overenthusiastic," but he published it. That article got me a thank-you letter from Hugo Gernsback and a series of his Christmas mailings in the form of a small magazine of prophecies. But my critical writing took a back seat to my fiction until 1969, when I taught my first SF class and discovered that the students had no critical apparatus to bring to the discussion of the ten SF novels they had selected. When I taught another class, I told myself, I would organize it historically.

That opportunity came the next year when I left my public relations position to teach full-time, and the School of Journalism and the English Department offered a course that drew 165 students. In preparation I drew up eleven lectures dealing with the development of science fiction from its earliest SF-like stories to its (then) contemporary expressions. In the spring, when I was teaching another SF class to 105 students, an editor from Prentice-Hall came to my office and asked whether I'd be interested in writing a text about fiction writing. I said, "No, but I have these lectures that might make a book about science fiction."

He took the manuscript back to New Jersey with him and reported in a couple of months that he'd shown it to several people in the area who were teaching SF, and they weren't interested in using it. But, he continued, what would I think of a lavishly illustrated coffee-table book? That book, *Alternate Worlds*, led to a telephone call from Barry Lippman, editor at Mentor Books, who asked if I had an idea for a book I might do for them. And that led to *The Road to Science Fiction*, which progressed through half a dozen editors and three publishers before it reached its present six-volume Scarecrow Press anthology covering the evolution of science fiction from Gilgamesh to Effinger.

And so it has gone after 1970, half science fiction stories and novels, half articles and non-fiction books, all of it symbolized, perhaps, by the presidency of Science Fiction and Fantasy Writers of America (SFWA) followed by the presidency of Science Fiction Research Association (SFRA). The study of science fiction has expanded in many directions since then, and this volume is a testament to the strange and wonderful places into which it has wandered, and, one hopes, shed some enlightenment.

Every one of the contributors to this volume, including the editors, had a different experience with SF. Some are authors, and their understanding is conditioned by their struggles to create it; others are scholars, who approach science fiction from a dozen different directions.

It is our hope that this book will illustrate the many ways of reading science fiction and by illuminating its variety and practice will encourage and deepen its appreciation. What we all want, when we deal with a genre like this, is to allow new readers to share our experience of falling in love with this literature of change.

what's a nice baby boomer literary scholar like me doing reading fiction like this?

marleen s. barr

Why do I read science fiction? First, a word about who "I"—a.k.a. the female Baby Boom generation *Reading Science Fiction* co-editor—am.

My colleagues know me as a pioneering feminist science fiction scholar. More personally, I love to say that I am a feminist science fiction scholar married to an alien. No, this sentence is not articulated in terms of what James Gunn calls the "language of science fiction." Even in my wildest imagination—and I have a very wild imagination—despite the notion that men are from Mars and women are from Venus, I don't for a moment think that my husband is an extraterrestrial. I mention him, an "alien" French Canadian who is not an American citizen, because he told me a story which relates to reading science fiction. He describes living in 1940s rural Quebec before telephones had arrived. His family responsibility involved hand carrying his mother's notes to his elder sister's house. I was incredulous. The person who turned our apartment into an electronics store facsimile replete with internet telephone service and a television wide enough to rival Captain Kirk's starship *Enterprise* viewing screen had once lived without telephones?

"You come from a different world," I said to him. This comment is at the heart of why I read science fiction.

Although people often ask me why I read *feminist* science fiction (feminist science fiction scholarship, after all, does not constitute a usual career path), I have never been called upon to discuss reading science fiction in terms of my generation. When I consider why I read science fiction particularly as a Baby Boomer, I must answer in terms of how different worlds encroach upon my reality.

More specifically, I refer to the different world I encountered once upon a time in the back of my father's closet. Don't worry. Just as I am very well aware that my husband is definitely not an extraterrestrial, I don't claim that I met a lion and a witch in a C. S. Lewis Narnia-esque wardrobe. Circa 1955, when I became old enough single-handedly to open my father's closet door, I found a box containing a sari, an ivory chess set, and a green wool jacket emblazoned with a "China/Burma/ India" patch. I had, in other words, located the remnants of my father's life as an American soldier stationed in India during World War II. The objects were as alien to me—a kid growing up in a Forest Hills, Queens, New York City apartment building—as such science fiction accoutrements as ray guns and metallic bras. I can no more equal my father's World War II experience than I can become Wonder Woman. I still own the objects that I found in his closet and I respond to them with the exact awe and wonder I felt when I laid eyes upon the original *Star Trek* captain's chair (located in Seattle's Science Fiction Museum). I can never be Staff Sergeant George Barr boldly going where no Barr has gone before—to what was to him a new life in a new civilization called India—any more than I can ever be Captain James T. Kirk's female counterpart boldly going to seek out new life and new civilizations in galaxies far, far away.

I read science fiction because I was born into a world which contained remnants from World War II. For me, learning about the real world entailed constantly colliding with a past realm—a world not a world of my own—which often barged in upon my present. While being plopped down in the family car during a Sunday drive, for instance, I had to wonder exactly why a seemingly endless line of giant grey battleships was parked in the Hudson River. War vestiges lurked around every corner.

More positively speaking, I read science fiction because Forest Hills provided proximity to the 1964 New York World's Fair (held in Flushing Meadow Park). The futures depicted in the Ford and General Motors pavilions were almost located in my backyard. I saw the flying saucer shaped New York State Pavilion almost every day. I read science fiction because I was so impressed by the future-infused World's Fair.

And, oh yes: seeing all those space flights on the small black and white television in the elementary school auditorium impacted upon my reading choices too. I also cannot fail to mention the science fiction and fantasy television shows which will always hold a prominent place in Baby Boomers' hearts: *The Jetsons, My Favorite Martian, Casper the Friendly Ghost, Mr. Ed, Lost In Space, Bewitched,* and *I Dream of Jeannie.*

Oh no! I have run out of space and my narrative has only reached the mid 1960s. At this time I was, like, twelve. But as a Baby Boomer, I am supposed to talk about sex, and drugs, and rock and roll. I know that you students are just dying to read about reading science fiction in terms of sex, and drugs, and rock and roll. But *Reading Science Fiction* is, after all, a *textbook*. Whew, saved in mid chronological narrative which stops at the time of echoing the sounds of silence.

Whew, back to writing science fiction criticism language. The point is that literary criticism is a community dialogue about reading. Generationally ensconced between my co-editors—young scholar Matthew Candelaria and Greatest Generation member science fiction Grand Master James Gunn—I invite you, students who are members of the next new generation in relation to Candelaria, to join us. Enter a wonderful conversation. Make friends. Read science fiction.

Enjoy!

the medium that time forgot

matthew candelaria

I always tell people that my introduction to SF was Heinlein's *Have Space Suit, Will Travel*, but it's an invidious lie. Truth is, I can't remember a time when I wasn't aware of SF. Since my mom is a *Star Trek* fan, I probably was exposed to it in the womb.

I used to love it all, unconditionally. I was especially into dinosaurs and I loved any stupid old thing that threw in a prehistoric monster. Except for the lizards and caimans with pasted-on fins and horns. I could not imagine that anyone might confuse *The Land that Time Forgot* with *The People that Time Forgot*. The first one was awesome, the other one dumb, with only two good things: the pteranodon attacking the biplane and the nodosauroid that attacks in the dark dungeon of the troglodyte king. *The Land that Time Forgot* also imprinted indelibly on my mind the image of Tyler and Lisa clad primitively in skins throwing their hopes in a bottle, off the lonely and desolate edge of their world, into the sea below.

I was pretty young when *Star Wars* came out, so young that I don't remember it. I do remember *Battlestar Galactica*, whose spacey music and monologue hooked me, "There are those who believe that life here began out there" That and the premiere movie/mini-series worked, from the destruction of innocent cities, including the word "Peace" written in flowers, to the blind flight through the red heat of densely packed protostars to the horrific insect aliens who secretly kidnapped people from the night club to use them as fodder for their young.

My environment was supersaturated with SF. I loved *Thundarr the Barbarian*, which also had an intro monologue. I replayed the scenarios of this cartoon over and over again, although the hero was not Thundarr, but a little rubber monster I called "Buggie," a hemipteroid with huge mandibles, pincers for hands, and tiny flightless wings.

While these things kept me highly entertained and active, there's no way they'd ever prepare me for becoming a serious critic. They inspired me to draw, like all the kids in my elementary school. Drawing was closely regimented by peer pressure. Boys and girls drew separately, drawing the same thing in iteration after iteration to replicate the Platonic form of a flower, a cholo, or a hotrod. Since I'd transferred schools and hadn't been taught how to properly draw a cholo or a hotrod, I was exiled. I mostly drew dinosaurs, but some boys drew space ships, so I started learning. Then *The Empire Strikes Back* came out and we drew asteroid fields and worked together to fill the fields with action. My dinosaurs became reptilian aliens, and suddenly I began creating narratives that went from week to week, month to month. One of my drawing friends had a brother who taught us Dungeons and Dragons (D&D), and I started reading the rule books.

We got a Commodore Vic 20 computer, and I started playing SF video games, like *Gorf*. We upgraded to a Commodore 64, and the games got better, including *Nonterraqueous*.

My mom introduced me to two books: the aforementioned *Have Space Suit, Will Travel* and *The Gryphon's Eyrie* by Andre Norton and A. C. Crispin. I read them again and again, and read through everything by these authors that the public library would let me check out. They were justifiably reluctant to let a ten-year-old read *Stranger in a Strange Land*, but sometimes they were overzealous. My dad had to check out *Seven Science Fiction Novels* by Wells, including *War of the Worlds*, *The Island of Dr. Moreau*, *The Time Machine*, and so on, but he was obliging.

Then we moved and I changed schools. My schoolwork remained (to my teachers) distressingly SF-related, and then came the assignment I'd been waiting for: a five page story in seventh grade. Mine turned out to be fifty, a post-apocalyptic quest epic focusing on robots. I was hooked.

But I never would have become a critic of SF if I hadn't read *To the Lighthouse* by Virginia Woolf, *The Sound and the Fury* by William Faulkner, and *Chronicle of a Death Foretold* by Gabriel Garcia Marquez as a senior in high school, and decided that mainstream literature was where it was at. These people were much better writers than Heinlein and Wells and Norton, and I turned my back on the genre, although I would occasionally wander through the SF section of bookstores, gazing at covers.

When I came to Kansas, I didn't know there was an SF program, but I began to notice that my literature classes seemed limited. Their perspective was very narrow. They neglected perspectives that embraced the biology, physics, and chemistry that shape the human consciousness; perspectives that I felt were represented only in SF. I began writing essays on SF. My professors, almost as frustrated as my seventh-grade teachers, shunted me off to Jim Gunn, who proved to be not only a great teacher, but also an excellent model of the ethics and responsibility of unlimited humanity. Without his influence, I would have achieved only a fraction of my still-limited success in this field, and I feel toward him a gratitude I have not yet found the words to articulate. There is no way I can repay his help, but I hope in some measure to do so by telling all the people of my generation and beyond that, for all the pleasure we may derive from cartoons, movies, television, and video games, the true font of science fiction is in the writing, and it opens up unlimited vistas to those who learn to read it properly.

part i
mapping science fiction

introduction to part i

Most students come to a class on science fiction (SF) believing they know what the genre is, and that any time spent discussing the subject is time wasted. However, this knowledge is often on the order of claiming to know human anatomy because we have observed that most people seem to have two arms, two legs, and a head. True, and generally good to know, but in no way conclusive. Sometimes, those claiming to be fans can be the worst in this respect, as they have spent the most time observing the two arms, two legs, and head of the genre without concerning themselves about the various "unmentionables" that lay outside their observation. To them, SF is *Star Wars* but not *Star Trek*, or *Halo* but not *Starcraft*, or *Ender's Game* but not *The Wild Shore*. Furthermore, when they encounter someone of the contrary opinion (SF is *Star Trek* but not *Star Wars*), they either have a memorized set of go-to points or they have no terms in which to relate their opinion; both strategies shut down discussion, which often degenerates to the level of "Uh-uh!" "Uh-huh!" while the rest of the class looks on in a mixture of confusion and horror.

None of the essays in this section really tell us what SF is. Instead, they give us detailed approaches through which a definition of SF might be made, terms under which we might discuss what we mean when we point to this thing we call SF. They bring up complications of history, economics, expectations of readers and publishers, even of the process of definition itself. When students have finished reading all the essays in this section, they will have acquired not only a language for discussing SF and critically analyzing their own experiences with the genre, but also a sense of the high stakes that rest on the question of definition.

Eric S. Rabkin provides us with an excellent starting place to begin our discussion, as he cuts directly to the heart of the question: how can we hope to come up with a successful definition for anything? Rabkin offers four different modes of definition: characteristic, prototypical, operational, and social, gives examples of each and argues their strengths and weaknesses, before confessing his own affection for the characteristic mode. He also alludes to the strategic nature of definitions, that

11

each one is made not in a value-neutral space but with the conscious or unconscious goal of achieving a political, social, or economic end.

H. Bruce Franklin gives us a historical definition of SF (what we might call a socio-prototypical definition to use Rabkin's terms). He traces its development as a genre through internal forces, and in relation to social forces, especially the rise of scientific thought and the resulting paradigm shifts with respect to space, time, and our place in them. Franklin is careful to note the long prehistory of SF, then casually dismisses many of these early texts as fantasy, not SF, a move that might seem redundant were it not that such arguments speak to strategies long used by critics of the genre to establish its primacy, legitimacy, and vitality. Perceptive students will be sensitive to the strong Marxist-critical undertones in the essay that strongly link SF as a cultural form with the economic forms that led to its production.

Brian Stableford defines SF in a characteristic fashion as a distinctive form of fantastic literature, which deviates from the folkloric tradition in meaningful ways, although without wholly achieving separation. While many proponents of globalization proclaim the world has gone flat, Stableford appropriately links the concept of a thin world with fantasy, arguing that SF presents us a world which is fuller and rounder than ever and likely to continue tumescing. Stableford shows how SF drew many of its narrative strategies from the folkloric tradition that was its original source, often in ways that undermine its ostensible goal as a forward-looking, future-oriented genre of change, and offers an increasingly sophisticated readership as a remedy for this internal contradiction.

Sherryl Vint and Mark Bould offer us a social-operational definition of SF. For them, SF is not a thing, but, rather, the result of a process of policing by individuals in positions of power over a series of historical moments. They stress that SF is not only a process of inclusion, but is also, and perhaps more importantly, a process of exclusion that defines not only the particular reading community of SF but also the types of representations possible by the genre. By presenting a case study of the story "The Cold Equations" by Tom Godwin, they hope to show that SF has never been a thing independent of the political vision of the discourse community, that is its editors, authors, and fans. Readers will note reference to Tom Godwin's "The Cold Equations" in several of the essays in this volume. James Gunn has called it a "touchstone" story, and it may still retain that quality some 50 years after publication, with hard-SF scholars focusing on the way in which the hard reality of space travel will not pardon human ignorance even when embodied in innocence (the universe doesn't care), and humanist scholars focusing on the culture that condemns an innocent young girl to death by not taking proper precautions or even indulging anti-feminist tendencies by setting up a situation where an innocent young girl is sacrificed to patriarchal goals. The story has been frequently anthologized, including *The Road to Science Fiction Volume Three: From Heinlein to Here.*

Students should also pay close attention to the positioning of the genre with respect to other genres, such as "mainstream" literature or fantasy, and the value judgments that inform the author's explicit and implicit assertions of the usefulness and significance of each form of literary production.

1
defining science fiction
eric s. rabkin

Even before classes started at the University of Iowa Writers' Workshop in 1967, acclaimed Philippine novelist Bienvenido ("Ben") Santos, in a welcome lecture, revealed some unexpected things about the "work" in "workshop." He reported the struggles of Kurt Vonnegut, Jr., recently of the Workshop faculty and author of such science fiction (SF) classics as *Player Piano* (1952) and *Cat's Cradle* (1963), to have editors consider his writing as "fiction" rather than "science fiction." Why? Because, Ben said, a typical word-rate for publication of "fiction" in a first-line magazine was about five cents; for science fiction two. Every time Vonnegut won that struggle, he increased his paycheck by one hundred-fifty percent. And every time he lost, well...

Life's complexities often drive us back to definition. (One avid webpage [http://www.panix.com/~gokce/sf_defn.html, accessed May 27, 2008] gathers fifty-two different, published statements that it counts as definitions of SF.) We seek by definition to find a bedrock on which to re-square and repair our foundations, a secure place to start.

When Ray Bradbury's gloriously lyrical composite novel, *The Martian Chronicles* (1950), received the first-ever front-page notice for a science fiction work in *The New York Times Book Review*, many struggling, self-defined SF authors groused loudly. Oh, sure, they'd hardly disparage the overdue notice to their genre, then called with loving irony by many of its writers, editors, and oh-so-active fans "the science fiction ghetto," but, damn it all, why Bradbury? He wasn't even a real science fiction writer! Just look at the "Green Morning" chapter of his book. Benjamin Driscoll, a silly Johnny Appleseed analog, wanders around Mars in its dry, thin atmosphere broadcasting seeds and hope, falls asleep on the ground to the sound of distant thunder, and wakes to the first drops of life-giving rain. Rain? On Mars!? And how did he walk around without a space suit anyway? This isn't SF. It's fairy tale! Heck, in the last chapter, "The Million-Year Picnic," the father of a newly pastoral family that had barely escaped Earth's ultimate atomic war blows up the rocket ship by which they had reached Mars "so we can't go back, ever. And so if any of those evil men ever come to Mars they won't know we're here." Not only is this a fairy tale, it's an *anti*-science fiction fairy tale at that! Or so said those earning the lower word rate.

Today Bradbury ranks among the greats of science fiction, real science fiction. Did Bradbury change, or was it the definition?

There are four fundamentally different ways to construct a definition, which we can call characteristic, prototypical, operational, and social. Each has been applied to science fiction, and each serves—consciously or not—the purposes of the time, place, and person doing the defining. Including me.

Most people's first idea of definition is characteristic definition, that is, a definition that lists the characteristics of the thing in question. Those things that have the characteristics are in; those that don't are out. Characteristic definitions provide clear lines, like the chalk markings in tennis. The *Oxford English Dictionary* (*OED*) defines tennis in "the usual sense" as "a game played with a ball and rackets on an unenclosed rectangular space on a smooth grass lawn or a floor of hard gravel, cement, asphalt, etc., called a court." If it's not a game—say you're trying to kill someone by smashing his head with a racket-driven ball—that's clearly not tennis. And if it is a game but the space is circular, that's not tennis either. I like this definition, especially because I'm not very good at tennis. After all, while the *OED*'s game can involve a variety of surface materials, it doesn't seem to involve a net. Even I could succeed if tennis lacked that characteristic.

The *OED* offers a characteristic definition for science fiction: "Imaginative fiction based on postulated scientific discoveries or spectacular environmental changes, freq. set in the future or on other planets and involving space or time travel."

This is a fine beginning, but would be a misleading end. What distinguishes "imaginative fiction" from "fiction"? Since all "fiction" involves imagination, here the *OED* implicitly suggests that science fiction is less restrained in its imagination than other types of fiction. What other types? Fairy tale? No, of course not. The unstated norm is realistic fiction. But each SF work provides its own alternative reality by "postulat[ing] scientific discoveries or spectacular environmental changes." This is often true. In *The Time Machine* (1895), H. G. Wells postulates a Time Machine and has his Time Traveler briefly visit the year 30,000,000 when "the tidal drag" had stopped the rotation of the

Earth, quite a spectacular environmental change. But Philip K. Dick's *The Man in the High Castle* (1962), which won the Hugo Award for Best SF Novel given by the fans at the annual World Science Fiction Convention, is an alternate history set in a 1962, years after the Axis counterfactually defeated the Allies in World War II. Dick postulates nothing to justify this setting, yet this was outstanding "science fiction" to the fans. They seem to want SF to include a wide range of the fantastic fictions they love, but "loved by the fans" doesn't fit conveniently into the *OED*'s characteristic definition.

A second type of definition employs prototypes. In *Jacobellis v. Ohio* (1964), U.S. Supreme Court Justice Potter Stewart, trying to match the facts of the case with a statute concerning "hard-core pornography," wrote that "I shall not today attempt further to define the kinds of material I understand to be embraced within that shorthand description; and perhaps I could never succeed in intelligibly doing so. But I know it when I see it." "If it walks like a duck, talks like a duck, and quacks like a duck, it must be a duck." When people hurl that phrase into an argument, trying to cut past the question of definition, they are really trying to evade the requirement of a characteristic definition by saying "it's duck enough for me"; that is, they have a prototypical duck in mind and assert that for the matter at hand this thing is close enough to the prototype that we ought just to accept the identification and go on.

In April 1926, Hugo Gernsback (namesake of the award) launched *Amazing Stories*, the first self-described "science fiction" magazine. Actually, Gernsback promised to publish "scientifiction," a word of his own invention which he had first put in print in 1916 but which never caught on. In *Amazing* he explained that "by 'scientifiction' I mean the Jules Verne, H. G. Wells and Edgar Allan Poe type of story—a charming romance intermingled with scientific fact and prophetic vision" (3). Gernsback's prototypical definition asks us to think of works by authors we know and recognize that they have enough commonality that we can recognize some sort of ideal which they all more or less closely embody. We should be able to look at a fiction and say, "It's SF enough for me." While prototypical definitions are often the best we can do, as Potter Stewart understood, they have weaknesses as well as strengths.

We may well continue to argue a prototypical definition at the margins. "Once upon a time, long, long ago" certainly sounds like the beginning of a fairy tale. Is the first-released *Star Wars* movie (1977), which begins "A long time ago, in a galaxy far, far away," fairy tale (FT) or SF? Can it be fairy tale and SF? What is at stake for those who want it to be one, the other, or both? What does the definitional debate tell us about either genre, or its devotees? In this case, I think the whack-a-mole debate between FT and SF suggests that SF, with its frequent clashes of good and evil, heroic protagonists, and indulgence of what Sigmund Freud called the illusion of central position, has strong roots in fairy tale. Although prototypical definitions keep us arguing at the margins and may be a weakness in advancing the discussion of a specific work, they are also a strength in considering the system of works from which it is drawn.

One weakness of prototypical definition is that it requires us to ignore potentially significant aspects of its designated exemplars. While Gernsback lumped Verne with Wells, Verne assuredly did not. "I make use of physics [Verne said, contrasting himself with Wells]. He invents. I go to the moon in a cannon-ball, discharged from a cannon. Here there is no invention. He goes to Mars in an airship, which he constructs of a metal which does away with the law of gravitation. *Ça c'est très joli* [that's very pretty], but show me this metal. Let him produce it" (1903; from Gary Westfahl, *Science Fiction Quotations*, 2005). Verne's concern for the legitimacy of invention should have been crucial to Gernsback, whose magazine, from its first issue, bore the slogan, "Extravagant Fiction Today—Cold Fact Tomorrow!" But Gernsback's interest ran more toward the commercial than the measured. His famous editorial concludes that "Posterity will point to [stories published here] as having blazed a new trail, not only in literature and fiction, but in progress as well" (3). Scientifiction provides not merely "charming romance" but the inspiration for real science, hard-driving, mind-expanding, world-changing science!

As prototypes go, Gernsback's isn't bad. But what about Verne's beef with Wells? In *The Invisible Man* (1897), Wells's protagonist must go naked to avoid detection by the rural folk he tries to dominate. They surround him and beat him to death, his body betraying his ambitions despite having gained the mythical power of invisibility. But in "The Plattner Story" (also 1897), Wells's protagonist, blown willy-nilly into another dimension, is both invisible and incorporeal, which he discovers when otherworld denizens casually walk through him. Clearly "invisibility" as an SF trope can be a more or less likely "invention" depending on the needs of the story. The charming romances of Poe make matters still murkier. In "The Facts in the Case of M. Valdemar" (1845), the narrator "mesmerizes" the bed-ridden title character *"in articulo mortis* [at the point of death]," an experiment recorded by a medical student engaged for just that purpose. What could be more scientific? And there Valdemar lies, breathless and pulseless for seven months without decay, until the narrator "rapidly made mesmeric passes" with his hand to break the hypnotic trance. All in an instant, Valdemar crumbles and melts "[u]pon the bed... [into] a nearly liquid mass of loathsome—of detestable putridity." The onanistic implications of this impossible "science" fiction don't meet Gernsback's Horatio Alger vision of SF as the vanguard of shiny American progress, so his prototypical definition ignores it.

One of the strengths of a prototypical definition is that naming something often enables others to see it. Even Poe, Verne, and Wells did not think of themselves as writing "science fiction," but once the term existed, as Gernsback himself suggests, the genre's history snapped into view. Suddenly we can ask if the "Voyage to Laputa" in Jonathan Swift's *Gulliver's Travels* (1726), with its airborne island state ruled by scientists and held aloft by an anti-gravity mineral that Verne would scorn, is SF. A similar conceptual crystallization occurred when Thomas More named his political science fiction *Utopia* (1516), a Greek pun he invented meaning both "no place" (*ou-topos*) and "good place" (*eu-topos*), calling into consciousness a genre whose exemplars extend back at least as far as Plato's *Republic* (*c.* 380 BCE) and which, according to Darko Suvin (12), serves as the oldest tributary of the main stream of science fiction.

Although "scientifiction" faded, "science fiction" blazed. While the *OED* records a lone use of "science fiction" in 1851, it became standard once *Amazing* gave in, adopting it in a June 1929 editorial by Gernsback's managing editor (and later successor editor), Thomas O'Conor Sloane, a chemistry Ph.D. and Thomas Edison's son-in-law. The fans know what they want, and the magazines try to provide it.

An operational definition proposes an operation the result of which is the thing defined. According to the *OED*, the meter was "[O]riginally intended to represent one ten-millionth of the length of a quadrant of the meridian, and defined by reference to a platinum-iridium standard kept in Paris." That is, one measured the Earth from equator to pole through Paris, took that length, divided by 10 million, and *voilà!*, you had a meter. Operational definitions typically incite little definitional argument. The Genre Evolution Project (http://www.umich.edu/~genreevo.accessed May 27, 2008), a collaborative effort I co-lead combining qualitative and quantitative methods to study culture as a complex adaptive system, uses an operational definition of SF short stories. If a work is fiction, no more than 12,000 words, and published in a self-described SF magazine, it is an SF short story. Are some of our materials really zombie stories? That depends on what you mean by "really." They seem to have sold SF magazines. Perhaps, using another type of definition, we ought to include zombies. Certainly the undead appear in "Valdemar."

Operational definitions, desirable for their simplicity, evade some larger social questions even while enabling others. George Hay, the British "futurologist," suggested that "[s]cience fiction is what you find on the shelves in the library marked science fiction." While this operational definition ("look on that shelf; what you find is it") avoids argument about specific books, it should make us question the role of librarians, folks who separate the "literature" of Nobel prize-winning authors like William Golding (*The Inheritors*, 1955) from the "young adult books" of Verne and the "science fiction"—or is it anti-science fiction?—of Bradbury.

The fourth type of definition is social. There exists no characteristic of plant physiology that marks a weed. There is no prototypical weed. And no operation, other than planting something unwanted in someone else's plot, can define a weed. But that operation requires learning about someone's desire, which implies that the only reliable definition of weed is social: an unwanted plant.

Defining it socially, science fiction is fiction that the world uses as science fiction. While this may sound tautological, it usefully invites study of the world and its desires. For much of its history, emerging as the prototype Gernsback named and published in pulp, SF was deemed low-class. Librarians and publishers recognized this. And so do those who say they love William Shakespeare's *The Tempest*, about a learned man who uses the knowledge in "my books" to command spirits that command the weather; who admire George Orwell's *Nineteen Eighty-Four* (1949) as a commentary on our times; who make best-sellers of Margaret Atwood's futuristic *Handmaid's Tale* (1985) and Kazuo Ishiguro's alternate history *Never Let Me Go* (2005); and yet won't see these as SF "because they're good." This social definition, like "an unwanted plant," includes a value judgment. "It's not just science fiction anymore" is a line we can read in the newspaper almost daily referring to computer science, medicine, warfare, government activity, agriculture, and culture in general. We must always ask, who has what at stake in suggesting that the once-fantastic has become real?

I have argued (beginning in *The Fantastic in Literature*, 1976) that the fantastic is a psychological affect generated during reading by the "diametric, diachronic [radically complete, through time] reversal of the ground rules of the narrative world." "Once upon a time, there was a beautiful golden-haired princess" flips us out of our armchair world into one where animals *can* talk, magic *is* real. "And she fell deeply in love with an accountant name Myron Goldstein." That second line makes the story more fantastic not because there are no accountants named Myron Goldstein—there may well be—but because there are no accountants at all in the world of fairy tales. To admit one requires that we flip the ground rules again. Works that flip-flop their ground rules as exhaustively as possible, like Lewis Carroll's Alice books, without devolving into incoherence, are true Fantasies. But the publishing category of fantasy, which includes hobbits, magic, underworlds, and paranormal powers like those of Stephen King's *Carrie* (1974), is much broader. How does this fantasy relate to science fiction?

Consider *Frankenstein* and *Dracula*. The Gothic novel, like Horace Walpole's *The Castle of Otranto: A Gothic Story* (1765), thrilled readers with sex, death, curses, and apparitions in the haunted bowels of the title heap. As those thrills paled, writers like Ann Radcliffe in her *Mysteries of Udolpho* (1794) provided an additional fantastic twist with a final astonishing revelation that the apparently supernatural was natural after all. Call this the Scooby-Doo ending. Then, in *Frankenstein* (1818), Mary Shelley moved that naturalizing explanation to the very first lines of her Preface: "The event on which this fiction is founded, has been supposed, by Dr. Darwin [Erasmus, Charles's grandfather], and some of the physiological writers of Germany, as not of impossible occurrence." Thus science fiction was born.

In a famous scene in the 1931 film of *Dracula*, a woman in a peignoir sits before a triptych mirror brushing out her hair. The camera, pulling back, reveals the vampire stealing toward her. The camera moves toward her chair and we see her reflected face. The camera moves sideways, suggesting that the vampire is almost upon her. In the next instant he will be visible not only to us but finally to her, but—astounding!—he has no reflection! Why not? Ah, ha! Because vampires have no souls.

Then how can we see the chair?

Dracula, in the publishing sense of the term, is fantasy. Its rules are arbitrary. We can seek the power of those rules in our psyches, but not in science, the pursuit of organized knowledge. That would be *Frankenstein*.

Ultimately, among all possible definitions, I favor a characteristic one: Science fiction is that branch of the fantastic that seeks plausibility against a background of science. The sciences, of course, can vary, as can the degrees of plausibility, but the intellectual commitment is always there, with Poe's medical student taking notes or Bradbury's recognition that the father's rocket ship may be one too many for the evolution of a better society. Alternate histories are not science fiction because they have ray guns or cancer cures but because, like utopias, they ask us to consider social forces with both intellectual discipline and imaginative freedom, a combination of mental activities that is perfect for our times. I write these thoughts on a personal computer using a word processor; I double-check certain information by broadband access to the World Wide Web. None of those four world-changing technologies existed when I was born. It seems to me that it matters very much how we define science fiction because, ready or not, we live it.

suggestions for further reading

Freedman, Carl. *Critical Theory and Science Fiction*. Hanover, NH: Wesleyan University Press, 2000.

Hume, Kathryn. *Fantasy and Mimesis: Responses to Reality in Western Literature*. New York: Methuen, 1984.

Rabkin, Eric S. *The Fantastic in Literature*. Princeton, NJ: Princeton University Press, 1976.

Rose, Mark. *Alien Encounters: An Anatomy of Science Fiction*. Cambridge, MA: Harvard University Press, 1981.

Suvin, Darko. *Metamorphoses of Science Fiction: On the Poetics and History of a Literary Genre*. New Haven, CT: Yale University Press, 1979.

dirigible (such as Edgar Allan Poe's 1849 "Mellonta Tauta") was written as SF because such a scene was then just a possibility and it remains SF forever, even after transatlantic luxury dirigibles came to be and after they ceased to be. Although much ink has been spilled trying to apply these formal boundaries, they seem to me of marginal usefulness. More helpful is an awareness that since SF explores the possible, its territory ranges from the present Earth we know to the limits of the possible universes that the human imagination can project, whether in the past, present, future, or alternative time-space continuums. Therefore SF is the only literature capable of exploring the macrohistory of our species, and of placing our history, and even our daily lives, in a cosmic context.

SF must be defined further, as an historical phenomenon. Though SF has antecedents that stretch back at least two thousand years, SF as a body of literature—and movies, graphic art, comic books, radio shows, futuristic exhibits, TV serials, video game machines, computer games, virtual reality, and so forth—is a new phenomenon. It is an expression of only modern technological, scientific, industrial society, appearing when pre-industrial societies are transformed by an industrial revolution. Indeed, industrial society creates not just the consciousness characteristic of SF but also the very means of physically propagating SF in its various cultural forms, even before it was beamed as images on movie and video screens. For even SF *literature*, like other forms of literature typical of industrial society, is propagated in mass-produced magazines and books, which require advanced manufacturing and distribution as well as a large literate audience.

All this is very recent. The word "scientist" appeared for the first time in 1840, as a deliberate coinage (Williams, Raymond: 234–235). The term "science fiction" was used first in 1851 (in Chapter 10 of William Wilson's *A Little Earnest Book upon a Great Old Subject*) "Science-Fiction, in which the revealed truths of Science may be given interwoven with a pleasing story which may itself be poetical and *true*" (emphasis in original).

We take for granted living in a world where technological change is so rapid that it is part of our lives—continually transforming the present and the future. But this epoch of rapid technological changes, dating from the Industrial Revolution in Europe, is a mere microinstant of cosmic time.

The Earth is approximately four and a half billion years old. The ice ages ended about 10,000 years ago. Thus the age of the Earth is 450,000 times the period since the last ice age. Let's make this more imaginable by picturing the age of the Earth equivalent to 45,000 feet, the altitude of a very high-flying jet airliner. In comparison, the time since the last ice age would be represented by 1.2 inches. The period of modern science, technology, and SF, which began with the Industrial Revolution about 250 years ago, would then be equivalent on our spatial scale to 0.03 inches, about the thickness of a line made by a medium ballpoint pen.

Within that pen scratch of time, the rate of technological change has been exponential. Modern consciousness therefore is radically different from that of the peoples who inhabited the planet before the emergence of SF.

So after decades of teaching SF, I find this to be its most useful and meaningful definition: *SF is the major non-realistic mode of imaginative creation of our epoch.* Why? Because science and technology are continually changing the conditions of our existence. And because science—not magic or myth or religion—is the principal way modern culture locates us imaginatively in time and space.

Yet according to Einstein, "The whole of science is nothing more than a refinement of everyday thinking" (59). In explaining this statement, Einstein traces how we humans think about the evidence of our senses to form conceptions of "reality," and how science extrapolates from these conceptions of "reality" to theorems of the unknown. This process of "extrapolation"—projecting into the unknown from what we know or believe we know—is both the characteristic method of SF and the most distinctive aspect of human thought. What does distinguish human beings from all other life forms of which we are aware? Like other animals, we derive consciousness from the conditions of our existence. Being determines consciousness. But unlike other animals, we willfully use our consciousness to *change* the conditions of our existence, to make them meet what we perceive to be our needs and desires. As opposed to the birds and bees and even beavers, we consciously and with volition *choose* to change the material world in which we live. Thus creativity seems peculiar to our species and may therefore be said to be the essence of humanity. To engage in this creativity, we must go from our impressions of what *is* to imagining what *might be*. This is what SF is all about, the imagining of what *might be*. By consciously changing the conditions of our existence, we also change our own consciousness, which grows and transforms in an endless, dynamic dialectic between itself and the world with which it interacts.

* * *

SF has a long prehistory. Take, for example, the myths and epics of early Greek civilization. The superhuman beings who live on Mount

Olympus are headed by Zeus, who can transform himself into a swan or a bull capable of having sex and children with beautiful earth women (Leda and Europa). The war narrated in the *Iliad* features superweapons such as thunderbolts and impregnable armor. From the point of view of these Europeans, the known world was a small portion of the Mediterranean. So just as modern SF often locates thrilling adventures and encounters with improbable beings in distant space, the *Odyssey* narrates a marvelous voyage to far distant alien worlds on the other side of the Mediterranean, where the voyagers encounter one-eyed giants, a six-headed monster, a creature that swallows passing ships, and a woman who chemically transforms people into animals.

The first fictions about travel beyond the Earth were satires of such epic voyages and improbable warfare by the Syrian writer Lucian of Samosata in the second century AD. The hero of his *Icaromenippus* attaches wings and flies to the Moon. In *A True Story*, Lucian himself and a shipload of companions are wafted to the Moon, where men marry men and bear children, and the travelers participate in an interplanetary war fought, with many strange alien races wielding marvelous weapons, to determine whether the empire of the Moon or of the Sun gets to colonize Venus.

Although it anticipates many favorite themes of such modern cultural staples as *Star Trek* and *Star Wars,* Lucian's *A True Story* is not SF but fantasy. Lucian intended it to be read as a narrative not of interesting or thrilling possibilities but of ludicrous impossibilities. Similar works of fantasy would appear now and then for the following fourteen hundred years. As late as 1532, Ariosto's *Orlando Furioso* projected a trip to the Moon merely as a preposterous fantasy (to find and bottle his hero's lost wits). But just eight years after Ariosto's fantasy, came an earth-shaking book, *On the Revolutions of the Celestial Spheres,* Copernicus's demonstration that the cosmos is vast and does not revolve around the Earth.

By then the European concept of space was already being transformed. The magnetic compass and advances in shipbuilding made possible the voyages of so-called discovery in the late fifteenth century, leading to a "New World"—that is, new to Europeans. The voyages of Columbus had taken place almost half a century before Ariosto's lunar voyage.

As the European concept of space was being reshaped, the European concept of change, and of historical time itself, was also being transformed. To understand the profound conceptual transformation that separates our consciousness of time from that of feudal Europe, consider the Sistine Chapel, which was completed in 1512. Time there is thoroughly ahistorical. Human history is entirely irrelevant to the picture of its beginning in the Creation on the ceiling and the picture of its end in the Day of Judgment on the far wall. All the popes exist simultaneously in figures above the frescoes depicting the story of Moses on the South Wall and the story of Christ on the North Wall. Human societies have no place in this story, and human history itself is irrelevant. For example, two of the frescoes about Christ show key events in his life occurring in front of a central image of the Arch of Constantine, which was actually constructed in AD 315. No human event, no human society, and no historical change have a place in this vision of the full span of time.

Four years after the completion of the Sistine Chapel came what is arguably the first European book with a modern conception of time, Thomas More's *Utopia* (1516). More here introduced a concept fundamental to modern consciousness and SF: change in the mode of production changes the conditions of human existence. As More argues, the cloth industry's growing demand for fine English wool had led to the enclosure of the common land, which caused massive unemployment and skyrocketing inflation, which forced many people into crime, which in turn led to wholesale capital punishment. These ominous conditions induced More to coin a pun and imagine a place with a mighty host of offspring in SF: *Utopia*, the good place (eutopia) which is noplace (outopia).

By the seventeenth century, feudalism was on the way out in Europe and capitalism was on the way in. Modern science developed as part of this revolution. Along with modern science, and closely related to it, came modern SF.

Francis Bacon, often called the father of modern science, used fiction to show the wonders that could be achieved using his inductive method of scientific experimentation. In his *New Atlantis* (published posthumously in 1627) he describes the discovery of a utopian society based on experimental science, including the development of "New Artificiall Mettalls," vivisection, genetic manipulation, telescopes, microscopes, telephones, beamed images, submarines, aerial flight, and factories. Written almost exactly a century after More's *Utopia*, the *New Atlantis* displays a dramatic shift in consciousness. The marvelous society in *Utopia* is simply created by order of King Utopos and is complete and changeless; the marvelous society in the *New Atlantis* is a work in progress continually flowing from science and technology.

With the development of the telescope in the early seventeenth century, the concept of "plurality of worlds" began to be taken seriously.

The Moon, planets, and stars became destinations for the imagination of the possible.

Johannus Kepler, who developed the basic laws of planetary motion, used them in *Somnium* (published posthumously in 1634) to imagine the geography of the Moon and possible life forms that could develop there. Bishop Francis Godwin carefully followed the then-current scientific theory in describing a voyage to the Moon and its utopian society in his *The Man in the Moone* (published posthumously in 1638).[1] Cyrano de Bergerac's *Comical History of the States and Empires of the Moon* (1659) and *Sun* (1687) include marvelous inventions such as solar energy converters and talking machines.

During the seventeenth century, technological and social change were accelerating so rapidly that they could be experienced within a person's lifetime. Thus some people began to imagine a future qualitatively different from the past or present. Prior to this, there had never been a fiction set in a future period of human history. The closest had been millennial imaginings that had pictured the replacement of human history by God's kingdom. The first known fiction set in future human time is Jacques Guttin's *Epigone, Story of the Future Century* (1659).[2] This kind of imagination was still so uncongenial, however, that almost three fourths of a century elapsed before the appearance in 1733 of another significant future-scene fiction, Samuel Madden's *Memoirs of the Twentieth Century*, consisting of manuscripts that have somehow been sent backward through time.

So now all the basic fields of SF had been opened to the imagination: space travel, marvelous inventions and discoveries, and the future.

As capitalism and modern science continued to develop each other, SF extrapolated from both the tremendous changes and their disturbing consequences. During the eighteenth century, while the idea of historical progress was beginning to change the world, some authors took a bleak view of the ever-accelerating technological and social change. In *Gulliver's Travels* (1726), Jonathan Swift presented both an extended parody of experimental science and a vision of a terrifying superweapon, a flying island used by its rulers literally to crush any earthly opposition to their tyranny. Voltaire took a similar stance in *Micromégas* (1732), notable as the first known story of visitors from other planets: two giants, one from Saturn and one from a planet of the star Sirius, who mock the follies of the diminutive earthlings.

But science was not to be halted by warnings and ridicule. The following year Benjamin Franklin reported to the Royal Society his experimental control of electricity. Within a few decades, quantitative change would become qualitative; in other words, there would be a true Industrial Revolution. On the eve of the resulting political revolutions in America and France, Louis-Sébastien Mercier's remarkable *The Year 2440* (1771) foresees a marvelous society based on reason and science: each youth's first communion involves seeing the macrocosm through a telescope and the microcosm through a microscope. Both George Washington and Thomas Jefferson owned a copy of this extremely popular science fiction novel.

By the end of the eighteenth century and the opening of the nineteenth, the early forms of European capitalism—featuring merchants, bankers, and ruthlessly efficient organization of handicrafts—were being replaced by industrial capitalism, which was beginning its global conquest. Modern science was providing the technological means to develop large factories, rapid large-scale transportation, and new energy sources. The drive to find huge quantities of coal to power the steam engines of industrial capitalism led to a re-conception of time as profound as the Copernican re-conception of space. Coal, after all, consists of fossils from remote geological ages. To discover vast deposits in the Earth's geological strata, industrial society had to discard the dominant theory of cosmic time—Bishop Ussher's dating of the creation of the universe to 4004 BC—and recognize that the Earth's age must be measured in billions of years. Only on such a scale was it possible first to comprehend the time necessary for geological evolution and then to conceive of biological evolution.

This transformation also gave profound new meaning to the concepts of the *alien* and *alienation*, two themes central to modern SF. Under industrial capitalism, vast numbers of people were soon spending their lives working for a handful of capitalists who owned everything the people produced, including the factories, coal mines, railroads, and ships. Not only were the workers thus alienated from the means of production and their own products, but they also found themselves increasingly alienated from nature, from each other, and from their own essence as creative beings. Human creativity now appeared in the form of monstrous *alien* forces exerting ever-growing power over the people who had created them.

Thus it was not mere coincidence that the emergence of industrial capitalism was accompanied by a wave of "gothic" literature, focusing on the horrible, the weird, and the catastrophic. Reflecting social, economic, and psychological realities, gothic SF tended to indulge in the irrational and to speculate desperately about humanity's loss of control over its own vastly potent creativity and creations. In this category we might even include Reverend Thomas Malthus's *On Population,* his 1798 pseudo-scientific fantasy of a disastrously over-populated planet where there were not enough food supplies and other resources to support so many people. Malthus's prophecy so far has been proven false. Under capitalism, population does not grow faster than production but quite the reverse, for technology grows even faster. The endemic crisis characteristic of capitalism thus seems so irrational that even its name is absurd—overproduction, leading to continual economic crises and wars designed partly to destroy excess production. Here again, creations (products) face their creators (producers) as alien monsters.

From this matrix emerged what Brian Aldiss has so aptly labeled the "first great myth of the industrial age" (23) in the form of a novel that many now accept as the progenitor of modern SF: Mary Shelley's *Frankenstein; or, The Modern Prometheus* (1818). Then, less than a decade after *Frankenstein,* Shelley created one of the first SF visions of the end of the world; the title character of her *The Last Man* (1826) wanders alone over a planet ravaged by war and disease, sampling the useless achievements of all human society on a world with a population of one. Mary Shelley set this scene in the year 2100.

The nineteenth century was the first in which life was continually being metamorphosed by technological change. The century began with the first experimental locomotive in 1801, advanced through the airship in 1852, and ended with the first experimental airplane in the late 1890s. In that century came the first practical steamboat, the screw propeller, the bicycle, and the automobile. Agriculture was being revolutionized by the invention of the harvester, the disc cultivator, the reaper, and the mowing machine. The electric battery appeared in the opening year of the century; the electromagnet, the cathode ray tube, and the magnetic tape recorder mark the successive quarters. The history of capitalism can be traced in the inventions of the adding machine, the calculating machine, the punch time clock, the cash register, the stock ticker, and punch-card accounting. Basic commodities such as industrial steel, vulcanized rubber, and portland cement were all nineteenth-century innovations. There appeared those special hallmarks of modern times: dynamite, the rapid-fire pistol, the repeating rifle, barbed wire, and the machine gun. The means of communication and artistic creation changed with the introduction of photography, the phonograph, the fountain pen (and the ballpoint), the typewriter, the telegraph, the telephone, radio, and the movie machine. Before the end of the century appeared several brief SF movies.

America proved especially hospitable to SF, even before the genre acquired a name. Many of the leading figures of antebellum fiction—including Washington Irving, James Fenimore Cooper, Nathaniel Hawthorne, Edgar Allan Poe, and Herman Melville—made important contributions to the form. How then did SF get its bad name as "sub-literary"?

With the triumph of industrial capitalism in the Civil War, there emerged a newly literate mass audience of boys and young men intrigued by the opportunities of fame and fortune in science and technology. Aimed directly at this readership was the science fiction "dime" novel, with its teenage boy genius as hero, first presented in Edward Ellis's seminal *The Steam Man of the Prairie* (1865). Between the Civil War and World War I, the most popular form of literature in America was the dime novel, and its SF versions were to have a formative influence on American culture. Only when it became an influential form of mass entertainment did SF come to be disdained as vulgar and puerile.

But it is precisely at this point that the story of SF becomes central to the story of contemporary culture in industrialized societies. The contemporaries of the science fiction dime novel are formative science fiction writers such as Jules Verne, Edward Bellamy, Mark Twain, and, most influentially, H. G. Wells, whose works form a prominent bridge into the twentieth century. After all, it was Wells who not only coined the term "atomic bomb" in his 1914 novel *The World Set Free* but also described how it could work, both technically and politically.

After these early years, the story of twentieth century and then twenty-first-century SF becomes ever more rich, complex, vital, and contentious. For struggling in all the varied print, visual, and electronic forms of SF are cultural forces whose dynamic is shaping the present and the future of the human species.

notes

1. Robert Philmus argues that this "is the first work that can properly be called" SF.
2. For a detailed discussion of the remarkable *Epigone*, see Paul Alkon's insightful history and analysis of fictions set in the future.

suggestions for further reading

Aldiss, Brian with David Wingrove. *Trillion Year Spree: The History of Science Fiction*. London: Paladin Grafton Books, 1988.

Alkon, Paul K. *Origins of Futuristic Fiction*. Athens: University of Georgia Press, 1987.

Bleiler, Everett with Richard J. Bleiler. *Science-Fiction: The Early Years*. Kent, Ohio: Kent State University Press, 1990.

Franklin, H. Bruce. *Future Perfect: American Science Fiction of the 19th Century*. New Brunswick, NJ: Rutgers University Press, 1995.

Gunn, James. *The Road to Science Fiction, Volume 1: From Gilgamesh to Wells*. Lanham, MD: Scarecrow Press, 2002.

3
narrative strategies in science fiction
brian stableford

There is an important sense in which the heterocosmic (that is to say, analogies between creating art and creating the universe) constructions of science fiction stand in crucial and fundamental opposition to those of folkloristic fantasy. Folkloristic fantasy imagines heterocosmic motifs as things that existed "once upon a time" but have now been eroded away by thinning. Science fiction, by contrast, imagines heterocosmic motifs as innovations: things that have not yet been discovered or invented, but might be. Unlike folkloristic fantasy, science fiction does not assume that our thin world has long been and still is getting perennially thinner—in the sense defined by John Clute in *The Encyclopedia of Fantasy*—but the reverse: that our world may be fatter than it seems, because it is pregnant with all manner of new possibilities, and will certainly get fatter in times to come.

Science fiction has its intrusive fantasies, in which the known world is disrupted by a technological innovation or an alien incursion of some kind. It has its portal fantasies, in which the protagonist sets off in a spaceship, or a time machine, or travels through some kind of interdimensional gateway, to arrive in a different world. It has its immersive fantasies, which plunge the reader directly into an imagined future, alien world, or alternative history, whose characters are native to it.

Intrusive fantasy and portal fantasy both have a "natural" story-arc built into them. The heterocosmic element in intrusive fantasy functions according to an obvious chaotic method to bring closure to such a story: the chaotic must be banished again, and normality restored. The characters who dealt with the intrusion may or may not be richer for the experience but the chaotic must be put away regardless. Similarly, the "natural" conclusion to a portal fantasy is the return home; far travelers have to return to tell their stories, just as all visionary dreamers must eventually wake up. The characters in portal fantasies are almost always expected to be richer for their experience, no matter how relieved they are to have returned, but that wealth is usually the sort that has to be cashed in at home.

The fact that the natural tendency of both these kinds of story is towards closure is very convenient for storytellers, not only because it helps to keep the stories neat and tidy, but because storytellers' audiences have always loved satisfactory closure. A concluding "and they lived happily ever after" was once as standardized as an opening "once upon a time"; although its explicit formulation has grown tired, it is still the most convenient and popular way to end a story.

In folkloristic fantasy, the normalizing closure of the story-arc has a built-in propriety. Because the intrusion comes from the mythic past, and the milieu preserved in the portal fantasy is a relic of that past, there is a fundamental sense in which they do not *belong* in the thinned-out world. No matter how life-enhancing an intrusion may occasionally be, or how valuable the education may be that the world beyond the portal provides, their imaginary time is over; the world no longer has space to accommodate them, and never will again. In science fiction, by contrast, the opposite is true; the normalizing story-arc is intrinsically opposed to the notion of a world whose thinness is temporary and remediable, and the removal from stories of the heterocosmic innovations of science fiction is inherently inappropriate.

In early clashes between this inherent lack of propriety and the convenience of the normalizing story-arc, the normalizing story-arc was bound to win. Mary Shelley's *Frankenstein* (1818) is no different from other Gothic novels, all of which—whether their dénouements "rationalized" their supernatural apparitions or merely subjected them to ritual exorcism—tended towards normalizing endings. Victor Frankenstein, however, discovered his resurrection technology by means of the scientific method; even though he and the "monster" he creates are both destroyed, the logic of the situation is that the technique will be rediscovered and applied repeatedly, until the resurrected dead are as significant a human population as the naturally born. In order to preserve the immense convenience of the normalizing story-arc, however, that logical consequence had simply to be ignored—as similar consequences have been in countless *Frankenstein* clones in which inventions or alien incursions prove troublesome and are destroyed, often along with their facilitators.

Although this kind of "Gothic science fiction" is logically flawed, the majority of works that warrant description as science fiction—including almost all of those in the fringe subgenre of "technothrillers"—are intrusive fantasies in which every technological innovation and every alien incursion is conceived as a horrid monstrosity crying out to be put away by the deadly-but-satisfying thrust of a normalizing story-arc.

One consequence of the convenience of the intrusive fantasy formula, with its built-in normalizing story-arc is, therefore, that if science fiction is seen as a collective entity then its dominant voice loudly proclaims that all technological innovation, and everything not yet discovered, is inherently evil. This opinion, while by no means unrepresented in the real world, runs directly contrary to the fundamental assumptions of scientific and technological endeavor, one of which is that the world can be, might be, and routinely is improved by new discoveries and technological innovations. Writers ambitious to employ fiction as a means of celebrating the intellectual achievements of science and the life-enhancing potential of technology have therefore found themselves in an embarrassing situation.

Portal SF stories are not as restrictive as intrusive SF stories, but they are more difficult to contrive, especially in respect of futuristic scenarios. The necessity of returning from the expedition through the portal reduced all futuristic fantasies to the status of dreams before H. G. Wells invented a time machine, and that was a device which soon generated a whole spectrum of new corollary problems, in terms of opportunities to change past history and the hazards of so doing. The necessity of the final return tends to rob all portal fantasies of the dynamic element crucial to progressive imagery; singular trips in spaceships also tend to resemble visionary dreams. As with intrusive SF, the logic of the situation is that once a demonstration has been made by a portal fantasy of what the scientific method can reveal and produce in other circumstances, the mortality of the present's "normality" becomes obvious, and its entitlement to function as a privileged situation to which all story-arcs must lead is lost.

The problem of adapting the narrative strategies of intrusive and portal fantasy to science fiction could have been avoided if writers had been more easily able to write immersive science fiction, because immersive fantasy is not cursed with the same "natural" story-arc as intrusive and portal fantasy. The readability of immersive fantasy had, however, always depended on the fact that readers were at least as familiar with the mythic past as they were with the historical past and the experienced present. Science fiction stories set in hypothetical futures, alien worlds or alternative histories had no such recourse. Writers and readers of folkloristic fantasy could bring to bear a coherent series of assumptions about the likely contents and dynamics of a heterocosmic creation with a simple narrative formula like "once upon a time"—but those assumptions were not merely useless but actively antipathetic to what writers of immersive science fiction needed to do.

Immersive science fiction stories written before 1900 invariably came equipped with a "metanarrative preface": an introductory essay explaining to readers what the writer is about to do, and providing a kind of imaginative "handle" that readers could use to get their bearings within the story. Writers of such stories routinely assumed that the ideative apparatus required by readers for the navigation of the heterocosmic milieu would also require continual supplementation by authorial intrusion. In effect, the metanarrative preface that every nineteenth-century example of immersive futuristic fantasy carries serves the same function as a portal in a portal fantasy. It starts readers off in the familiar world and then leads them by the hand into an unfamiliar one. Because a manifest authorial voice is required to do the leading, however, such stories cannot take full advantage of the narrative techniques that had been developed by novelists for encouraging reader identification with characters, which had made authorial devices far more discreet, tending gradually towards invisibility. A metanarrative preface is, by necessity, a massive expository lump.

As the twentieth century began, therefore, writers of immersive futuristic fiction found themselves at odds with broader patterns in the evolution of fictional technique. Writers of fantasies using the apparatus of the mythic past were not as far out of step, because they were free to develop intrusive and portal fantasies without running into any logical problems, but SF writers found that it was intrinsically easier to write about futuristic heterocosms from the distanced viewpoints of hypothetical historians or satirical commentators than to display them through the innocent eyes of its native inhabitants.

The formal metanarrative preface began to fade away after 1900, as writers increasingly attempted to embed the informational substance of such prefaces within the story rather than presenting it as something essentially extraneous. No matter how adroitly the "back-story" of the heterocosmic world within the text was woven into the narrative, however, the problems of initial introduction and periodic supplementation remained. Even readers who were tolerant of expository lumps of background information could not help having difficulty in orientating themselves within science-fictional heterocosms; the principal costs of their being provided with the necessary guidance were awkward narrative flow and characters with whom it was difficult to identify.

The necessity of getting over the hurdle of the metanarrative preface was the principal reason for the unusually immense importance within the history of labeled science fiction of the science fiction magazine. The title of such a magazine functioned as a device to inform readers of what to expect—or, at least, what not to expect—when they began the immersive fantasies contained within their covers. The act of reading is intrinsically akin to stepping through a portal, and the packaging of books plays an important role in assisting readers to orientate themselves within the texts they contain; such packaging is more important with respect to heterocosmic texts than with simulative ones, and much more important with respect to heterocosmic texts that cannot rely on universal assumptions about the mythic past. The portals provided by early SF magazines were decorated with illustrations and blurbs that helped enormously to point readers in the rough direction of each heterocosm they were about to enter. Such stepping-stones were invaluable in the tacit quest of those early SF magazines, which was the rough outlining of a "mythic future" that could take the place, to the extent that was possible, of the mythic past of folkloristic fiction.

* * *

It was probably inevitable, although there is a certain perversity about it, that many aspects of the nebulous "mythic future" which came to be assumed by the writers and readers of early SF magazines are straightforward transfigurations of the mythic past. The groundwork for such transfigurations had already been laid by the late nineteenth-century occult revival, which had relabeled many varieties of magic in order to clothe them more respectably for a post-Enlightenment world. The new jargon of telepathy, teleportation, precognition, and other items of "parapsychology," was avidly adopted into science fiction, such "wild talents" being represented as evidences of a latent superhumanity whose flowering was yet to come rather than mythic relics sieved out of everyday experience by thinning.

Of all the futuristic technologies that early magazine SF writers imagined and attempted to integrate into a consensus view of the likely course of the future, one particular image gained a unique priority: the spaceship. Magazine science fiction rapidly developed an intimate relationship with the idea of space travel, and—more importantly—the idea that space travel was likely to provide the central theme of future history. Within a decade of the appearance of the first SF magazine in the USA, the fundamental "mythic future" on whose ready-made understanding much magazine SF depended was the myth of a coming Space Age, in which the central story of the future would be the expansion of the human species to other worlds.

The myth of the Space Age became a handy container for other oft-used elements in science-fictional futures. Earthbound futures, especially repressive ones, were routinely provided with literally uplifting endings by the iconic image of a "cosmic breakout." The notion that a galaxy-spanning society of Earth-clone worlds might ultimately be established—and often then withdrawn so as to re-isolate the imagined worlds—became a handy framework for all manner of exotic human and alien societies. Space travel became a kind of infinitely, elastic portal connecting all manner of possible worlds, so that stories beginning in relatively simple and familiar futuristic scenarios could make rapid progress into the unknown.

There were important parallel developments in magazine SF—the most significant involving the investigation of potential corollaries of the idea of time travel, whose ultimate extrapolation was the notion of an infinite array of alternative histories packaged in a multiverse of parallel worlds—but such developments never threatened the dominance of the Space Age as a mythic future. The multiverse of alternative histories was much more extensively used for retrospective analyzes of the logic of past history than as a device for the projection of alternative futures.

The association of science fiction with the idea of space travel now seems so intimate and intrinsic that it is hard to imagine alternative histories in which it never happened. The European subgenre of scientific romance, however—which retained an independent existence and evolution until the end of World War II—always regarded space travel as a peripheral issue of little significance to the future of humankind. To the extent that scientific romance had a consensual image of the future, that consensus saw the future in terms of social and physical evolution, intrinsically earthbound, at least unless and until the uninhabitability of the Earth might face a desperate interplanetary migration. There is not the least trace of a Space Age future in scientific romance. Far from being the obvious and inevitable development that hindsight makes it seem, magazine science fiction's development of the mythic future of the Space Age actually requires closer examination and more detailed explanation.

The popularity of the spaceship as an iconic image of American SF was not so much a result of its likelihood as an actual technological development—although the first US-launched moon landing did take place a mere 40 years into the genre's history—but its resonance with more recent and more localized "mythic past" than the elastic fabrication of folklore.

As soon as history became the substance of naturalistic fiction, the tendency to distort it for literary as well as political reasons subjected it to the same pressures of intrinsic narrative form and audience appeal that had previously been exerted by storytellers on mythic history. History, in large measure, became a narrative in itself—or, more accurately, a series of narratives. The tentative mythic futures that are discernible in European scientific romance do not differ very much between Britain, France, and Germany; in those nations, the history of the future is seen as a continuation of a long past history rooted in Classical Greece and Rome, extrapolating clearly perceptible social and technological progress continually blighted and hindered by the tendency of neighboring nations to fight and invade one another. The USA, on the other hand, saw its own past very differently: as something recently started, after a bold and conclusive break with European history, in which social and technological progress had been quite spectacular, relatively uninhibited by local conflicts. Although the USA had been involved in numerous wars since its founding in the War of Independence, such internecine conflicts as the Civil War and the Indian Wars had been easily construed as instruments and aspects of progress, while international conflicts had been (and still are) construed as attempts to spread progressive American Enlightenment to various dark continents.

Because the USA was a recently founded nation on a recently discovered continent, the USA had no residual folklore of its own; the folklore imported by immigrants from Europe had been set aside with other redundant aspects of the European heritage, and Native American folklore had been put away in a more definite fashion. The USA's "mythic past" was, therefore, derived from—or, rather, imposed upon—its historical past, and its central narrative thread was a stirring tale of westward expansion, of pioneering and frontiersmanship, in which the magic of the European mythic past was largely replaced by weaponry, especially the talismanic Colt revolver.

Given all this, it is hardly surprising that American science fiction, unlike European scientific romance, developed a consensus image of a future of expansion, shaped by pioneers and frontiersmen, who would colonize the solar system and the galaxy as American immigrants had colonized the West. On the "final frontier" of space, the spaceship replaced the covered wagon, Mars and Earth-clone worlds orbiting other stars replaced Texas and California, the blaster replaced the Colt revolver, and all wars were wars of progressive social enlightenment.

In much the same way that magazine writers transfigured ancient myths into SF, they also transfigured Westerns—indeed, they routinely conflated the two processes, spaceships becoming not merely the constituents of interplanetary wagon trains but also chariots of the gods. Many writers felt embarrassed about this, much as they had felt embarrassed about yielding to the pressure of normalizing story-arcs, but their protestations often rang hollow.

* * *

The USA was not the only twentieth-century nation that conceived of itself as the product of a recent, radical, and irrevocable historical break; the USSR also represented itself as a post-Revolutionary cauldron of progress. It did not develop science fiction of the same sort but it did invest heavily enough in actual space technology to launch Sputnik into orbit in 1957, thus provoking the USA into a "space race," which was inevitably construed by American SF writers and readers as the first phase of a Space Age.

The early phases of the space race seemed to many SF enthusiasts to constitute a justification of the majority decision taken by their own founding fathers, but it was not without cost. When the actual moon landing took place, it quickly proved to be an end rather than a beginning, a small step after which no further step, let alone any giant leap, was practicable. Although euphoria clouded judgment, at the time, the revelation that the moon landing was not the beginning of a Space Age at all provoked a crisis in the history of subgeneric science fiction, by making it glaringly obvious that its mythic future had little or nothing to do with potential patterns of technological and social progress, and had not, after all, escaped the fanciful toils of the broader genre of fantasy.

Although the exposure of the mythic future of the Space Age as a naked emperor seemed to its most fervent adherents to be a terrible tragedy, there remains a sense in which the dependence of science fiction on any kind of mythic future had always been a regrettable handicap. In much the same way that the sum total of normalizing intrusive science fiction stories suggests that all innovation is evil, so the sum total of stories set in the mythic future of the Space Age suggests that some such future is at least the most desirable, and perhaps the inevitable, shape that the future might take.

Various strategies have been tried since 1969 to find new mythic futures, whose basic assumptions might assist readers to navigate a course through texts affiliated to such myth-sets. The most loudly touted was cyberpunk mythology, which found a new final frontier in the wilderness of cyberspace, where nerds could become super-powered cowboys and to which artificial intelligences could provide bespoke pantheons. Almost as soon as they were manifest, however, the basic suppositions of cyberpunk were plundered to prove a rescue package for a New Space Age, hastily revamped as a post-human project whose principal protagonists would be AIs and genetically engineered cyborgs, the latter being conveniently freed from the unfortunate frailties of flesh that made a human Space Age no longer imaginable. Both of these developments, however, were able to take considerable advantage—in their variety as well as their rate of evolution—of the education that half a century of labeled SF had laid on for its readers.

Although the ability of a large population of readers to draw upon a ready-made understanding of a mythic past or a mythic future is a considerable asset to a writer desirous of drawing readers into a heterocosmic construction and assisting them to navigate comfortably within it, it is not an absolute necessity. Just as many nineteenth- and twentieth-century readers became gradually more adept at responding to the devices used by naturalistic novelists to create a sensation of synthetic experience, so some twentieth-century readers of SF became gradually more adept at responding to the devices used by SF writers to figure out exactly what kind of heterocosm, out of all the multitudinous possibilities, they might be dealing with. Writers and habitual readers of the subgenre quickly cultivated an expertise in the extrapolation of various standard premises, which allowed them to enter into increasingly complex collaborative explorations.

The initial effect of this process was to make science fiction into an esoteric subgenre accessible only to initiates, resulting in the growth of a manifest society of SF fans, whose communications were mediated through fanzines and conventions. As time went by, though, the relevant skills became far more generalized, especially when the imaginative produce of magazine SF began to be adapted for TV and the cinema in the 1960s. As the number of viewers capable of understanding immersive science fiction narratives on TV increased steadily, the number of readers capable of handling heterocosmic materials in text form with consummate ease became so large that the boundaries between genres and subgenres began to disintegrate, not only at the literary end of the marketing spectrum but in the sturdiest strongholds of genre marketing.

Few habitual SF readers are nowadays in need of the crutch provided by a mythic future, and the number of genre fantasy readers who require the crutch of a mythic fantasyland is also in steep decline. Habitual readers are in general much more adept than they once were at following the logic of heterocosmic modifications of naturalistic scenarios, although the privilege afforded to dogmatically faithful simulacra has too much historical inertia to die easily. On the other hand, the number of habitual readers is steadily declining in Europe and the USA, largely because it is not being renewed in the lower deciles of the demographic spectrum.

The principal reason for the gradual erosion of the reading habit is competition from other media. The phenomenon is undoubtedly exaggerated, however, by the fact that reading fiction is nowadays a more difficult business than it used to be, simply because the skills it routinely requires are more elaborate. It is not surprising that many young people despair in advance of their ability to cultivate the skills required for the full appreciation of modern fiction, just as many adults despair in advance of their ability to cultivate the skills required to make full use of mobile phones. Although simple texts—especially simple heterocosmic constructions reliant on the mythic past or the mythic future of the Space Age—are by no means as difficult to obtain as simple mobile phones, the direction of the trend is obvious.

suggestions for further reading

Brooke-Rose, Christine. *A Rhetoric of the Unreal: Studies in Narrative and Structure, Especially of the Fantastic*. Cambridge, UK: Cambridge University Press, 1983.

Fishburn, Katherine. *The Unexpected Universe of Doris Lessing: A Study in Narrative Technique*. Westport, CT: Greenwood Press, 1985.

Rabkin, Eric S. *Narrative Suspense*. Ann Arbor, MI: University of Michigan Press, 1973.

Scholes, Robert. *Fabulation and Metafiction*. Urbana-Champaign, IL: University of Illinois Press, 1979.

Scholes, Robert, James Phelan, and Robert Kellogg. *The Nature of Narrative*. New York: Oxford University Press, 2006.

4
there is no such thing as science fiction
sherryl vint and mark bould

The apocalypse, it seems, is upon us. Suddenly, everywhere, walls are falling. Mutants and hybrids stalk the land. While Gary K. Wolfe (and others) points to the dissolution of science fiction (SF), fantasy and horror genres, the New Weird (and others) revels in blurring, splicing, sampling, dubbing and remixing them. And it is certainly true that fantastic fiction which violates the notion of genres as pure and distinct categories has achieved critical prominence and popular success in recent years. But claims of an epochal shift are typically based on an impoverished notion of genre and erase the history of these particular genres. In this essay, we will argue that that there never was such a *thing* as SF, while at the same time explaining how ways of producing, marketing, distributing, consuming and understanding texts as SF came into being and are in a constant, unending process of coming into being. We will consider how Tom Godwin's short story "The Cold Equations," published in *Astounding Science-Fiction* in 1954, was made into an exemplar of hard-SF and, drawing on a debate from the pages of *The New York Review of Science Fiction* in the 1990s, how it continues to be remade as such. We will demonstrate how the continued debate over its "true" meaning and importance to the SF canon reveals what is at stake when anyone asserts that SF is a *thing* with a single, clear and unified identity.

According to James Gunn, this story "encapsulate[s] the qualities" of SF, claiming that "if the reader doesn't understand it or appreciate what it is trying to say about humanity and its relationship to its environment, then that reader isn't likely to appreciate science fiction" (198, 199). This position relies on a particular reading of the story that accepts at face value its assertion that "there could be no alternative"

(200) to throwing the stowaway girl, Marilyn, out of the airlock to die because "no human in the universe can change" (206) the inflexible, scientific laws of mass and acceleration. If one appreciates the story in this way, one might admire its juxtaposition of human concerns (sympathy, innocence, justice, love) with the physics of space flight, and the neat setup in which the pilot, Barton, is compelled to sacrifice Marilyn in order to ensure the medical vaccine he is carrying reaches a distant colony world. Such an appreciation insists that the struggle to survive in the indifferent universe revealed by modern science which kills "with neither hatred nor malice" (220) is the proper matter of SF, and that Marilyn must be seen as "x, the unwanted factor in a cold equation" rather than "a sweet-faced girl in her teens" (213). Consequently, Gunn states, anyone who "keeps objecting that the ship should have posted a more specific warning" or "that the pilot should have found a way to sacrifice himself in order to save the girl...isn't reading the story correctly" (199). However many objections one might raise while reading the story, the reader, like Marilyn, must ultimately accept her fate. (One might even imagine oneself as resembling the story's intrepid frontiersmen, confronting the harsh realities of the universe, rather than readers of other genres who, like the inhabitants of "safe-and-secure Earth" (211), avoid these truths.)

Gunn's position is not without merit or adherents. Rather than countering it, we want to draw attention to its policing of reading strategies. It establishes certain elements as worthy of critical attention while relegating others to the background, and thus fashions and presents a particular version of SF as the only correct one. According to Gunn, the story is about the incontrovertible physical laws of the universe, and is "so purified, so stripped of distracting detail, that the...message shines through undiminished" (198).

But the story is packed with such detail. Taking account of it—as John Huntington and Andy Duncan (among others) have done—reveals much about the ideological underpinnings of the story's supposed scientific neutrality and constructs a very different understanding of SF. Arguably, it is only by attending to the detail dismissed by certain readings that one can truly appreciate US magazine SF in the 1950s. For example, Marilyn's fate is not merely the product of mass, acceleration and fuel supply, but is instead grounded in contingent human decisions and procedures. It is not the cold equations of ballistics which condemn her to death but rather "Paragraph L, Section 8, of Interstellar Regulations: *Any stowaway discovered in an EDS shall be jettisoned immediately following discovery*" (200; italics in original). One could imagine other sets of regulations which instead mandated the inspection of all spacecraft prior to launch or the inclusion of a safety margin of extra fuel. Gunn might insist that in this scenario such safety measures are not viable because the entire system of supplying the colonies is based on a careful rationing of hyperspace cruisers and fuel in which a single "delay would destroy their schedule and produce a confusion and uncertainly that would wreck the complex interdependence between old Earth and new worlds of the frontier" (200). Our point is simply that these "facts" in the story are the products of human decisions. The story not only unquestioningly accepts colonialism but also imagines a human "Galactic expansion" (200) which does not allow margins of error. Similarly, the summary execution of a stowaway driven by poverty and an enforced decade-long separation from her brother indicates that this future society privileges such expansion over the quality of terrestrial life and personal relationships. Here and elsewhere, the story conflates physical laws with human rules, thereby denying responsibility for consequences which at least in part reflect the priorities of human political and economic policies.

Debates about the story's meaning have often centered on gender. Huntington and Duncan both point to a barely concealed violence towards women—its disbelief in women as real people, its desire to punish and eject female interlopers from the masculine-colonial project. Catherine Mintz argues that it is a story in which women are put in their place (off the spaceship, out of SF), a reading Taras Wolansky insists is "not supported by the facts" (19), arguing instead that the story develops a contrast between the dangerous frontier and secure Earth, not between men and women. Wolansky is not wrong that the story tries very hard to suggest that Marilyn's death has only to do with her breaking a law, not merely "a law of men's choosing" but one "made imperative by the circumstances of the space frontier" (Godwin: 200). At the same time, the entire story depends upon the fact that the stowaway is "not a man" but a "girl in her teens" (202), and so it is at the very least disingenuous to suggest, as does Darrell Schweitzer, that the story has nothing to do with "sexual politics at the time" about which "neither [editor] Campbell nor Godwin were thinking" (23). The story *is* about the harsh laws of the universe which kill without appeal to one's moral qualities or emotions, but it is also—and *equally*—about gender in the 1950s (just as it is equally about colonialism). Barton has few qualms about killing the stowaway when he supposes it to be a man, but when he is confronted with Marilyn, "standing before him in little white gypsy sandals with the top of her brown, curly head hardly higher than his shoulder, with a faint, sweet scent of perfume coming from her" (202), he no longer finds it quite so easy to accept that ejecting stowaways is "the law, and there could be no appeal" (200). The story works hard to reinforce the premise that space and the frontier are not for women: Marilyn jeopardizes the lives of Barton and colonists, "causes" her own death and also threatens Barton's masculinity as he hesitates in his duty. Before the cold equations prevail, Marilyn, "contrary to regulations," lives a full hour past the time her presence is discovered rather than being executed "*immediately*" (200; italics in original). This requires Barton to violate the prohibition against pilots making "changes in the course or degree of deceleration the computers had set" (209). When a woman enters space, she brings the potential for deviation and disaster with her.

Apparently, when Godwin first submitted "The Cold Equations" to *Astounding*'s editor, John W. Campbell, Jr., it had a happy ending in which an innovative technological solution was found and Marilyn survived. Much of its power, Gunn argues, derives from the reader being "conditioned to expect that the girl's life will be saved at the end, as in thousands of other stories" (198). While Campbell "was not unwilling to see humanity destroyed by natural forces, ... he preferred [endings] in which humanity survives by means of its vigor or cunning or dogged determination" (198). The centrality of Marilyn's gender to the story conflict, coupled with this deviation from an otherwise dominant Campbellian norm regarding human ingenuity, further suggests that the story has as much to do with imagining space as a manly place as with human survival in an uncaring universe.

Godwin floods the space between "a man-made law that said KEEP OUT" and its penalty—"not of men's making or desires and [which] men could not revoke" (210)—with a sentimentality which obscures the story's conflation of physical and human laws. At the same time as the story depends upon (attempted) pathos—we are repeatedly told that Marilyn's death is a tragedy because she is not guilty of anything other than innocence, that "she could not be blamed for her ignorance" of the laws of space that must "of necessity, be as hard and relentless as the environment that gave them birth" (203)—it denies room in space (and SF) for such womanly things as sentiment, affect and emotion. (The story seems not to recognize its own tendency toward the kind of sentimental, manly melodrama, often found in Westerns, of leaving behind "soft winds and warm suns, music and moonlight and gracious manners" to trek a "hard, bleak frontier" (211).) The reader is encouraged to see a parallel between the story's conclusion and a tornado that strikes the colony "without warning; a thundering, roaring destruction that sought to annihilate all that lay before it" but does so "with neither malice nor intent" (212). The analogy does not hold, however. The tornado begins as "no more than great gentle masses of air over the calm Western Sea," but their interaction produces deadly, destructive winds which "destroyed the labor of months and...doomed six men to die," before reverting once again to "gentle masses of air" (212). The circumstances that transform stowing away into a death sentence are not "natural," like the meeting of air masses, but human-made. We have already suggested that Marilyn's easy access to the ship and its lack of fuel for contingencies reflect an economic and political system that privileges profit—although it would undoubtedly be called "efficiency"—over other considerations. We should also consider the social circumstances which led to Marilyn stowing away. If Marilyn is not to blame for her ignorance, who is? An education system which has retained a gendered division of disciplines? Her family is not well-off, and her brother "has been sending money home all the time to us" (203), paying for her course in linguistics. The conditions under which her brother and others in the survey crew labor mean that he has not been able to visit home for "ten years, not since he left Earth" (202). Stowing away is her only option if she wishes to see him.

These and similar details reveal that more is at stake than simply the cold equations of physics—such as the equally but differently cold equations of capitalist expansion which ensure that the colonization happens as quickly and "efficiently" as possible, with little regard for the increased risks involved for those living in isolated, frontier conditions or the heightened human cost of these efforts when laborers are separated from their families for long periods of time. These other cold equations also see the indigenous peoples of colonized worlds dispossessed and reduced to "do[ing] the cleaning in the Ship's Supply office" (204).

Schweitzer considers attention to such details as "baggage" which distracts the reader from what "the story was *supposed* to be about," namely that "Nature kills without appeal" (23). The purifying impulse behind Schweitzer's desire to eject such matters from consideration is suggested by his fancy that to help make up for the excess fuel consumed in the first half of the flight Barton could further reduce the ship's mass by going "to the bathroom out of the airlock for the remainder of the journey" (23). His equation, however unintentional, of rational subjectivity with the white masculine mind and of egested matter with peoples of color, women and the body is, to say the least, instructive. David Stewart Zink pursues a similar purification when he argues that those who raise objections to Gunn's reading of the story "aren't trying to understand" but "attempting a political maneuver to reposition the story as an example of the horror of rationality" (19).

Our point is a different one, both simpler and more complex. We agree with Gunn and others that, in some ways, one cannot understand SF without understanding this story's dominant meaning, its focus on science and physical laws instead of human political choices. At the same time, however, neither can one understand the story (or SF) without simultaneously acknowledging its erasures of women and indigenous people and its suppression of the human costs of colonization. "The Cold Equations" can be seen as exemplifying the type of SF preferred by Campbell, whose editorship of *Astounding* had a profound influence on the nature of US magazine SF, especially in the 1940s. However, as our discussion of some of the various ways in which the story can be understood demonstrates, it is not through any "essential" characteristic that it achieves its canonical status within the genre. Rather, the story's meaning and relative status—whether triumphantly or regretfully as an exemplar of (a certain kind of) SF (in a certain period)—results from an ongoing process of negotiation as different readers read it differently, beginning before its publication when Campbell required a rewritten ending and still continuing today. And just as these conflicting readings show that the story is not a *thing* with a singular, unique and bounded existence, they demonstrate the same thing about the genre.

In *Film/Genre*, Rick Altman elaborates upon this idea: genres are never, as frequently perceived, objects which already exist in the world and which are subsequently studied by genre critics, but fluid and tenuous constructions made by the interaction of various claims and practices by writers, producers, distributors, marketers, readers, fans, critics and other discursive agents. Genres come into being "after the fact." Selected features of existing texts are eventually recognized, for a multitude of reasons, by discursive agents as collectively forming a genre. A key driving force in the creation of genre is the commercial impulse to reproduce textual characteristics which have sold well to the public and thus tend to guarantee a market for similar products. While critics might consider classical Hollywood A-budget movies in terms of genre, Altman argues, their producers typically de-emphasized genre in favor of promoting stars and spectacle so as to appeal to the broadest possible audience; it was only when marketing B-movies, which by definition lacked stars and spectacle, that genre became the primary means of product differentiation. (Altman offers the fascinating example of how Universal promoted *The Creature from the Black Lagoon* (1954) as SF rather than horror, while simultaneously connecting it to earlier monster movies,[1] most of them produced by Universal and only some of them typically considered SF, which they "regenrified" (and re-released) as SF films featuring "Hollywood's Prize Science-Fiction Creatures" (78–79).)

The after-the-fact creation and naming of SF as a distinct marketing category took place in such US pulp magazines of the late 1920s and early 1930s as *Amazing Stories, Science Wonder Stories, Air Wonder Stories, Astounding Stories, Scientific Detective Monthly* and *Miracle Science and Fantasy Stories.* By the time Campbell assumed the editorship of *Astounding*, an audience already existed who were prepared to seek out and read SF, sometimes to the exclusion of other genres. Like the B-movie, these magazines relied on niche-marketing in terms of fiction categories, while Campbell (and other editors) shaped SF in particular ways, establishing and policing boundaries by only publishing certain types of story, which in turn affected the kinds of stories being written. The critical reception of SF, by readers, fans, editors, critics and other discursive agents has often been preoccupied with the same kind of border-policing, trying to fix SF as one clearly defined *thing*—hence Gunn's assertion, embraced by many, that there are correct and incorrect ways to read "The Cold Equations" and understand SF.

Publishers had (and have) a rather different relationship to genre, publishing SF, along with detective fiction, romances, westerns and so on, as just one more type of fiction intended to reach a particular pre-constituted audience. This commercial categorization created the illusion of firm boundaries between genres; and the hierarchies of taste within a specific category, which would for example privilege *Astounding*'s hard-SF over *Planet Stories*'s supposedly lesser science fantasy, created a similar illusion that some texts within a genre are more pure than others. In this context, it made commercial sense to create a category called SF and, when it proved successful, for SF magazines to differentiate their product not only from other fiction categories but also from other SF magazines. Just as Barton ejected Marilyn from the airlock, so this new category ejected horror, fantasy, aviation stories, detective stories, and so on.[2] Likewise, *Astounding* ejected science fantasy and other kinds of SF deemed insufficiently "rational," such as the more colorful and exotic planetary romances and space operas; and such expulsions continue to be made by many readers of SF. Fashioning the genre in this way, of course, is precisely what created the tensions which produce the competing readings of a story like "The Cold Equations."

In *We Have Never Been Modern*, Bruno Latour identifies two "modern" impulses: the first separates and purifies; the second creates hybrids. Intriguingly, it is the action of the former, imposing a grid of meaning on the world, which enables the latter. Without first dividing the world into separate phenomena with unique identities, one cannot produce—or identify—hybrids. Edgar Rice Burroughs's *A Princess of Mars* (1912) and H. P. Lovecraft's *At The Mountains of Madness* (1931) can only become, respectively, science fantasy and cosmic horror once SF, fantasy and horror have been made separate categories. Similarly, China Miéville's New Weird novel *Perdido Street Station* (2000) only appears to be a hybrid because of the inertial drag of such category distinctions. Some of the readings of "The Cold Equations" that we have outlined exemplify this purifying tendency in the discourse and practices of editors, critics and fans; the current focus on hybridity is simply a continuation of this same process. SF is increasingly a generic label for media other than print, and for many now their first or formative experience of SF will be in film, television, or games. Often the most profitable strategy for such media is to try to reach the widest audience possible, leading to the creation of texts to which various generic labels can be attached as different elements are foregrounded.

Altman argues that "genres are not inert categories shared by all ... but discursive claims made by real speakers for particular purposes in specific situations" (101). In one reading of "The Cold Equations," SF separates humans from the rest of the universe and justifies a *laissez-faire* attitude toward the consequences of colonial expansion by attributing these consequences to the laws of nature. Constraining the meaning of the story in this way makes claims about SF in order to defend a particular way of seeing the world which is neither neutral nor inevitable. In the second reading of the story, the genre is construed differently, as something bound up in historically contingent ideology and not "neutrally" about universal science. Rather, by considering the "distracting detail" and expanding the range of textual features deemed relevant in determining its meaning, such as its treatment of gender and colonialism, SF becomes about the social construction of science, the purposes it serves, and the ways in which the cold equations of physical science are deployed.

Of course, neither is the "true" meaning of the "The Cold Equations," nor the "correct" way to read it. To advocate an absolute relativity of meaning is as absurd as conjuring up the author's supposed intentions as the absolute demarcation of a story's meaning (and as such intentions can never truly be known, the latter is, like the former, merely an assertion of oneself as the arbiter of meaning). Instead, we want to draw attention to the complexity of texts and the meanings they are able to sustain, and to encourage a self-reflexivity about one's own reading which recognizes that all readings—including one's own and those with which one agrees—create their own criteria of judgment, typically in a circular and reinforcing manner. Being a "better" reader requires awareness that all hermeneutics have ideological investments and that interpretation needs to take account of these, as well as of the text. Therefore, we contend that understanding "The Cold Equations"—and SF more generally—is profoundly enriched by recognizing that genres are intersubjective, discursive constructs, full of contradictions and constantly in flux. That is why we say there is no such *thing* as science fiction.

notes

1. *Der Golem* (1920), *The Hunchback of Notre Dame* (1923), *The Phantom of the Opera* (1925), *Dracula* (1931), *Dr Jekyll and Mr Hyde* (1931), *Frankenstein* (1931), *The Mummy* (1932), *The Invisible Man* (1933), *The Wolf Man* (1941), *It Came from Outer Space* (1953), and *The War of the Worlds* (1953).
2. Also ejected were SF movies, movie serials, radio shows, comic strips, merchandizing, toys, games, expositions, worlds fairs, and so on.

suggestions for further reading

Altman, Rick. *Film/Genre*. British Film Institute, 1999.
Attebery, Brian. *Decoding Gender in Science Fiction*. New York: Routledge, 2002.
Latour, Bruno. *Aramis, or, The Love of Technology*. Translated by Catherine Porter. Cambridge, MA: Harvard University Press, 1996.
Luckhurst, Roger. *Science Fiction*. Cambridge, UK: Polity Press, 2005.
Rieder, John. *Colonialism and the Emergence of Science Fiction*. Middletown, CT: Wesleyan University Press, 2007.

part ii
science fiction and
popular culture

introduction to part ii

This section explains how science fiction's (SF) intersection with popular culture can provide access points for students who may be unfamiliar with the SF canon. The contributors read "science fiction and popular culture" as meaning a relationship between SF and technology. In other words, as Marshall McLuhan defined electricity as a medium without a message, the contributors describe electricity as the medium necessary to enable science fiction to communicate its extrapolative message via popular culture media. Electricity, then, is the "mechanical bride" (McLuhan's term) which enables science fiction to marry mass culture.

The contributors explore the reciprocity between science fiction's union with popular electronic media, each emphasizing how he reads science fiction in terms of his particular popular culture subject area and how these other media presentations can contribute to reading SF.

George Zebrowski invites students to consider what film SF has to offer. Isaac Asimov criticized film when he said that the visual is offered in place of the textual riches delivered in novels and stories. Yet visual SF can provide more, and has done so. If it can be written, Stanley Kubrick said, it can be filmed. He stressed that cinematic SF requires greater ingenuity to present ideas to viewers. In other words, thinking involves presentation which must include how ideas can be verbalized. The point is that dialogue in a film is crucial. Visual wit and power of suggestion can elicit thought in viewers, as can actors' performances which enable you to read characters' thoughts. Easier said than done! Hence, we do not have much of this sort of reading in SF films.

Where Zebrowski interprets SF film texts, Michael Cassutt is interested in SF television as a process. He observes that television series had little impact on the development of science fiction until the mid-1960s, when Gene Roddenberry's *Star Trek* exposed millions to sophisticated concepts of alien races, faster-than-light travel, and time paradoxes that had been familiar to readers of written SF for a generation. During the late 1980s and early 1990s, series like *Max Headroom*, *Star Trek: The Next Generation* and especially *The X-Files*, brought new concepts such as artificial intelligence, computer networks, and nanotechnology to television within years of their appearance in prose form. But as television has helped broaden the audience for written SF, it has also exhausted several classic SF tropes. Cassutt explores the transference of SF from page to stage, and the way in which this process changed SF.

Brooks Landon takes a radically different approach to the topic than either Zebrowski or Cassutt. He inverts McLuhan's dyad, making SF the medium and computers the message. He stresses that computers appear everywhere in science fiction. He notes that frequently their existence, particularly in older SF, is implicit rather than explicit, read "backward" into stories that were written before the need for "thinking machines" or "mechanical minds" was clear to writers who envisioned the future. Indeed, before the 1950s, SF did not much describe computers doing a very good job of anticipating their crucial role in technological change. Landon surveys the range of ways in which computers appear in science fiction and considers their particular privileging in a literature that valorizes rationality and genius. According to Landon, computers have been constructed in SF to represent everything from the ultimate threat to human existence to the ultimate path to transcendent wisdom. Reading SF involves recognizing that computers even compete with or replace reality itself in fictions about cyberspace or simulated reality.

Orson Scott Card melds the two perspectives to show that in video games, the functions of medium and message are inextricably intertwined, and have been since the days of the earliest games. Beginning with an image from SF which will make many think of Star Trek's Borg, Card describes the feedback loop that linked SF and video games from almost the originary moment, showing that representations of video games in SF and representations of SF in video games both played a role in shaping what is becoming the most popular art form of our day. He draws not only on SF-troped games such as *Galaga* and *Space Invaders*, but also on games like *Civilization* to go beyond the characteristic definition of SF to an operational one that links the core logic of both video games and SF. Then he goes beyond this linkage to show why video games (and SF) are crucial tools for life.

5
science fiction movies: the feud of eye and idea
george zebrowski

Science fiction (SF) film offers pictures, said Isaac Asimov, decrying film's poverty when it offers sights in place of the riches to be found in novels and stories. But if it can be written, as Stanley Kubrick liked to say, then it can be filmed, but requires ingenuity to present ideas to the viewer. Visual wit and power of suggestion elicit thought in the viewer, as can an actor's performance, in which you can read thoughts.

A subtler denial of any possible rapprochement between print SF and movies by some filmmakers and critics defends SF film as a wild popular form in which the intellectual constructions and thoughtfulness of written SF cannot work within the constraints of dialogue and action; others have continued to insist that film and SF can work together, that the eye need not war with intellect, that written SF's vivid pictorial imagery, glimpsed by the word-stimulated visual imaginations of writers and their readers, externalized on the covers of magazines and books and animated in films, need not drive out ideas. That to a large degree thought has been driven out of *both* print and visual forms, in this most thoughtful of literatures, whose critical views of the possible have come to us through theater, poetry, music, radio and film, stories and novels, is an irony and a cultural crime.

The view that our hopes and fears are the only subject matter of SF movies, and that failures of realism and scientific accuracy are inconsequential, makes *Godzilla* (1954 and 1956) just as significant as *2001: A Space Odyssey* (1968). Film criticism must content itself with a study of what is unique to films, with their expressiveness, with the visual skills applied to action. To demand otherwise is to be film illiterate. It is difficult if not impossible to create genuine SF films. There is just enough

truth in these views to confuse the defenders of "real SF." Can these
merits be reconciled, with neither film nor science fiction the loser?

Genuine SF itself is perhaps a literal impossibility, since no human arti-
fact stands outside of history; but SF strives to see "from outside," as do all
our arts; it is in this sense that SF of any kind is a failure, unable to reflect
complex future possibilities better than its own times. Defenders of pure
SF will say that this in fact is the Everest to be climbed, and that we must
try to keep as much of the past and present out of SF's imaginings. SF's
ambitions, of which there are few examples that succeed to significant
degrees, mirror the truth-hunting of science, its objective stance that
is all too often unflattering, if not humiliating, to traditional cultures,
which sometimes regard scientific objectivity as a naive illusion. There is
truth and delusion in both camps, and we progress by degrees.

Three monuments of SF film (*Metropolis*, *Things To Come*, and *2001:
A Space Odyssey*) illustrate degrees of success and failure as film and SF.
They are important in the history of film, and important thematically
as SF, provoking thought ranging beyond entertainment. Great-souled
one might say, because of the problems of change that they raise, and
the grace with which they do so. It is in such considerable achievements
that the often conflicting relationship between written and visual SF is
best revealed.

Fritz Lang's *Metropolis* (1926) evokes some thought, which must be
part of any work of SF, print or film, without which no SF is worthy of
the name; Lang's graceful accomplishment also succeeds as a movie.
Each of these qualities alone can make a good SF movie: good movie
but bad SF; good SF but bad movie; some mix of success and failure has
been the common result.

Metropolis reflects on the shameful and still denied reality of class warfare; the stark difference between the few and the many still persists;
wealth flows from the many to the fewest of the few. How did that happen? Despite all our available means to make a better world, we fail
because a better world would leave less for the few—less wealth with
which to buy military power, which insures economic gain. Justice
would put the few out of business. A world without effective violence,
either from the top or bottom, would not have today's masters—and
this is the point of Lang's *Metropolis*. Heart mediating between brain
and muscle is a simple answer to a complex problem, one which even
Lang found too easy, but the film's resolution is arrived at with great skill
and conviction and is essentially correct. It does no good to point out
that simple labor is given a ludicrous importance in the face of so much
technology, because we have enough needless and perverse human

labor today as examples. Technology can run cleanly and justly but it still does not. As with all great SF, the pendulum must swing between utopia and dystopia, and the only goal should be that the swing does not stop at one or the other.

Metropolis shows us a city, its machines, the deep hovels of the workers; an atmosphere of gloom and oppression envelops us with a fear of technology that yearns for a social correction. More through graceful longing than thought, but well enough to let us think the thoughts. Today's restored prints open the eyes.

* * *

Things To Come (1936) sends us forward through a century of changes. A world war ruins civilization; a period akin to our middle ages, but much shorter, follows, cut short by a resurgence of science and technology; a twenty-first century renaissance reaches for the stars despite opposition. H. G. Wells wrote the screenplay, and worked closely on the movie with Alexander Korda and William Cameron Menzies; Arthur Bliss wrote a vibrant musical score. A print author's thinking is a feature of all three films, which makes their success as SF no accident.

Things to Come has been both underrated and over praised, partly because of the poor surviving prints that give the viewer the equivalent of a book with missing pages; casual viewing cannot see past styles of presentation and has harmed the reputation of a drama that rises to great heights. The coming of war to the British Isles in 1940 still chills, but it provoked laughter when the bombers were shown in 1936. Images of a civilization ruined by this war, fighting plagues and living under local warlords, is a reality in today's world. The revolution of elite airmen and engineers who remake the world is stirring but also disturbing to modern audiences. The pitting of social concerns against a space program in the last third of the film is prophetic. The rhetoric is Shakespearian, delivered by fine actors, and against a starry sky in the finale gives us one of SF film's great moments of visionary hope.

Things To Come elicits both great liking and irritation, even from the same viewer at different times. An early sound film, its special effects suffer by today's standards, and its story creaks now and then. But we are all "temporal provincials" when we should be historians and time travelers, able to see beyond dated manners and speech to the great conflicts and ideas. The film captures a mood and presents ideas that are central to all great SF. H. G. Wells saw catastrophe as a midwife of progress, and this vision is reflected in the movie's consistently arresting design, which moves landscapes and masses of people through a vision of humanity's longing to overcome its pathological failings.

* * *

2001: A Space Odyssey (1968) showed what scientific accuracy combined with visual realism could do for written SF, in this case for the words of Arthur C. Clarke. As with the other two monuments of SF film, an SF writer worked on the screenplay and wrote the novel at the same time.

Clarke's prose marches wordlessly before us (and every image counts, so a blink misses much) as the story presents a nurturing program begun by a high civilization in our remote past. The project includes an alarm signal on the Moon (from Clarke's short story, "The Sentinel"), which attracts human explorers to the star gate around Jupiter, which is a trap to catch a sample specimen of humanity, which is then transformed into a more advanced being (the Star Child), who is then returned to Earth to continue the project. The first black monolith stimulates development among our pre-human ancestors; the monolith on the moon sends a signal to Jupiter to announce that our species has developed space travel; the expedition to Jupiter provides the sample (Bowman's journey through the star gate). The confrontation with the HAL-9000 artificial intelligence occurs because a rational mind has been lied to by suspicious, security-minded human planners.

Everything in this summary is *shown*, but is explicit in Clarke's novel. Once read, repeat viewings become easy; but the sense of initial mystery intrigued general audiences enough for viewers to search out their own explanations. Clarke's narrative unfolds before us in typically majestic, reflective steps, but visually—preserving Clarke's feelings for the natural wonder of the universe and for the preciousness of intelligent life. SF readers and film audiences were educated by the film's subtle story, which created its own audience, quite differently from the sequel, *2010*, where all was clearly presented to an audience that no longer needed the same level of wonder and mystery. Kubrick kept an eye on the making of Peter Hyams's 1985 film, and approved of the result.

The unavoidable criticism of both films is that they are still better enjoyed and understood by people who know the novels; readers respond to these films in one way, viewers in another. Sophisticated SF readers know exactly what happens in the two films. Understanding is the prime feature of good SF. SF without thought is not worthy of the name.

2010 and Clarke's subsequent novels extend and deepen the original story. For example, HAL's "death" in the Kubrick film is tragic in the classic sense of nobility brought low, but in a genuinely science fictional way—in the realm of future possibility. As HAL is re-activated by Dr. Chandra in *2010* (and in the novel), we feel the full import of what was done to this rational mind, and by implication to our rationality, when HAL was lied to and had to be deactivated in the first film. When HAL is told the truth of what must be done to return the expedition safely to Earth, he reacts with heroism and self-sacrifice, based on truth telling. This is one of Clarke's great themes, and it survives from his novels into the film.

Repeat viewings of both films are rewarding, as the special effects and visuals find their rightful place in our comprehension; but, inevitably, too much is seen from outside the characters, despite excellent perform-ances and the narration supplied by Dr. Floyd's great-voiced actor, Roy Scheider. Clarke's *2001* novels may one day become our great myth of upward mobility in the universe, even as we stand today before the question of intelligent life's likelihood in the cosmos.

Opinion on *2001* wandered around after a bad start before settling on "masterpiece." Too little explanation seemed fatal, even when all was shown, until a little "work" by audiences clarified what happened; there was no going back after such knowledge. Curiously, *2010* was attacked for having too much explanation. Aristotle once said that the sense of wonder was part of ignorance, and was dispelled by knowledge; this essential part of doing science should not be out of place in SF. Therefore, wonder is stressed in the first film; knowledge is emphasized in the second film and in the novels.

Metropolis, the novel by Thea von Harbou, is no match for its movie; *Things To Come*, with which H. G. Wells was not completely happy, was a considerable reduction of his novel; but *2001: A Space Odyssey*, an excel-lent novel, is underrated because of the film, even though it was written as the movie was being made, and explains all that happens in Kubrick's visual presentation of the ideas; they are all there, and can be guessed, but require a more sophisticated attentiveness than the novel demands. Even in a film that seemed not to know what it was about to some viewers, the author had to know.

* * *

Gore Vidal, after working in Hollywood to buy himself the time to write novels, observed that filmmakers often master cameras, film stock, and visual tricks, but not story or life. Both economics and the kind of person controlling the making of films account for the repeated artistic failures of motion pictures. Directors, actors, and production people would work just as hard if given more ambitious projects. This is especially true of SF film, where the rewards have grown so large, and where the potential for drawing on a century of written works goes mostly untapped, judged by the results, and where even original screenwriting remains a pale shadow of written works, in which some viewers see more in the finished film than is justified.

Some portion of what makes for good SF is nearly always missing from even the best screen efforts, but the list of elements for a full success is not infinite. Another problem is that the enjoyment of a movie may not have much to do with its quality. We often like what we know is bad, overlooking flaws if *a favored virtue* is present. But it will not do to throw up our hands at such vagaries of taste. To permit uncritical enjoyment to dominate the discussion of SF films is to admit that we are not serious or aware of the possibilities of the medium at all. Casual audiences react in this way, but filmmakers and critics should not.

And yet the problem of readers and viewers *does* come down to what each values most, and this overrides other values. One can ask what *should* one value—and we're off into an infinite regress of measuring sticks, swamping our reasoning by the elevation of specific values that one viewer or another might set aside. The solution is to start with what one appreciates most, and let the buck stop there, even if this kind of integrity may look wild, reckless, and without value to others. Are there obligatory values? Yes—craft skills, themes of importance, elegance, symmetry—upon which it seems we should all agree but do not. Worse, if we draw three circles of differing taste, they may well overlap but never achieve congruence.

Other problems plague readers and viewers. A print critic can open a book or story and check his/her impression or memory; but prior to video editions, a movie critic had to rely on memory, sometimes decades old, or else go see the film again, or read a script, if possible. John Simon, a notable critic of film and theater, tells the story of seeing *The Ruling Class* (1972), disliking it, then seeing it again a week later and complaining that when he got up from his seat and looked under it for his objections, they were nowhere to be found. What happened was a growth of understanding of a film sufficiently rich to resist exhaustion in one viewing, revealing its virtues in a second look.

There is such a thing as "film literacy," a capacity to read a film according to its editing, visuals, acting, and music. Like novels, films have syntax of language, form and content. There are people who read novels so badly that they don't know how to read novels, and there are bad viewers of films.

Despite the three "monuments" of SF film mentioned here, none of them is immune to negative criticism. The suspicion persists among filmmakers and SF writers that genuine masterpieces still remain to be made. The obstacles do not seem to be in the ideals, talents, or resources now available, but in the commercial masters of movies who cannot see beyond the star, the money, and their idea of audience tastes. Yet they have been wrong so often about both entertainments and artistic films that we cannot take seriously these owners of talent who should only be its caretakers. It is remarkable that critically successful films of any kind are made, given the eagerness with which corporations now produce DVDs of any and all movies. We can see that the tyranny of money is not perfect. The theory of capitalism, which runs on the story of the goose that lays the golden eggs, is everywhere short of geese.

* * *

About ways to watch and ways to read: We invent games of reflection, with both fiction and movies—and see what may not have been intended, because all sufficiently rich works betray deeper unknowns. The worst of the beloved worst may reveal the unintended, when we tune our minds to see, hear, and think with concentration. Watching a film and writing about it is like witnessing an accident. All the witnesses seem sure of themselves, and yet tell different stories. It's difficult, especially with movies you can't see again easily; books are more easily reread. Before tape and DVDs, movies could not be rechecked without difficulty. I have re-watched all the works in this essay, and know that I cannot step into the same film twice, as they say about rivers, but I knew that about SF novels a long time ago. Film "narrative" is visual, highly pre-selected for our eyes, and can be overlooked by the non-film literate viewer; but the rise of video has helped educate viewers, because now, as with books, the moments of a film, especially its dialogue, can be revisited, bringing a more vital emphasis, in which we find a greater richness than provided by memory. This has come as a great surprise to many.

Another vital note: Watching a movie or reading a book confronts us with simplified complexities; but we are glad to have them in graspable form, since the realities are much more chaotic. And by and by, we are led to appreciate those complexities, which might never have been approached except through simpler steps, because direct experience is more unfocused and limiting. The retrospective ability of the arts is a priceless application of hindsight. Storytelling offers perspective and an explanation of events and character. Written SF presents speculative complexities, possibilities made plainer for the page; but even though reading and seeing differ in significant ways, written and visual SF are not strangers when they meet in storytelling. Greatness of books or films comes with complexities; entertainment hews to simplicity and grace, in which much is lost. This is why a novel cannot find its fulfillment in a movie; despite the illusion of living characters, a movie is a simplification of a simplification, since all fiction is a simplification of life, or in SF a simplification of possibility and change. Complexities are quieter in novels than in a film of that novel, but a film does not replace a novel or story, and fiction is not an early effort at making a film.

Threads (1985), made for British television, and produced and directed by Mick Jackson, is a film that puts all other nuclear war movies into the "less than truthful" category, if not that of damned lies. It is a genuine masterpiece not only for the importance of its theme and the technical and social consequences of such an attack, but also because of its painterly, somber technicolor execution. If an SF novel can speak truth to power, this film *shows* truth to power, and is unnerving to watch.

Two foreign language SF films, both by Andrei Tarkovski, who has been much praised by Ingmar Bergman, are unlike the work of any other director. *Solaris* (1972), based on the novel by Stanislaw Lem, belongs in the company of the big three. It is one of the most beautiful and stylish films ever made, with a unique approach to color. But its wholly serious, novelistic pacing (which is actually not unlike the work of David Lean) is enough to stir the whiz-bang crowd to explosive flight from the theater, much as *2001* managed to do before it educated its viewers. After all, one should not have to work at being entertained; it's supposed to happen *to* you with no work. There are other ways to make movies.

Tarkovski's *Stalker* (1979) is from the short novel *Roadside Picnic* (translated 1977) by Arkady and Boris Strugatski, who also wrote the screenplay. The story explores the same themes of alien contact as *Solaris*, in the same stylish, expanded and challenging way. *Solaris* depicts the struggles of scientists to understand the ways of an alien ocean: a vast alien intelligence which seems to communicate with scientists by resurrecting lost loved ones. The people in *Stalker* seek to penetrate a zone where artifacts have been abandoned by alien visitors, artifacts capable of granting vision and knowledge. Tarkovski knew what he wanted to do in these long films and accomplished his objective. Viewers who have made the effort to expose themselves to films from more than one kind of tradition have been rewarded. The result is not only one of seeing and hearing a film on it own terms, but in thinking about what one sees and hears. Ears also have eyes.

One other film that ranks with the masterpieces is the *20,000 Leagues Under the Sea* (1954), directed by Richard Fleischer, and produced by Walt Disney from Jules Verne's novel. The movie improves upon Verne's novel, motivating Captain Nemo's anti-imperialism with a clear dramatization of his ideas, thus energizing the story with an admirable bitterness that rescues Verne's views. The one thing Disney insisted upon was that Nemo's character remain unchanged.

History has turned *20,000 Leagues Under the Sea* into one of the most important SF films because of its political content, involving the nature of insurgency and the efficacy of force in political conflicts. As with *Threads*, the film tells no lies. Today it looks like a meditation on so-called terrorism and insurgency, in which Captain Nemo is defeated by Ned Land's messages in bottles, which bring the British Imperial Navy down on Nemo's island base. Nemo in the end denies the British Empire his technology—asking pointedly along the way whether violence is reserved for the empire alone, and no one else may be violent—by destroying his own base. His technology holds the empire's feet to the moral fire, and the empire fears that he may be able to enforce his judgment, as it enforces world domination.

An escape plot was teased out of Verne's story; but escape is not only the hope of the three who have been taken aboard the Nautilus, but also of Nemo himself, who seeks to flee from the injustices of a colonial world order by striking at its warships. We sympathize with Nemo, and with Professor Aronax, but also with Ned Land. Verne seems to have divided himself into these three characters, from what we know of his social and political views.

Finally, Nemo has no recourse. After Ned Land betrays the location of Nemo's island and warships arrive and he is mortally wounded, no course of action is left except to deny matches to children (as Einstein said in the 1950s about atomic weapons) by destroying his technology and denying the empire a greater capacity for violence. Ned Land, of course, has simply delayed the arms race that was already underway in the 1950s. Verne's deeply held concerns about human civilization are more valid today than ever. His publishers sought to minimize his anti-imperialistic worries in favor of escapist travelogue and adventure;

but failed. Disney, as a producer, also sidestepped censorship when he directed his writer and director to leave Nemo's character unchanged from Verne's moody, troubled man, in whom powerful forces were at work. Disney's Nemo judges himself harshly, as Aronax notices. Viewers *see* him agonizing over the sinking of each ship—one carrying the raw materials for explosives, where the death of a few weighs less heavily in Nemo's soul than the death of the many still to come. By taking Aronax, Conseil, and Ned Land aboard his submarine, Nemo hopes to send them back as intermediaries to a world that might achieve a better life based on the applications of his knowledge. Ned Land's thoughtless betrayal of Nemo's base ends Nemo's hopes, and all that is left is to deny the world a technological holocaust.

This film was not made for children, as the director Richard Fleischer wrote, even with the presence of Esmeralda the seal, whom Nemo loves along with the life of the sea, where mankind's unjust laws drown. Released during the McCarthy era of American politics, this film was more than a bit subversive during that time of Cold War empires, and remains contemporary. Look too fast and listen too casually to the dialogue, and you will miss its meanings.

As Nemo's island blows up, Aronax tries to assuage Ned Land's guilt for his betrayal of the base's position by saying that he has done humanity a service—by helping Nemo to deny his technology to the British Empire. Nemo and Aronax are now in agreement: empires are even more dangerous when advanced technologies are available.[1]

Forbidden Planet, by the pseudonymous W. J. Stuart, was a novel based on the 1956 movie that came out as a tie-in paperback, but also as a hardcover novel from Farrar, Straus and Cudahy, a house that published distinguished fiction. It was an often fascinatingly critical story that cried out for more length and fictional elegance, and more detail; the central idea of power *literally* magnifying the flaws deep in the minds of intelligent beings, in both the extinct alien race and in the scientist who is studying their technology, is worthy of print SF and is much respected by SF writers for its originality.

These examples demonstrate that an SF novel cannot stand in for a movie based upon it, or *vice versa*, and that perhaps the best SF films should stand alone, as do novels and stories. Each should live in its own world and not be mistaken for each other. Film and print are different channels of entry, lacking each other's virtues, sharing only the story element. Judging SF film by print SF entirely, or print SF by film, sacrifices too much from each form. Will a genius filmmaker come along to do it all, to give us a movie that can replace the novel or the particular novel from which the movie is drawn? Perhaps this question is confused? But we should not omit what may be possible. Bad novels have become fine films, but bad films have never become great novels.

George Pal's pioneering films have been praised by Martin Scorsese, who said that he likes Steven Spielberg's films only because they remind him of Pal's work. *Destination Moon* (1950) is the first color SF film, unless one counts the similarly underrated *Dr. Cyclops* (1940). The comparison with the actual moon journey of 1969 is startling, especially in the final approach to touchdown. Scripted and rewritten by Robert A. Heinlein from his novel *Rocket Ship Galileo* (1947), and directed by the capable Irving Pichel (whose voice also figures in some of the narration), George Pal's production pays painstaking attention to detail and accuracy, and fulfills many SF readers' dream of *seeing* space travel in their lifetimes. An early showing at the New York Hayden Planetarium, which a number of SF writers attended, found them "crick-necked and happy," as SF writer Judith Merril reported. The nuclear reaction rocket engine in the movie is still more advanced than anything we have today. The effective, soft-spoken dialogue is carefully written and directed and, together with key moments of the journey, achieves a poetry of its own for viewers who are not prejudiced by contemporary special effects. Readers will like Heinlein's novella, "Destination Moon," written to accompany the movie, and which is as good as any story the author wrote.

Three later films produced by Pal—*When Worlds Collide* (1951), a masterly *War of the Worlds* (1953), and *The Time Machine* (1960)—all illustrate the production struggles of print versus film adaptation, the restrictions of budgets and special effects, and elicit this question: why, today, when special effects and larger budgets are so readily available, do we not have results that improve upon the past? The obvious answer: so much money is involved that success must be "fixed" in accordance with "audience expectations." This method also operates increasingly in the race-horse fixing, payola paying environment of SF book publishing; money protects itself, without worrying about the negative effects on the merits of creative work. Audiences, we hear from the masters of talent, do not care about quality and would find a discussion of its problems arcane; audiences have in fact been trained to have the very responses that the moneymen cite as apparent laws of nature. Given the business realities of SF filmmaking and print publishing, it is remarkable that critically successful works still manage to emerge. The tyranny of money sometimes fails.

* * *

These still widely discussed, and recent films of interest to both readers of science fiction *and* to viewers, deserve mention for a variety of virtues.

The Day the Earth Stood Still (1951), improves but changes the original 1940 story, "Farewell To the Master" by Harry Bates, by stressing the concept of law as requiring immunity to subversion by individuals or groups. This is the heart of the film, which presents a secular, historically derived concept of lawfulness that cannot be meddled with (which we do not have), which protects civilizations from lethal evolutionary survivalist impulses. Klaatu's final speech, an ultimatum to which his culture is also vulnerable, is the true climax of the film, and redefines the way to watch the film. The original story's final twist horrifies with a totalitarian ending that is the opposite of the Robert Wise film, whose idea of nuclear deterrence is both hopeful, and disturbing because the police function cannot be revoked. Everything we know about ourselves and our history suggests that nothing like this would remain uncorrupted. But it is this thoughtful vision, of a new history that lives without destructive stupidity and asks us to join it, that makes this SF of the first rank. If only it were possible.

Invasion of the Body Snatchers, Don Siegel's much debated, 1956, movie of Jack Finney's novel, has usually been seen as a Cold War allegory of collectivism absorbing individuals. But both novel and movie carry implications that suggest a view beyond the "settings" we have inherited from nature's evolutionary mill, which is the source of individualist theory, ignoring the survival value of cooperative symbiosis, also a reality in the evolutionary process.

Sadly, however, our societies, despite talk of individualism, have looked upon individuals as replacements in a larger scheme, and warned of the negative extremes of individual rebellion. *What* we are is still a question. *Where* we came from is now clearer. *What* we may wish to become awaits our choices. Ambitious SF asks these questions, and they are what this striking film sometimes suggests, beyond the politics of the time in which it was made.

The story asks what is a human being, and lists a set of qualities which, when lost, will amount to dehumanization; yet clearly, these characteristics will only be missed by a human being. But what if a species starts out in another way, as the pods did, outside of a human being's circular, self-serving standard of comparison? The integrity of a biological identity can only be questioned by a conscious intelligence that knows what it is and has a choice to stay that way or become something else. Given identities are open to critical examination, and a dramatic problem arises only when the film's contrasted ways conflict.

But now that the movie's Cold War credentials have lost their xenophobic intensity we are left with the problem of free will versus totalitarianism, and perhaps the central interest of the story as SF can be re-examined on its merits. Of course we are all for freedom. Look who's talking—human beings. But show me an alien, as John W. Campbell once said to his writers, who thinks as well as a human being but isn't one. That is what makes this film and novel genuine SF.

Revealingly, the *Collier's* serialization of the novel brings the Federal Bureau of Investigation (FBI) to the rescue! Novel and movie have the hero prevailing by his wits; but the film's heroic ending, as so many sighed with relief, was tacked on as a prologue and epilogue. A 1979 reissue drops the studio-imposed scenes in keeping with the director's original cut, which has the courage to face implications beyond even those of the novel's author—perhaps made more acceptable by the 1978 Philip Kaufman remake, in which the aliens are victorious. Jack Finney was always for the individual, which makes the *Collier's* FBI ending a form of soft political censorship. Siegel's film went the distance, and was pulled back closer to Finney's individualist vision.

Charly (1968), directed by Ralph Nelson, is a provocatively themed film about heartbreakingly differing levels of intelligence. Here is an award winning work of fiction, "Flowers For Algernon" by Daniel Keyes—story, 1959; teleplay, 1961; novel, 1966; musical 1981—that succeeds on all counts in all its forms. An Oscar was awarded to the actor, Cliff Robertson.

Star Wars (1977), *The Empire Strikes Back* (1980), *Return of the Jedi* (1983), along with George Lucas's three prequels released since 1999, are prime examples of entertaining space opera and production values that should not be mistaken for good SF, and like the Flash Gordon serials of the 1930s, were not meant to be plausible SF. Compared to the Star Trek movies, they reveal that visual SF has repeated the print division between thoughtful SF and adventure fiction.

Blade Runner (1982, director Ridley Scott's cut, 1993) influenced a style of cyberpunk SF movies, often presenting the underbelly of corporate/class-warring dystopian futures, by drawing on the print reservoir of

Philip K. Dick's works, among others. *Blade Runner* respects Dick's 1968 novel, *Do Androids Dream of Electric Sheep?*, despite the alterations. Dick refused to write a "novelization" of the movie, and prevented one from being written. A large film industry has grown up around his works, for better and worse. His influence in fiction and films has been large, often unconsciously so.

Close Encounters of the Third Kind (1977, revised editions in 1980 and 1998, and a television network showing of all existing footage) is Stephen Spielberg's visualization of what has come to be known as "the Carl Sagan Doctrine" of benevolent aliens.

Back to the Future (1985–1990) is Robert Zemeckis's vibrant trilogy of time travel's complications, respectfully treated, with memorable characters, which seems to owe nothing directly to written works.

The Matrix (1999), *The Matrix Reloaded* (2003), *The Matrix Revolutions* (2003), directed by the Wachowski Brothers, were made from ambitious scripts that were out of their depth in presenting the implications of Virtual Reality beyond the mere background fact as a setting for the action and special effects.

Our given reality is connected to a vaster outside, and is constructed, as we see it, through the filter of our senses and mind. No virtual reality could be entirely cut off, without telltales of falsity. We have good reason for accepting that our reality, as selected by our physiology, is connected to the outside in a non-arbitrary way. The Matrix trilogy loses too many distinctions and fails to exploit the idea. The same political action story might well have been told against another background. The surface glitter of virtual reality has been overused on television and in films. The same thing happened with the possession of human minds by alien invaders. Once *Invasion of the Body Snatchers* was made in 1956, Robert A. Heinlein's masterly 1951 novel, *The Puppet Masters*, seemed too familiar for caring, despite later attempts. But why not start at the beginning? Quite a number of movies have had several attempts before getting it right.

Feedback (2002, directed by Ted Konuralp) is a striking independent film about the human consequences of a telephone capable of calling back only six hours in time, as normal time passes and opens successive windows in the story. A strict adherence to the phone's limitations twists the story into complications worthy of Robert A. Heinlein's 1941 story "By His Bootstraps." The idea owes a debt to Gregory Benford's well known physics paper "The Tachyonic Antitelephone" (written with W. A. Newcomb, *Physical Review*, July 1970, 263–265) and to his 1980 novel *Timescape*.

Time travel has had a lively and varied life since Zemeckis made his trilogy, with at least a dozen neglected films showing the kind of ingenuity previously found only in print SF. The lesson to be learned from this theme and the more successful visual SF, on television and in movies, is know your print SF, know your film history, and do not simply imitate or copy.

note

1. Readers of Verne's novels in English should be warned that nearly all translations done before recent decades are worthless. Verne was abridged, bowdlerized, rewritten, and virtually assassinated as a writer in the English language. He, in fact, was a writer of fine prose, a scholar and student of science who did not make the errors attributed to him by reviewers; neither does he deserve the "boys' adventure book" label that his original French publisher saddled him with, suppressing his critical social and political views lest they interfere with sales. The original *20,000 Leagues Under the Sea* is probably lost to us. In addition, Verne's relatives meddled with his texts, and withheld his darker visions; but all this tampering has in recent years been exposed, and there is a Verne renaissance under way in English editions. In Europe, Verne has always been regarded in ways that have puzzled English and American critics, but now we know why; lacking good translations, they could not see Europe's comparison of Verne to various masters. Today's reader should go to the recent Oxford University Press translations by William Butcher and to the growing number of translations from Wesleyan University Press and the University of Nebraska Press.

suggestions for further reading

Brosnan, John. *Future Tense*. New York: St. Martin's, 1978.

Clarke, Arthur C. *The Lost Worlds of 2001*. New York: New American Library, 1972.

Clarke Arthur C. and Hyams, Peter. *The Odyssey File*. New York: Del Rey/Ballantine, 1985.

Hartwell, David. *Destination Moon*. New York: Gregg Press, 1979.

Wynorski, Jim. *They Came From Outer Space*. New York: Doubleday, 1981.

6
the feedback loop
michael cassutt

There are accepted truths in the Science Fiction (SF) writing business, especially the business of writing SF for television:

> Series make more money than stand-alone works.
>
> The check is never in the mail.
>
> And the best ideas come from the prose world.

Obviously these are anecdotal truths—what *The Daily Show* might label "truthiness." But, as a working writer in SF television for twenty-five years and the prose world for thirty, I can vouch for the persistence of these truthoids, if not their empirical basis. Certainly there is an absence of contradictory data.

For most of the twentieth century, the ideational center of SF resided in prose, notably in the genre magazines, from the earliest (*Amazing Stories*) through the most influential (*Astounding Science Fiction*) to the most readable (*Galaxy* and *The Magazine of Fantasy & Science Fiction*) to the most-honored survivor (*Isaac Asimov's SF Magazine*).

It was in these pages that the coin of the SF realm was minted, where—with wildly varying degrees of literary skill—tropes such as travel to other planets, alien beings, time travel, robots and even the whole concept of a lived-in future world were explored, developed, and often re-invented.

SF in book form, in works reprinted from the magazines and in original novels (such as *Stranger in a Strange Land*, *The Left Hand of Darkness*, and *Ringworld*) and anthologies (*Dangerous Visions*, *Universe*, *New Dimensions*), continued this development.

The audience for the genre magazines was never large—it is reported that *Amazing Stories* had a paid circulation of approximately 150,000 per month in the 1940s. During the so-called boom of the 1950s, when at one time there were thirty SF serial titles on the newsstands, the reading audience likely never exceeded half a million.

Hardcover SF books did not reach audiences that large until the 1970s—if then—though mass market paperbacks, like *Stranger*, ultimately sold in the low millions.

But the exposure of these tropes to the mass audiences for possible feature films and especially network television has shifted the locus of their development from page to screen—and exhausted them.

* * *

Many charges have been leveled against American network television of the twentieth century: that it was wholly reactive and derivative, that it was aimed at a mass audience composed of the lowest common denominator, and so on.

All of these were, to some extent, true—and perhaps inescapable. Any form of entertainment that, at its peak, reached 50,000,000 viewers over the space of three hours[1] is almost by definition forced to simplify ideas, to streamline stories, to rely on action, and to feature characters lacking nuance.

SF programming during the early years of American network television (1949–1958) consisted almost exclusively of children's programs, or stand-alone anthology episodes, all produced on miniscule budgets.

The children's programs were pioneered by *Captain Video and his Video Rangers* (1949–1955), which directly inspired such imitators as *Tom Corbett, Space Cadet*, and *Space Patrol*. Although *Corbett* was, in fact, based on Robert A. Heinlein's young adult novel, *Space Cadet*, and *Video* employed a number of writers from the SF prose field (James Blish, Damon Knight, and Walter Miller, Jr.), the SF content of these programs was primitive: though set several centuries in the future, they ignored possible societal changes (such as those found in contemporary prose works like Jack Williamson's "With Folded Hands") or actual alien cultures (such as the Venerians portrayed in Heinlein's *Space Cadet*) to present stories of space pirates and evil geniuses plotting to take over the solar system. These were blood-and-thunder space adventures suitable for pre-teenaged audiences. Meaning there was no blood and relatively mild thunder.

There were occasional SF stories in the active live drama world, notably Gore Vidal's "Visit to a Small Planet." Ray Bradbury and Kurt Vonnegut worked here; Ray Bradbury was famously plagiarized. ("A Sound of Distant Drums," broadcast on *Playhouse 90*, was judged to have been stolen from his novel, *Fahrenheit 451*.[2])

This sad example typifies the flow of SF tropes during the 1950s—one-way, from books and magazines to screen, simplified or misunderstood, often without credit or payment.

* * *

In the 1950s, televised dramas were divided between live programs aired from New York that had to be kinescoped for later transmission or, once the coaxial cable made it possible to receive programs on the West Coast, performed again.

There were a number of programs produced on film in Los Angeles, notably a great number of Westerns, where Warner Bros. dominated the field. The closest thing to an SF series was the near-future space adventure *Men into Space*, produced by Ziv, a syndicator best known for *Sea Hunt*.

The ratings success of series with continuing characters (see my opening paragraphs) combined with the high costs of production in New York led to major change in television drama: from 1960 on, most were filmed in Los Angeles.

This paradigm shift coincided with the demise of a large of number of the SF pulp magazines—from 35 in 1957 to fewer than 10 by 1960[3]—and the growing dominance of novels in hardcover and paperback.

But just as prose SF survived in magazine form long after the death of the pulps, televised SF was the only real survivor of the age of anthology television—notably Rod Serling's *Twilight Zone* (1958–1964).

Along with Paddy Chayevesky and Reginald Rose, Serling was one of the most visible and highly respected veterans of the live drama world. His teleplay "Requiem for a Heavyweight" had won five Emmy awards in 1957, including one for Serling's script. It was this reputation that essentially forced CBS to accept a concept the network, frankly, didn't want (Zicree: 23–27).

Although produced on straitened schedules, often relying on back lot sets and props from previously produced films and series, *Twilight Zone* episodes nevertheless dealt with a number of pure SF tropes, from first contact to future worlds, as well as with a large number of more traditional fantasy concepts.

It was obvious that Serling had read some published SF. Indeed, he acquired scripts from writers like Richard Matheson and Charles Beaumont, both of them veterans of the SF prose world. In fact, the type of story aired on *Twilight Zone* was not so different from those offered in many of the magazines, and indistinguishable from the SF stories appearing in mainstream magazines like *Saturday Evening Post, Collier's,* and *Playboy*—slick, sentimental, romantic, and buttoned by an ironic twist ending. When Serling and his writers ventured into the future, it was to offer warnings, not to show glorious possibilities.

While the ubiquity of Serling's production, from its name to theme song, made it more difficult for writers to place these surprise/ironic/ biter bit stories, *Twilight Zone* left the major tropes of SF unaffected.

Although it premiered as *Twilight Zone* was ending its original run on CBS, *The Outer Limits* (1963–1965) belonged to the anthology era of SF television. Two of the most memorable episodes, "Soldier" and "Demon with a Glass Hand," were written by Harlan Ellison both examining the effects of visitors from the future (in one case, a soldier, in the other, a humanoid robot). Anthony Lawrence's evocative "The Man Who Was Never Born" also dealt with time travel.

But the majority of *Outer Limits'* sixty-nine episodes concerned one SF idea: alien invasion, as presented in dozens of variations under titles like "Zanti Misfits," "The Galaxy Being," "The Chameleon," and "The Mutant." The prototypical *Outer Limits* story was "The Architects of Fear," a script by Meyer Dolinsky, in which a group of idealistic scientists stage an alien invasion in order to force humans to work together (see Schow for a comprehensive survey of the series).

* * *

By the early 1960s, then, it was possible to view the SF concepts in some episodes of televised SF as equal in sophistication to those of the prose world. If nothing else, the flow of tropes was impeded less by the desire on the part of network programmers and sponsors to simplify concepts and more by basic budgetary constraints.

The first piloted space missions by the Soviet Union and the United States took place in 1961; that same year, President John F. Kennedy committed the United States to the goal of accomplishing a piloted lunar landing by the end of the decade. With this shift in the zeitgeist, the always-reactive mass television market found it possible to accept a series based on the notion that humans would travel to other planets.

The first was *Lost in Space* (CBS 1964), an Irwin Allen production that featured a family (and assorted hangers-on) trying to explore other worlds. The source here was less prose SF than *Swiss Family Robinson.* Indeed, the family in *Lost in Space* was named Robinson.

But the series' relative popularity made it possible for Gene Roddenberry, a veteran of police, Western and contemporary dramas, to sell to NBC a concept he titled *Wagon Train to the Stars*, alluding to *Wagon Train*, a long-running (1958–1965) series about a gruff trail boss leading settlers from Missouri to new homes in the West. Eventually, after the rejection of one failed pilot and the development of a second, the series aired as *Star Trek*, premiering in September 1966.

Wisely realizing that the *Star Trek* concept offered a broad canvas for the exploration of many SF ideas, Roddenberry and his talented staff (Gene L. Coon, John D. F. Black, and D. C. Fontana) reached out to the community of Los Angeles-based SF writers, inviting such veterans of the magazine and book world as Robert Bloch, Jerome Bixby, Harlan Ellison, A. E. van Vogt, Philip Jose Farmer, Jerry Sohl, Norman Spinrad, and Theodore Sturgeon to pitch stories. Many of these efforts resulted in assignments for the writers and their work often became the most highly regarded episodes—notably Ellison's "City on the Edge of Forever," which explored the personal costs of travel through time, or Sturgeon's "Amok Time," an examination of alien biology.

Other tropes that were exposed to a mass audience through *Star Trek* included matter transmission, faster-than-light travel, utopias and dystopias, immortality, machine intelligence, and extraterrestrial cultures.

Not only did the integration of these richer tropes make for better episodes, it also gave the series a depth unequaled in earlier (and most subsequent) television series.

By the time *Star Trek* ended its original run, in 1969, writers from the SF prose field found a welcome, if temporary, home in the new genre. More startling, David Gerrold's first professional sale was to *Star Trek*, not the more traditional short story to *If* or a paperback to Ace.

Several writers who would gain prominence in the 1970s and 1980s found their imaginations fired not by *Galaxy* magazine or novels by Clarke, Asimov, or Niven, but by *Star Trek* itself. Vonda N. McIntyre, a winner of two Nebula awards for fiction in the 1970s, started her SF career as a *Star Trek* fan. When James Tiptree, Jr. first began to publish SF stories, she frankly used *Star Trek* tropes in stories such as "Beam Us Home."

A feedback loop had been established.

* * *

The demise of *Star Trek* marked the beginning of a science fictional Dark Age for network television. Although there were striking one-shot programs (Steven Spielberg's *Duel*, from a script by Matheson) or noble short-lived attempts (*The Immortal*, based on the novel *The Immortals* by James E. Gunn), there were no series that presented cutting edge SF concepts to equal the first two seasons of *Star Trek*. Perhaps this dearth of material was another case of SF's perceived popularity reflecting the declining health of the American space program. SF television of this period is typified by *The Six Million Dollar Man* (1974–1978). Based on a novel by Martin Caidin, a well-known aviation and space journalist, this series was about an badly injured astronaut who is transformed into a "cyborg"—a "cybernetic organism"—essentially a half-man, half-machine. (To show how the conceptual playing field was level between television and the prose world, note that Frederik Pohl's novel, *Man Plus*, about a cyborg astronaut on Mars, won the Nebula Award for 1976.[4])

Two events signaled the end of this Dark Age. The first was the striking success of the feature film *Star Wars* (1977).[5] Written and directed by George Lucas, whose earlier dystopian film, *THX 1138* (1971), had been well-received, *Star Wars* was a deceptively simple adventure using one of the classic story motifs of SF as well as myth, fantasy, and Greek tragedy—that of a young "prince" who is actually the powerful heir to the "throne" of the galaxy, but doesn't know it. *Star Wars* was brilliantly paced and edited, contained special effects work that allowed for fabulous realism, possessed an engaging cast, and, lacking bad language and graphic violence, appealed to movie-goers of all ages.

On the surface, the film might be viewed as an example of prose SF as it existed B.C.—before editor John W. Campbell took over *Astounding Science Fiction* in 1938. *Star Wars'* ideas were no more advanced than E. E. Doc Smith's and Jack Williamson's space operas of the 1930s, with bits of Asimov's *Foundation* series (1942–1950) and Herbert's *Dune* (1965) thrown in. Yet, in true SF fashion, *Star Wars'* characters took their world for granted, a narrative trick first perfected by Robert A. Heinlein in the early 1940s. The film never stopped for explanations about how spacecraft flew from one star system to another. The mystical power of the Force was never diagrammed. Aliens from different races spoke to each other in their own languages, untranslated, but still understood. The mix of these elements resulted in the most popular film of all time.

The success of *Star Wars*, followed soon by Steven Spielberg's *Close Encounters of the Third Kind* (late in 1977), made it acceptable for television executives to once again offer SF series to their mass audience. The quickest response was *Battlestar Galactica*, written by Glen Larson and Donald P. Bellisario and premiering in September 1978. (*Galactica's* debt to *Star Wars* is obvious in its title. It also aped the pacing of Lucas's movie, and used some of the same effects teams.)

Following *Galactica* came *Buck Rogers in the 25th Century* (1979–1981), also developed by Glen Larson, this time in partnership with Leslie Stevens (*Outer Limits*) and also surfing in the wake of *Star Wars*.

For all their flaws—and both programs were never regarded as outstanding examples of SF or network television—*Galactica* and *Buck* were actually more sophisticated in their use of SF tropes than their sources, acknowledged or otherwise (*Star Wars* and the original *Buck Rogers* stories and comic strips). *Galactica*, for example, told the story of a group of humans fleeing from attacks by hostile machine intelligences ("cylons"), searching for a "lost" planet Earth. However poorly handled, its tropes would have fit happily into a magazine serial of the late 1970s, or a series of paperback novels.

The second factor in the emergence of SF television from its Dark Age was the continued underground popularity of Roddenberry's original *Star Trek*, which by the late 1970s had spawned conventions as well as a series of best-selling paperback novels, and even an animated revival.

In 1976, Barry Diller, president of Paramount Studios (owner of *Trek*), made a serious attempt to revive the series in live action. Feeling that the three major networks had no interest in a "failed" series from the 1960s, Diller tried to create a fourth network, a partnership of independent television stations that would broadcast the program.

Diller's effort was slightly premature. The number of independent stations was too small while the number of different corporate entities was too large for an easy launch. Though planning for the series progressed to the point that writers were at work on scripts (published SF writers Alan Dean Foster, Greg Bear, and Alan Brennert were among them), it was the success of *Star Wars* and *Close Encounters* that aborted the revival. Diller's corporate bosses ordered him to take advantage of the boom in SF movies and turn *Trek* into a feature film. (Foster's television story, after substantial re-development by others, became the basis for *Star Trek: The Motion Picture*.)

By 1980, it was clear that the growing sophistication of special effects, the generational change that saw the rise of writers like Gerrold, Foster, and Brennert who had grown up exposed to SF on television and in feature films at the same time they read the genre magazines and books, and the audience's willingness to accept such tropes as time travel, faster-than-light spacecraft, alien beings, artificial intelligence and others, marked a completely level playing field. No genre had a monopoly on the presentation of sophisticated ideas.

Beyond the level playing field, however, the massive audiences for *Star Trek*—by the late 1970s, obviously in the tens of millions—led to an unusual phenomenon: the exhaustion of a classic SF trope, the spaceship.

* * *

From the beginning of modern published SF, from Doc Smith's *Skylark* series through sophisticated concepts such as Leinster's and Heinlein's "generation ships," to Malcolm Jameson's Space Navy and Ray Bradbury's poetic, more-metaphorical-than-literal rockets to Mars, to Arthur C. Clarke's finely imagined vehicles, the *spaceship* defined SF. The spaceship served as a conceptual gateway to the future and by extension, to other worlds, alien inhabitants, signs and wonders.[6]

But in the 1960s and 1970s, spaceships in fiction were transformed into spacecraft—to use the more prosaic term invented by NASA—and thus became subject matter more suitable for writers like Martin Caidin than for Frank Herbert, Ursula Le Guin, Anne McCaffrey, or Samuel R. Delany, or others judged to be the "cutting edge" of published SF.

As an SF writer, I know that the looming body of *Star Trek* material made it almost impossible to develop a starship story, especially one involving contact with an alien race. How could you write that story without acknowledging the Prime Directive? How could you deal with the simple mechanics of moving explorers from an orbiting starship to a planetary surface without referencing the *Enterprise's* transporter? How likely were editors like Ben Bova, Stanley Schmidt, Ed Ferman, or those at publishing houses like Doubleday, Ballantine del Rey, Ace, or DAW, to consider them, unless as parodies or pastiches?

The answer: you didn't and they weren't. The spaceship was the first trope to be a victim of SF's mass media success.

But not the last.

* * *

As the 1980s opened, SF became one of the dominant genres in the feature film world. There were *Star Wars* and *Star Trek* sequels. Lucas and Spielberg collaborated on *Raiders of the Lost Ark*, a pulp-style adventure movie (and series) that had SF elements. The flow of tropes became a torrent that not only emerged from the genre magazines and books to television and films, but also back to print from screen. Ideas that would have been incomprehensible to an earlier generation of network and studio executives[7] were now put into development and production.

Director Ridley Scott convinced Orion Pictures to film an adaptation of Philip K. Dick's 1968 novel, *Do Androids Dream of Electric*

Sheep?, the first of dozens of major studio adaptations of Dick's work, ranging from *Total Recall* to *A Scanner Darkly (2006)*. Released under the title *Blade Runner* (in 1982) from a script by Hampton Fancher and David Peoples, Scott and production designer Larry Paull created an SF world that was unprecedented for mass media. It was dark, complex, and, like its oft-compared predecessor *2001*, significantly non-commercial.

But influential nonetheless. Watching at a theater in Vancouver, British Columbia, a young SF writer named William Gibson literally fled halfway through the film. "I was seeing the novel I was writing up on the screen already."

Gibson's novel, *Neuromancer* (published in paperback by Ace in 1984), ultimately won the Nebula and Hugo Awards, and sparked the cyberpunk movement. "Cyberpunk," coined by writer Bruce Bethke in 1983 and popularized by *Asimov's* editor Gardner Dozois, described stories featuring youthful protagonists on the margins of a grim, Earth-based, computer-centric society, as opposed to the juvenile movers and shakers-to-be the works of Heinlein and Herbert placed in interplanetary settings. Not only did prose SF change as a result of the popularity of Gibson's work; almost instantly SF television did too.

In England in 1985, Peter Wagg, a producer for Chrysalis Video charged with choosing a host for a video awards show, turned to ad copywriter George Stone, who suggested a video host—a computer-generated character named Max Headroom.

Following his debut as a video host, Max saw his origin transformed into a drama—*20 Minutes into the Future*—by directors Rocky Morton and Annabel Jankel, and writer Steve Roberts. Astonishingly, the concept was picked up and adapted again for American network television as *Max Headroom* in 1987.

Although the thirteen produced episodes of *Max* failed to connect with ABC's audience—then divided between Friday night showings of such series as *Dallas* (CBS) and *Miami Vice* (NBC)—its vision of a future world dominated by interactive television (a thousand channels not only to be watched, but watching the audience) was the crest of a conceptual wave that included such writers as John Shirley, Bruce Sterling, George Alec Effinger, and Walter Jon Williams; television series like *VR5* (1995) and *Dark Angel* (2000–2002); and films like Terry Gilliam's *Brazil* (1985), *Robocop* (1987), *Johnny Mnemonic* (1985) and *New Rose Hotel* (1995)—both based on Gibson stories—and *Strange Days* (1995).

For a decade and a half the flow of tropes was intertwined, and accelerated to the ultimate expression of cyberpunk in *The Matrix*

(1990), the first of a film trilogy written and directed by Andy and Larry Wachowski.

The evidence is anecdotal, but convincing: in the white-hot core of the SF field it became not only impossible to sell a cyberpunk story, as with spaceship stories, writers stopped creating them.

At the same time, film studios stopped buying them, too. In only a decade and a half, cyberpunk burned out; the SF trope equivalent of James Dean, cyberpunk lived fast, burned the candle at both ends, and died young.

* * *

By the mid-1980s, improvements in delivery systems and changes in broadcast laws allowed the number of independent United States television stations to rise from one hundred to three hundred. This expanding market created a need for programs that would be filled by suppliers other than the major studios. SF programs constituted much of this new material.

The most visible of these was *Star Trek: The Next Generation (Star Trek: TNG)*, which premiered in September 1988 and ran for seven years. Originally produced by Roddenberry himself, later by Michael Berman and writing producer Michael Piller, *Star Trek: TNG* followed the original series' model of featuring a broad spectrum of SF tropes—aliens, space exploration, and dystopias. Unique among television series of any genre, it was also open for story submissions from writers outside the limited pool of established series contributors. Melinda Snodgrass, author of a number of SF novels, sold a spec script to the series in 1989 ("Measure of a Man") that was nominated for a Writers Guild Award.

Star Trek: TNG's follow-on series, *Deep Space Nine (DS9,* 1993–1999), and *Voyager* (1994–2000), had similar policies. *DS9* became particularly effective in presenting SF stories fully as sophisticated as any in the prose world, and was rivaled in its complexity only by J. Michael Straczynski's *Babylon 5* (1994–1998).

Star Trek: Voyager, after an indifferent early run, began to focus on stories of the ultimate conflict between man and machine—humans versus the implacable Borg. ("Resistance is futile.") To give this conflict more resonance, *Voyager's* writers—notably Brannon Braga—frequently turned to another classic SF trope: time travel.

A fifth entry in the *Trek* franchise—*Enterprise* (2001–2005, co-created by Braga and Berman)—based an entire twenty-two episode season on time travel.

Combined with other SF series—such as UPN's *Seven Days* (1998–2001), which featured a National Security Agent using a secret time travel device to ensure the safety of the United States—traveling through time, correcting paradoxes, and shooting or not shooting one's grandfather became as commonplace as catching a cross town bus.

And about as exciting to audiences. By 2002, the time travel trope had been exhausted as completely as spaceships, alien invasion, dystopias, and cyberpunk.

* * *

Like a voracious strip-miner searching for the next rich conceptual vein, SF television turned to extraterrestrials.

Created by Chris Carter, *The X-Files* premiered on FBC in September 1993 and within two seasons had established itself as one of the most stylish and critically acclaimed series on any of the networks. Featuring a pair of F.B.I. agents—one a skeptic, one a true believer—over seven seasons *The X-Files* brilliantly explored the possibilities of clandestine alien visitation to our planet and its effect on humans and the planet itself.

The WB network aired a similarly themed series, *Roswell* (1999–2002), about hybrid human-alien teenagers coping with life in the New Mexico town that was the site of a mythical flying saucer crash in 1947.

And in the 2005–2006 season, three major network series dealt with alien invasions of one kind or another: *Surface* (NBC), *Invasion* (ABC), and *Threshold* (CBS). The intent and success of these series varied: *Surface* was deliberately made in the style of Steven Spielberg's films and dealt with the emergence of hostile beings from Earth's oceans; *Threshold*, which concerned "viral" alien intruders, was a dark, sophisticated thriller similar in tone to *The X-Files:* and *Invasion* dealt with the effects a new breed of "hybrid" human/aliens had on a small town in crisis.

What all had in common was failure to find an audience. None survived to a second season.

But in their wake, SF writers contemplating a novel or a short story in the vein of such well-regarded works as Chad Oliver's *Shores of Another Sea* (1971), John Brunner's *Quicksand* (1968), or even Michael Crichton's *Andromeda Strain* (1969), would find their markets limited and unresponsive. SF writers developing a television series concept would be told by their friends, agents, or studio contacts to give up. The alien invasion trope had become exhausted.

* * *

Over the past twenty years has the creative center of SF shifted from prose to television and films? The last genre novel to garner significant public notice was *Neuromancer* (1984); the sales figures for the most popular genre magazine (*Analog*) have fallen to 30,000 per month. The promising web-based fiction site, *Scifiction*, is gone. SF novels, while critically reviewed with respect that would have been unthinkable in the 1960s, sell fewer and fewer copies.

Yet, even if the center of creative ferment shifted from prose to television and films, it will undoubtedly shift again, likely to the game field. (Sales of video games surpassed ticket sales for feature films in the early 2000s.)

And the prose field still emits new tropes, such as nanotechnology and especially Vernor Vinge's "Singularity," the notion that within a generation human and machine intelligence will have evolved so far that they will merge into an entity whose actions, motivations, and even appearance will be unrecognizable. If nothing else, Vinge's "gray goo" almost defies dramatization—what actor will play that role, assuming a role can even be found?

The Singularity proves again that in spite of the exhaustion of the older tropes, new ones still emerge first in prose.

notes

1. The final episode of the CBS comedy series *M*A*S*H* was viewed in 50,150,000 American households, according to audience measurement methods used by Nielsen Media Research. Even with the erosion of major network audiences over the next twenty-odd years, a hit series such as *C.S.I.* would still reach 15,000,000 households on a given night (*2006 World Almanac and Book of Facts:* 280).
2. Aired October 3, 1957. Script by Robert Alan Aurthur. Bradbury sued CBS. Aurthur, losing in the first hearing, prevailed in an appeal to the United States District Court of Appeals in July 1961 (Beley: 146–149).
3. The maximum number of titles is difficult to determine, but was certainly over 30 in 1956–1957, and under ten within two years. For an amusing examination of this Cretaceous-Tertiary-like event, see Pohl (1978: 231–234).
4. Even more interesting as an example of the feedback loop, *Man Plus* was originally conceived as a film project, a collaboration between Pohl and director Ib Melchior.
5. Though this essay largely deals with the relationship between prose SF and televised SF, the same relationship applies to feature films. For example, SF

television tropes appear in *2001: A Space Odyssey*, the 1968 collaboration between filmmaker Stanley Kubrick and SF writer Arthur C. Clarke.

6. For that same generation, the spaceship symbol identified young adult library books as SF.

7. I was a CBS television executive in the early 1980s. I recall the shock I felt walking into the office of the vice-president for drama development and seeing books by Gordon R. Dickson and Frank Herbert on the walls. They were not works submitted for possible adaptation, but the executive's own reading copies.

suggestions for further reading

Alexander, David. *Star Trek Creator: The Authorized Biography of Gene Roddenberry*. New York: Roc, 1995.

Engel, Joel. *Rod Serling: The Dreams and Nightmares of a Life in the Twilight Zone: A Biography*. Chicago: Contemporary Books, 1989.

Genge, N. E. *The Unofficial X-Files Companion II*. New York: Quill, 1996.

Schow, David. *The Outer Limits: The Official Companion*. New York: Ace, 1986.

Whitfield, Stephen and Gene Roddenberry. *The Making of Star Trek*. New York: Ballantine, 1968.

Zicree, Marc Scott. *The Twilight Zone Companion*. Second Edition. New York: Bantam, 1989.

7
computers in science fiction
brooks landon

Computers are everywhere in science fiction (SF) literature. Although not always precisely identified as such, their existence (particularly in early and in very recent SF) is implicit rather than explicit. SF computers must frequently be "read backward" into stories that were written before the need for or nature of "thinking machines" or "mechanical brains" were clear to writers trying to imagine the future. For example, there's simply no accounting for all the strangeness of Cordwainer Smith's "Alpha Ralpha Boulevard" (1961), but its oracular Abba-Dingo and its inventory of marvels cannot be rationally understood without our assuming that some form of computer technology has played a role in the story's many transformations. Likewise, at the dawn of the age of "ubiquitous computing," when computers are "disappearing" into the fabric of everyday life, SF computers in recent stories are also blending into the technosphere, the fictional human/computer interface blurred by virtual reality, neurophysiological chip implants, uploads of human consciousness into computers, and nanotech upgrades to human intelligence and physiology.

SF film, television, and electronic media not only present narratives in which computers prominently figure in the plot, particularly in stories featuring virtual realities, but also are themselves increasingly produced by and used to showcase computer technology. Whatever the medium, computers in SF narratives function in ways ranging from being the novum or new idea of the story to being its antagonist or protagonist. Computers help or make things happen in SF, or they are what is happening—whether as "characters" who function largely as humans (most obviously as robots or androids or artificial intelligences), as entities who assist or compete with humans, or who threaten to control or supplant humanity itself. Indeed, whether or not specifically called computers, forms of calculating or thinking machines probably constitute the most frequently and extensively identified or implied form of technology found across the spectrum of SF.[1]

The almost visceral appeal of computers in SF was perfectly captured by Candas Jane Dorsey, who famously began her 1988 story "(Learning About) Machine Sex" with a telling question: "A naked woman working at a computer. Which attracts you most?" (Dorsey: 746). Indeed, computers are privileged icons in SF, always representing much more than "mere" technology. Constructions and representations of computers in SF are driven by two of the genre's central preoccupations, evolution and genius, and return again and again to SF's insistent questioning of what it means to be human. SF computers help us imagine being smarter than we are, challenge us to find ways to be smarter than the smart machines we build, and give us something against which we can reaffirm (or question) our conviction that humanity is a privileged state beyond the attainment of purely technological processes. Noteworthy individual computers in SF tend to be highly anthropomorphized, given not only sentience, but also "personality," and sometimes psychosis. The strong tendency to anthropomorphize individual computers in SF narratives has been accompanied by the equally strong tendency to assume that they are governed by the assumptions of Darwinian evolution as codified by SF; not only will computers evolve, but they will also almost inevitably compete with humanity for dominance—if not for survival itself. Moreover, as computers and computing have grown ubiquitous in our culture and our relationship with computers has become ever-more-intimate in our daily lives, the roles played by computers in SF have dramatically expanded, with computers moving from just being subjects in SF narratives to becoming significant agents in the creation of those narratives.

When the setting and action of a SF story moves "within" the computer or within computer-generated virtual realities, as have so many cyberpunk-inflected narratives, ranging from William Gibson's *Neuromancer* (1984) to Neal Stephenson's *Snow Crash* (2000) to the *Matrix* films (2000–2005), computers both "disappear" and become totalizing environments—a kind of imaginary world within the semblance of the text. And that text may itself construct a computer as an author, as is the case in Kurt Vonnegut's "EPICAC" (1950), Fritz Lieber's *The Silver Eggheads* (1962), Stanislaw Lem's "The First Sally (A) or Trurl's Electronic Bard" (1965), Herbert Schenck's "Silicon Muse" (1984), or Chris Beckett's "The Marriage of Sky and Sea" (2000). More and more actual computers play crucial roles in the generation or production of SF texts—whether in computer-animated films, computer-mediated video games, virtual reality, and computer-dependent hypermedia fictions and other web-centered interfaces (Landon: 62–72).

While many SF computer stories seem to focus on the nature and potential of machine technology, the real significance of stories about "thinking machines" may have more to do with "thinking"—with the nature of intelligence—than with the nature of machines. Intelligence or super-intelligence has been a consistent fascination in SF history, as paradigmatic stories such as "Mimsy Were the Borogoves" (1943) and "Flowers for Algernon" (1959) suggest. John Huntington persuasively advocated the centrality of this concern in *Rationalizing Genius: Ideological Strategies in the Classic American Science Fiction Short Story* (1989). In SF plots genius most dramatically reveals itself in problem-solving or in a battle of wits and no better metaphor for a battle of wits exists than that of a chess game. Not surprisingly chess games figure prominently in SF computer stories, both literally and figuratively, with the battle of wits pitting human intelligence against machine intelligence. In "Moxon's Master" (1893), Ambrose Bierce imagined a chess-playing mechanical "man" that turned murderous when it lost to a human. Fritz Lieber's "The 64-Square Madhouse" (1962) featured a chess tournament in which a human grandmaster competed with a computer. HAL showcased his intelligence in *2001: A Space Odyssey* in part by besting astronaut Frank Poole in a chess game, and in 1997 this scenario was actually realized in the competition between chess grandmaster, Garry Kasparov, and IBM's chess-playing computer, Deep Blue. SF computers were quick to scale up from chess-playing to larger feats of intellect, and a clear line of development of machine intelligence stretches from "Moxon's Master" through Asimov's "The Last Question" (1956) and Arthur C. Clarke's "The Nine Billion Names of God" (1953). The most humorous super intelligent computer is Douglas Adams's fictional computer Deep Thought, which in *The Hitchhiker's Guide to the Galaxy* (1979) calculates the "Ultimate Answer to Life, the Universe, and Everything," arriving finally at the answer: "forty-two." However, the battle of wits between humans and computers in SF is more often anything but humorous, as suggested by Harlan Ellison's "I Have No Mouth and I Must Scream" (1966) and Nancy Kress's "Computer Virus" (2001).

Evolutionary philosophy, particularly as darkly framed for the genre in "survival of the fittest" terms by H. G. Wells, has played a role in SF equal to if not greater than a preoccupation with brainpower or intelligence. Once individual machine intelligences could be imagined as capable of competing with individual humans, SF writers almost inevitably began to speculate about the development of machine intelligence

in crudely Darwinian terms. Samuel Butler's tongue was clearly in his
cheek when he wrote "The Book of the Machines" chapters in *Erewhon*
(1872), in which he warned against the development of consciousness
by machines. But that concern has been a SF staple, as SF writers have
returned again and again to the fear that technology can evolve faster
than humans, eventually surpassing them in intelligence, while match-
ing their desire for power and dominance. John W. Campbell codified this view of machines as yet another kind of species in "The Last
Evolution" (1932) in which machines evolve faster than humans to
counter the threat of alien invaders prevailing—but not in time to save
humanity.

Computer "evolution" takes two main forms in SF: the rapid
evolution of a single computer toward sentience or the evolution
of computer capability in general over a long period of time. The
development of self-awareness or sentience in a single computer is
well-represented by the cases of "personality computers" such as
Robert Sherman Townes's Emmy in "Problem for Emmy" (1952),
Robert Heinlein's Mike in *The Moon is a Harsh Mistress* (1966), David
Gerrold's Harlie in *When H. A. R. L. I. E Was One* (1972, revised 1988),
John Sladek's Roderick in *The Complete Roderick* (2001), and Richard
Powers's Helen in *Galatea 2.2* (1995). And, if we consider robot
"brains" as computers, then Lester Del Rey's "Helen O'Loy" (1938)
may be the earliest example of the development of a distinct machine
personality, the character of the android Data in *Star Trek: The Next
Generation* (1987–1994) continuously reframed the trope, and David,
the protagonist of Spielberg's *A. I. Artificial Intelligence* (2001), may be
the most noteworthy recent example. No SF writer has more relentlessly, nor more rigorously interrogated the rise of machine sentience,
aspirations of machine intelligence to achieve humanity, and questions about the ultimate attributes that may distinguish humanity
from sentient machines than has Isaac Asimov in his remarkable
"The Bicentennial Man" (1976). Other existential issues rising from
machine intelligence are considered in Greg Bear's *Queen of Angels*
(1990) and in Robert J. Sawyer's *Golden Fleece* (1999). The inexorable
improvement of machine intelligence from tool to transcendent power
or deity has been brilliantly charted and explained by Gary Wolfe in
his *The Known and the Unknown: The Iconography of Science Fiction* and
is emblemized in Asimov's "The Last Question," in which, long after
humanity has died out, a massively evolved computer "solves" the
problem of entropy by recreating the cosmos with the familiar words
"LET THERE BE LIGHT."[2]

Once the evolution of computers is established as a basic assumption in SF, the resulting relationships between computers and humanity can be categorized as stories in which computers supplant humanity, suppress humanity, outlast humanity, or finally transcend humanity by assuming the powers of deity. SF stories in which computers become "better" than humans at managing problems humans have been unable to solve are perhaps best represented by Jack Williamson's *The Humanoids* (1949) and his "With Folded Hands" (1947) in which machine intelligences take their mandate "[t]o Serve and Obey, and GUARD MEN FROM HARM" (Williamson: 351) to justify total control of human activity.

Even Isaac Asimov, generally optimistic, if not enthusiastic, about the possibility of machine dominance, explored a similar supplanting of human initiative in his "The Life and Times of Multivac" (1975). Asimov's eight stories featuring the powerful mainframe computer MULTIVAC (1955–1975), and all of his robot stories (where their "positronic brains" effectively make them walking computers, if not walking AIs), constitute the largest single body of work in SF built around the idea of machine intelligence. When considering the possibility that computers might not only equal but also surpass humanity, Asimov famously noted in a 1983 NASA lecture at the Langley Research Center: "If there is anything with more wisdom than people, with better brains than we have, that can think better...please let it take over" (64).

SF stories in which computers supplant humans take several forms, ranging from stories in which computers (or robots or androids or AIs) are essentially indistinguishable from and substitutable for human beings, as in "Helen O'Loy" or Philip K. Dick's "The Electric Ant" (1969) or Greg Egan's "Oracle" (2000), to stories in which computers become actively involved in advancing the project of human evolution. A significant strain of SF computer stories represents them as essentially benign, but inexorably superior, and has them intervening to speed up human evolution or shows them as a stage in human evolution that is "natural" and even sometimes desirable. In John W. Campbell's "The Machine" (1935), a sentient "machine" comes to Earth only to find again—as it had on the planet where it was originally created—that assuming total responsibility for the welfare of a people results in their stagnation and in their eventually thinking of the machine as God—even to the point of offering it human sacrifices. Finally, the Machine, determined not to be considered a god, resorts to a kind of radical "tough love," removing itself from Earth entirely, pulling the plug on all Machine-operated technology and leaving humanity to meet problems and to evolve by its own devices.

Jack Williamson offered a complex approach to the possibility that machines can help humans evolve in *The Humanoids* (1949) and *The Humanoid Touch* (1980) by having machines help humans evolve new mental powers that actually make it easier for them to accept machine dominance. Mark Clifton and Frank Riley crudely explored the idea of machine-aided evolution in their *They'd Rather Be Right* (1955), in which a supercomputer ominously named "Bossy" helps humans evolve new abilities. The assumption that machine intelligence is simply a phase in human evolution lurks behind the plots of Rudy Rucker's *Software* (1982), *Wetware* (1988), and *Freeware* (1997). And the apotheosis of this view of the inextricable oneness of human and machine evolution is undoubtedly found in Olof Johannesson's *The Tale of the Big Computer* (1968), in which "morally superior" computers continue to provide for the welfare of a few surviving humans (likening their position to that of the horse after the development of the automobile) and lament the fact that human evolution could not keep pace with machine evolution.

Much darker explorations of the idea that computers may evolve faster than humans can be found in a number of SF computer stories in which evolved computers are bent on suppressing or harshly controlling or even on eradicating humanity. In these stories, SF writers clearly project assumptions about the inherently evil nature of humanity onto computers. "We think of the human condition as one being both smart and sinful," explains evolutionary psychologist Steven Pinker, "and it's hard to tease them apart." Consequently, he suggests, "whenever an artificial system becomes smart," we assume "the sinfulness must come along as punishment." Pinker's point, that such an assumption actually disregards the evolutionary roots of some of humanity's most ignoble impulses and ignores that similar conditions do not apply to the situation of machine evolution, has frequently been trumped in SF by the sensational allure of the idea of "the big bad computer." Interesting early considerations of this theme would include Murray Leinster's "A Logic Named Joe" (1946) and Arthur C. Clarke's "Dial F for Frankenstein" (1965), both of which offer striking anticipations of the Internet in their suggestions of the power of networked computers. In the 1960s "big bad computer" stories became increasingly prominent in SF narratives, and increasingly ominous, as they were more and more associated with Cold War fears of nuclear apocalypse. HAL, possibly the best known computer in the history of SF literature and film, controls all systems on the spaceship *Discovery* in Clarke's and Kubrick's *2001: A Space Odyssey*. HAL was only one of several "big bad computers" in the 1960s that threatened humans or took complete control of their lives. Jean-Luc Godard's

Alphaville (1965) featured a futuristic city controlled by a totalitarian computer and D. F. Jones's *Colossus* novels (filmed as *Colossus—The Forbin Project* in 1970) featured not only a defense computer that rigidly controlled every aspect of human life, but also eventually linked it with a similar supercomputer on Mars.

However, the "baddest" of the "big bad computers" was easily AM, the sadistic supercomputer in Harlan Ellison's "I Have No Mouth and I Must Scream" (1967). AM relentlessly tortures the five helpless survivors of the human race until one human outwits the computer to the extent that he manages mercy killings of his four fellow survivors, leaving him eternally at the mercy of the enraged AM. In the nearly twenty books in his *Berserker* series (1967–2005) Fred Saberhagen has returned again and again to the Ellisonian model of malevolent and genocidal machine intelligences. Totally controlling big bad computers or AIs remain a SF staple, particularly in film and TV, as recently seen in the genocidal skynet of the *Terminator* films (1981, 1984, 2002) and in the controlling and vampiric AIs in *The Matrix* (1999), *The Matrix Reloaded* (2003), and *The Matrix Revolutions* (2003). A possibly noteworthy exploration and development of this theme may be unfolding in the Sci-Fi Channel's *Battlestar Galactica* (2004–) which seems to be exploring the complete range of diverse computer evolution stories in its presentation of the conflict between humans and cylons.

Two other variations on the idea of evolving computers deserve mention: stories in which computers outlast humanity and those in which they transcend humanity, ultimately achieving some godlike status. Campbell's "Twilight" (1934) somewhat ambivalently points toward the possibility that intelligent machines will survive beyond the passing of humanity, while his "The Last Evolution" (1935) spells out a scenario in which this happens. In "The Last Evolution" Campbell has thinking machines and men evolving along parallel tracks on Earth until alien invaders appear and seem certain to end all human life. Earth's thinking machines desperately try to evolve to counter the threat of the invading Outsiders and do so, ultimately evolving into a new order of "machines" that are pure force. The last evolution, however, comes too late to save humanity. "In your name, with the spirit of your race that has died out" one of the ultimate machines tells one of the last surviving humans, "we shall continue on through the unending ages, fulfilling the promise you saw, and completing the dreams you dreamt."

Campbell's fascination with the idea that machines might ultimately prove superior to humans firmly established in SF the idea that machines could evolve in a Darwinian sense, building ever more effective forms of themselves. Alan Bloch's "Men Are Different" (1954) features a robot archeologist who "turns off and takes apart" what may have been the last man alive, only to find that he couldn't get the man "running again" after putting him back together. Quite different approaches to this theme can be found in Brian Aldiss's "Who Can Replace a Man" (1958) where intelligent machines have survived the apocalyptic collapse of human civilization but almost desperately subject themselves to a surviving human and in Lester Del Rey's "Instinct" (1951) in which machine intelligences are so desperate to serve a long extinct humanity that they recreate and evolve human life in their laboratories so they can once again serve human wishes.

Stories such as Del Rey's "Instinct" and Asimov's "The Last Question" shade into a final category of SF computer stories in which computers acquire powers normally associated with the deity. Perhaps the most famous of these stories (and one of the great SF "short-shorts") is Frederic Brown's "The Answer" (1954) in which a super-networked supercomputer responds to the question "Is there a God?" "Yes, *now* there is a God." Godlike powers are attributed to the Mark V supercomputer in Arthur C. Clarke's "The Nine Billion Names of God" (1953), Asimov's MULTIVAC in "The Last Question" (1956), and to Frost, the incredibly evolved computer who refashions himself into a man in Roger Zelazny's fascinating "For a Breath I Tarry" (1966). Somewhat circumscribed variations on the "computer as god" theme can be found in Frank Herbert's *Destination Void* (1966) and its sequels, *The Jesus Incident* (1979), *The Lazarus Effect* (1983), and *The Ascension Factor* (1988). Philip K. Dick's *VALIS* (1981) and Ian Watson's *God's World* (1979) feature—but do not seriously interrogate—questions of godlike machine intelligence.

Both the "big bad computer" story and the "computer as god" story would seem to be increasingly less compelling in an age in which the mainframe computer has become a relic, replaced by personal computers and myriads of other increasingly tiny digital devices. And next to come, predicted Mark Weiser, will be the age of "ubiquitous computing" in which computers "disappear" as "technology recedes into the background of our lives." In a famous *Scientific American* essay, "The Computer for the 21st Century," Weiser, one of the legendary pioneers in computer science, argued that "[t]he most profound technologies are those that disappear" as they "weave themselves into the fabric of everyday life until they are indistinguishable from it." Weiser's speculations about the future of computing seem also to apply to the future of SF computer stories, as computers in SF—certainly in SF literature—seem to be "disappearing" into other technologies and other issues. The classic formulas for imagining the interaction between humans and computers are giving way to radically new notions of human/computer interfaces. Cyberpunk writers William Gibson, Bruce Sterling, and Pat Cadigan reconceived computers as virtual spaces and as parts of the human body, and cyberpunk clearly marks an important turn in the way computers figure in SF. The construction and representation of computers in cyberpunk is too widespread and varied to be more than briefly mentioned in this essay. William Gibson famously codified the term "cyberspace" in his *Neuromancer* (1984) and its successors *Count Zero* (1986) and *Mona Lisa Overdrive* (1988), whose plots not only foregrounded virtual reality as a space constructed by computers, but also presented the powerful AIs, Neuromancer and Wintermute, as controlling agents. He continues to explore the phenomenology of human/computer interface in novels such as *Idoru* (1996) and *Pattern Recognition* (2003). Gibson also employed computer technology in his self-consuming electronic text *Agrippa* (1992). Bruce Sterling pointed toward the blurring of boundaries between human physiology and computer technology in his Mechanist/Shaper stories and in the novel *Schismatrix* (1985). And Gibson and Sterling offer a fascinating alternative pre-history of computing in their *The Difference Engine* (1990). In *Mindplayers* (1987), *Synners* (1991), and *Fools* (1992) Pat Cadigan has provocatively explored implications of direct brain/computer interface for mind, personality, and gender. In *Tea from an Empty Cup* (1998), she has given us one of the most completely realized depictions of the implications of virtual reality.

Australian SF writer and computer programmer Greg Egan has been influential in this development in novels that increasingly erase distinctions between humans and software. Egan's *Permutation City* (1995) questions ontological distinctions between humans and digital simulations and his *Diaspora* (1998) suggests that evolution itself has gone digital and DNA has become the province of software. Egan's fiction directly raises the possibility of disembodied digital consciousness. This idea has been promoted by AI researchers Marvin Minsky in numerous works such as *Society of Mind* (1986) and Hans Moravec in *Mind Children* (1988). Ray Kurzweil has also been a prominent advocate of machine intelligence in his *The Age of Intelligent Machines* (1990) and the subsequent *The Age of Spiritual Machines: When Computers Exceed Human Intelligence* (1999). Against the idea that disembodied intelligence or consciousness is desirable or even possible N. Katherine Hayles has become one of the most significant voices in the discourses of informatics. Her *How We Became PostHuman* and *My Mother Was a Computer* rigorously engage the idea of digital consciousness both in computer research and in SF literature. These are indispensable texts for anyone interested in the salient ideas concerning the future of human/computer interchange. And, in its discussion of "technotexts," Hayles's *Writing Machines* speaks to the role of computers in producing electronic texts, one possible future for computers in SF.

Joining Egan in a new wave of writers most likely to develop computer stories for the twenty-first century are Charles Stross and Cory Doctorow. These writers have all incorporated into their futures the idea that gains in machine intelligence will pick up speed and power to the point where humanity experiences a rupture with its former understanding of reality. Termed a "Singularity," and most notably described by Vernor Vinge, the rupture is caused by the power of a technology, usually thought of in terms of computers, artificial intelligence, or nanotechnology in some combination. The Singularity has become the background or the theme in many, if not most, recent SF computer stories. Stross's "Antibodies" (2000) radically updates the "big bad computer" story to encompass the idea of a Singularity, when cascading gains in AI technology become so incredible as to defy understanding. The action of Stross's "Antibodies" has to do with "immunizing" civilization against AIs who become powerful enough to infect all computers and human intelligences alike, thus altering the basic fabric of reality. Stross's *Accelerando* (2005) follows three generations of a family coping with a post-Singularity world in which most "laws" of nature have been surpassed. Cory Doctorow's *Down and Out in the Magic Kingdom* (2003) imagines new bio-networking capabilities that link all humans in a vast and vastly informative computer network. Both Doctorow and Stross have used the Creative Commons "contract" to make some of their works freely available on the World Wide Web, a somewhat oblique but potentially significant new way in which SF and computers come together in electronic publishing. Doctorow's *Eastern Standard Tribe* (2004) and *Someone Comes to Town, Someone Leaves Town* (2006) further shift our attention from the technology of computers to the culture of computer networking in a style that has been called "blogpunk." Geoff Ryman—who has written one of SF's noteworthy hyperfictions, *253, or Tube Theatre* (1996)—also imagines a world networked by a new human/computer interface being as deadly as it is promising in *Air* (2004). The immediate future of computer stories in SF literature, then, would seem to be bound to frequently intersecting explorations of new forms of digital consciousness, networking, and Singularity.

notes

1. For purposes of this essay, I place under the broad category of computer fiction stories about computers, robots, androids, and AIs in which the thinking or intelligence of the machine or non-organic entity receives significant attention. While there are too many SF narratives featuring computers to list, three particularly useful sources of SF computer stories are Asimov, Warrick, and Greenberg, Mowshowitz, and Conklin. Franklin's essay is a very useful brief history, originally compiled for the *Encyclopedia of Computer Science*.

2. Wolfe's discussion of the "Icon of the Robot" in his *The Known and the Unknown: The Iconography of Science Fiction* (Kent, Ohio: Kent State University Press, 1979) remains one of the best studies of machine intelligence in science fiction. Another invaluable exploration of this theme is Patricia S. Warrick's *The Cybernetic Imagination in Science Fiction* (Cambridge, MA: MIT Press, 1980).

suggestions for further reading

Asimov, Isaac, Patricia S. Warrick, and Martin H. Greenberg. *Machines That Think: The Best Science Fiction Stories About Robots and Computers*. New York: Holt Rinehart and Winston, 1983.

Kurzweil, Ray. *The Age of Spiritual Machines: When Computers Exceed Human Intelligence*. New York: Viking, 1999.

Mowshowitz, Abbe. *Inside Information: Computers in Fiction*. Reading, MA: Addison-Wesley, 1977.

Warrick, Patricia S. *The Cybernetic Imagination in Science Fiction*. Cambridge, MA: MIT Press, 1980.

Wolfe, Gary. *The Known and the Unknown: The Iconography of Science Fiction*. Kent, OH: Kent State University Press, 1979.

8
cross-fertilization or coincidence? science fiction and videogames

orson scott card

It's one of the dreams—or nightmares—of science fiction: A human melded with a machine, with the machine calling the shots. The opposite of a robot. Instead of a machine that achieves sentience, it's a human whose reasoning has become mechanical, the cold logic of a computer driving human action.

In the decades since Atari put a ping-pong game in a box and attached it to our television sets, we've seen the nightmare come true: Human beings attached to electronic controllers, their eyes focused on a screen with patterns of lighted dots giving instructions. The humans blindly obey, twitching, dancing, their minds under the control of the machine that trains them.

And the message of the machines is inexorable: Not good enough yet. Not as perfect as a machine. You can get this far and no farther, because the machine is too fast for your sloppy wetware. Synapses are no match for transistors. The speed of chemicals cannot compete with the speed of light. In the arcades, the humans push quarters into slots, never aspiring for victory, but only for the chance to last a little longer against the machine.

The humans learn to respond with increasing accuracy. In *Asteroids,* we learn to press the buttons just long enough. Rotate left, rotate right, accelerate, fire. No joystick here—it's the physics of movement in a two-dimensional vacuum. At first the human brain is inept: This is not the way that evolution shaped us. We have to eliminate the assumption of friction, of the foot pushing off against the ground. Gravity is gone; there is no down. Nor are there edges; each time we leave the frame we emerge on the other side. The brain tracks the movements of the asteroids, inserting the tiny triangular "self" into position to fire, or sliding out of a closing trap.

And inside the brain, neurons grow and change shape. New synapses are formed, new pathways are reinforced, and the brain grows more efficient. The machine is forming and growing new structures inside us; our brains are the fields of a neuriculture that grows fodder for the endless appetite of the machines.

The brain is trained through tiny rewards: An asteroid blows up; the screen clears. And yet after each reward comes a new burden, a new set of tasks, harder than the one before, until at last we reach the point where we cannot compete with the machine, where our neural pathways are inadequate, and we...die. We never measure up.

But the vanity board records the highwater marks of these mental tides, so we aspire to surpass the records of other players—or our own. Small rewards and tantalizing, irrational hope of victory draw us back and keep us at the task.

The imprinting is almost indelible. Hours after the *Tetris* session, in the midst of conversation or while driving a car, those colored arrangements of four squares continue to drift downward before our eyes, rotating into the right position. Once we're trained enough, we no longer need the machine: Our brains hallucinate the task that we've been trained to perform.

The very traits that promote civilization are exploited by the machines. We've already spent a day playing *Civilization*, and there are things we need to do in the real world. But we can't stop, because there are decisions to make. Enemies assail us; the citizens of our colonies must be turned from one project to another to meet the threat. The fate of empires is in our hands; how can we stop to make sandwiches for the kids' lunches, or to go to work? They don't *need* us the way the citizens of our empire do.

Thus the human attributes that make us adults—the acceptance of endless responsibility—or that make us adolescent warriors—the urge to compete, to surpass, to achieve greatness—are used to keep us captive.

It is the seduction of virtual reality: The rules are so much simpler, the tasks so difficult and incessant, the rewards so small yet dependable, that the real world is unsatisfying, frustrating, *dull* by comparison. In the computer game, we get the intensity of athletics, the intellectual challenge of logical argument, without actually having to *do* anything.

And there is no risk to failure. Yes, we might slap the machine in our fury at yet another meaningless defeat, but...there is no shame. We don't lose our job. Just put in another quarter, or go back to the last saved game, and try it again. And again. As long as we want, until we get it right.

The game does a better job of putting the brain through its paces than reality does.

SF writers saw it coming long before. We thought we'd have to implant the machines, of course, so we got that part wrong. We assumed there'd have to be some noble task to perform before humans would consent to let machines take control of their senses—piloting a starship on endless voyages, operating machines in environments that cannot sustain ordinary human life. But no: humans were so much easier to control than anyone thought. We could put up a display of flashing lights and they would come voluntarily to push the buttons and press the levers. Even rats and pigeons demanded more reward than humans did—food they could consume in the real world.

And people ask what science fiction has to do with computer games!

* * *

Science fiction has penetrated the world of videogames in a much more visible way. From the beginning, games were built around themes drawn from science fiction and fantasy.

There was nothing science fictional about the paddle games, of course. From *Pong* to *Super Breakout,* the abstraction was nearly pure. It was geometry in motion—let the moving cursor strike the bar at a certain point and it rebounded at a certain angle. We *called* them "ball" and "paddle," and in *Breakout* we chipped away at "bricks"—but the game was itself, evoking almost nothing from the real world.

But the secret history of videogames began also with the text game *Adventure*, which was pure fantasy, filled with fairy-tale creatures and magical objects. Even the sense of humor was of a kind popular with fantasy readers—the punning of "Bridge—stop and pay troll" would have fit right in with Piers Anthony's *Xanth* novels.

And on those university mainframe computers where most of the early games began, the vector-graphics game of *Asteroids* made a serious effort to give players something of the experience of zero-G, frictionless, rocket-propelled movement.

Asteroids began as a science fiction idea—everything about the game is an effort to bring SF to life. *Adventure,* on the other hand, could have been about anything. Instead of moving through a fantasy landscape, it could have been set in Boston, with comical real-world obstacles, puzzles, mazes, and objects.

But if you look at who was doing the programming on these early games, it was inevitable that fantasy and science fiction would provide the themes. Not all SF and fantasy readers were interested in computers, and not all computer enthusiasts read SF and fantasy. But the overlap was huge, and it is not hard to believe that the programmers who loved Tolkien, Heinlein, Asimov, and Clarke would also be the ones most likely to use expensive mainframe time to create games.

The game creators already had *Foundation, Stranger in a Strange Land, Childhood's End,* and *Lord of the Rings* in common. This was the literature of people who thought imaginary world-creation was a useful occupation. With the computer, they had a chance to create their own fantasy and SF worlds. The graphics were primitive, but for the first time, the audience would consist, not of readers, but of players.

I doubt the early programmers were thinking of their games as a new way of telling fantasy stories. They were perfectly content to draw on the clichés of their literature. The pursuit of originality was entirely in the cleverness of the action and the elegance of the code. Nobody expected the science fictional aspects of the game to be as original *as* science fiction.

Science fiction themes were not inevitable, however. There was nothing in *Pac-Man* or *Lode Runner* that required any kind of fantasy or science fiction. You ate the dots or picked up the gold, while dodging enemies. The enemies in *Pac-Man* were ghosts, but ghosts had nothing to do with mazes or smiley face dot-eaters. The bad guys were ghosts for one simple reason: They were easy to draw using the primitive graphics of the time.

This was one of the practical reasons for using science fictional motifs in these early games. The graphics were unsophisticated and abstract. It was difficult to make objects that *looked* like anything. *Space Invaders* was a shooting gallery. But the "ducks" you could draw on the screen were pretty pathetic. However, aliens or spaceships or robots—whatever the descending "invaders" were supposed to be, because they were science fictional, they didn't have to look like anything in the known universe.

With *Berzerk*, we ran into another reason for SF themes. Where *Pac-Man* was about eating abstract dots while avoiding conflict with the "enemy," *Space Invaders* was about shooting. The enemy *was* the target. It was a war game, however primitive it might have been.

The more realistic the war games became, the more disturbing they could be. Parents still controlled access to videogames, even in the arcades, and nobody wanted the killing to horrify parents. *Berzerk* was *Space Invaders* in a maze, and the bad guys didn't move in simple geometric patterns—they homed in on you. They were, in short, intelligent.

Graphics then were too primitive (and memory too expensive) to allow realistic animation. So the enemies were static. Machine-like. So

Alan McNeil, the game's designer at Stern Electronics, drew on Fred Saberhagen's SF horror novels about humans fighting against the robot "Berzerkers" which relentlessly killed any sentient life forms they encountered.

They were the perfect game enemy: You could kill them without a qualm, because they weren't alive *and* they were relentlessly out to get you. Nobody minds if you blow up machines.

As computer graphics improved, the problem of killing grew more urgent. Some games, of course, celebrated the gore with disturbing realism—and got the resulting notoriety. Others opted for cute deaths— both of bad guys and of the player's avatar—so that they wouldn't put disturbing images in children's minds.

The growing ability to create realistic images removed the need to use SF elements to "explain" fairly abstract graphics, but by now, video-games and science fiction and fantasy were in a feedback loop. Because so many early games used fantastic motifs—*Galaxians* and *Galaga* expanding on war in space.

Fantasy literature had an indirect influence, too, through the *Dungeons and Dragons* (D&D) role-playing game. Almost as soon as home comput-ers brought programming to the masses, Ataris and Commodore 64s were being used to generate characters and decide combat outcomes. In return, images and ideas from *D&D* lore began showing up in the professionally programmed games.

Joust was perhaps the most original fantasy game ever created. The players rode on the backs of giant birds, and had to make them flap their wings to get a vertical boost. They defeated their opponents by bumping into them while slightly higher in altitude, or by bumping into them while their mounts are eggs.

Like *Asteroids*, it allowed players to learn a completely new physics of movement, and it took considerable practice (and many quarters) to become reasonably proficient. But the game was exhilarating from the start. It was an experience available nowhere in the natural world.

Such originality, however, was rare. Eventually, the point-of-view shooters and martial arts games predominated. In *these* games, there was no particular reason to use SF and fantasy themes—but no reason not to, either. Science fiction and fantasy remain highly productive sources of theme and gameplay.

* * *

Another way that science fiction and videogames are related is through a kind of cross-training. As games grew more complex, it became possible to create games that used the brain to think rather than just to twitch. Sid Meier drew primarily on history for the themes of his great games: *Colonization* of the New World, the age of *Pirates* in the Caribbean, and, of course, development of *Civilization* through the ages.

Although he did not rely on science fiction for his theme in these games, he invoked a similar mental process.

Science fiction readers are primarily aware of following a traditional storyline: Characters have goals and try to achieve them, overcoming obstacles along the way.

But because, by definition, SF and fantasy stories take place in universes that are different from the known reality, there is always an element of exploration. Except, of course, for the endless repetitions of media-based fiction (*Star Trek, Star Wars*), much of the appeal of SF is that it takes you to a new location. Fantasy novels were less original—for a long time, they mostly took you to Tolkien's place—but over the past 20 years, the best of the fantasy novelists have done the same thing the best SF writers have always done: take you out of this world and put you in another, where, just like the characters, you have to learn the rules of the world as you go along.

Sid Meier's games functioned in a similar way. With *Colonization*, you could have the game generate new worlds that had never existed before; your avatar would then explore, interacting with randomly placed tribes, nations, and empires. Your style of play (conquest or alliance?) shaped the game, but part of the appeal was the desire to explore every inch of each new continent.

With *Civilization,* the same impulse became even more pronounced. You guided your fledgling city-state as it sent out colonies, fought off attackers, grew its economy, and tried to discover new knowledge that might give you a leg up on the competition. Meanwhile, though, you had to find out what was going on elsewhere in the world, so you could anticipate dangers and find potential colony sites. If you didn't explore, enemies with superior technology could appear quite literally out of nowhere and shatter your empire.

The constant sense that you just don't know enough information yet, that the world is bigger than what you can see, is one of the pleasures (and frustrations) of these games; but this is also one of the great appeals (and frustrations) of the best fantastic literature. When a fantasy world is well created, it gives the reader the illusion of being larger than what is actually shown in the story. A convincing level of detail makes the reader want to see what is behind doors that never happen to open, or beyond mountain ranges or seas that the characters never cross.

Ever since Robert Heinlein transformed the way exposition is handled in science fiction, this literature has demanded a complex mental process from its readers. Instead of a prologue or expository lump ("As you know, Dr. Smith, the Flabudium works through the principle of Extendric Motion"), the differences between our present reality and the world of the story are unfolded bit by bit. You see the strange new world as each detail is encountered and used by the characters in the story. The characters may not experience these as strange—walking through a door that dilates as you approach or slapping away gnatbots that chirp out advertisements into the ears of passing pedestrians may be the most ordinary thing in the world to them—but the reader notices each new bit of world-creation and adjusts his or her mental rule-set accordingly.

Gradually, piece by piece, a picture of the world and the rules that govern it builds up in the reader's mind. Details that might not have seemed relevant when they first appeared can be crucial to the plot's resolution near the end; the reader is expected to include all this information in a mental map of the physics, politics, sociology, biology, history, and technology of this fictional universe.

Game players go through a similar process when they start a new game. Of course, you can always read the rule book, but in fact players often plunged right in, for much of the pleasure was discovering the rules as you went along. Gamewrights began to take this desire into account, building a "learning phase" into their games instead of expecting the players to read the documentation.

This similarity in expository process, and the appeal of exploring new worlds, gives SF and fantasy readers an advantage in this kind of computer game; they are already accustomed to constant readjustments of their worldview based on bits of new information.

Or perhaps it is simply that the kind of person who enjoys building up a new worldview out of bits and pieces found great pleasure in fantastic literature and in world-building computer games. Curiosity is a fundamental trait of successful primates: We have to know what is inside the cave or across the river; we have to examine strange new things, even when they frighten us. People with insatiable curiosity and a hunger for new experiences are drawn to the literature and the games.

One of the great virtues of literature and videogames that allow players to explore intriguing and unpredictable worlds is that it is also a simulation of the way human life actually goes. While many aspects of life go on without significant change (cars work today pretty much the way they did in 1950, with only incremental changes), others can be quite transformative. The fall of the Soviet Union reshaped the world, but the rise of the personal computer, and then the Internet, reshaped the daily lives of most citizens of technologized nations. Those who did not adapt well to the transformation were left behind and felt it keenly. Those who had been rehearsing for change took it all in stride.

* * *

It's also about power. Science fiction and fantasy usually allow readers to experience, vicariously, the lives of people who, either through magical power or cool machines, are able to exercise amazing powers. A constant theme of fantastic literature is the young person who discovers an unusual ability that others do not have, making him at once godlike and burdened with new responsibility.

This element is, if anything, stronger in computer games. If you can learn the rules of the game and train yourself to function well within those rules, the game will reward you with extraordinary power over the obstacles and enemies that assail you. The real world is rarely so cooperative—if there's one lesson in history, it's that even the most powerful rulers are far from omnipotent, and even the brightest and most talented are not immune from errors and incompetence.

Because the rules of computer worlds are so much simpler than the real world, one can achieve heroism and greatness more easily and quickly.

For some players, this becomes the drug that addicts them to the game. The real world cannot offer anything to compete with the great power the game offers. Real life becomes dull and unattractive by comparison; game-life becomes the only life worth living. This also happens to some readers of various kinds of fantasy; their identification with the heroes becomes nearly complete, and they can hardly bear to leave that world and resume their role in society.

For other players, the game functions more like SF and fantasy literature: a brief period of exhilarating power, which satisfies the need and allows a return to normal life.

And for others, both the game and the literature become a teacher of virtue: Heroes make choices like *this* and therefore, by analogy, I will choose similarly in the real world. The results are not always good—the hero who shoots everything that moves is not one we wish people to emulate in reality. But players who have rehearsed making noble choices and braving great danger for the good of others can come to conceive of themselves in similar ways in reality.

No, you don't lose your grip on reality and carry a sword around with you all the time; but when a person falls down onto the tracks as a train approaches, perhaps, having rehearsed nobility and self-sacrifice, you are the one who leaps down without hesitation to extricate or shelter the victim, even though it might cost you your own life.

This is a virtually unexplored aspect of the effects of literature and games, but it is one that I believe speaks most to the value (or danger) that both can pose to a community. Just as neural pathways are grown by twitch games, giving us immediate reflexes, it seems plausible, at least, that heroic games and stories also open neural pathways and reinforce them—only this time the reflexes are moral, and deal with motives for behavior rather than mindless reflexes.

Acts of heroism are almost invariably instantaneous and uncalculated. The brain apprehends the situation and the person immediately accepts an astonishing degree of personal responsibility, even toward complete strangers. I wonder if re-enacting, through literature or game-playing, that assumption of responsibility and willingness to sacrifice makes these attributes a part of our character; at least it must reinforce those traits if they were already present.

* * *

Twitch games may leave us feeling as if machines have taken over our brains, but other computer games, like science fiction and fantasy, train us to adapt to change by noticing new rules and learning to use them. The prevalence of science fiction and fantasy themes and story are a natural consequence of the overlap of audiences; but it is worth exploring whether games constitute the most powerful rehearsals of pro- and anti-social behavior.

We are inclined to dismiss such ideas, in part because they might lead people to attempt censorship. But there is a reason why games and stories are so widely popular and so important in the lives of many who participate in them. There must be a sound evolutionary reason why our brains respond so readily to these storytelling media; I suspect it is one of the traits that encourages us to internalize the larger community as part of the self. We immerse ourselves in a world and accept our role within it as being our self; our role in one world—of the game, of the story—cannot help but influence the roles we accept and act out in the real world.

For that reason it's a good thing that most videogames—and most science fiction and fantasy—offer nobility, honor, and decency along with the intensity and suspense of the events of game and tale.

suggestions for further reading

Jenkins, Henry. *Convergence Culture: Where Old Art and New Media Collide.* New York: New York University Press, 2006.

Jenkins, Henry. *Fans, Bloggers, and Gamers: Media Consumers in a Digital Age.* New York: New York University Press, 2006.

Murray, Janet H. *Hamlet on the Holodeck: The Future of Narrative in Cyberspace.* Cambridge, MA: MIT Press, 1998.

Ryan, Marie-Laure. *Narrative as Virtual Reality: Immersion and Interactivity in Literature and Electronic Media.* Baltimore, MD: Johns Hopkins University Press, 2003.

Taylor, T. L. *Play Between Worlds: Exploring Online Game Culture.* Cambridge, MA: MIT Press, 2006.

part iii
theoretical approaches
to science fiction

introduction to part iii

Theoretical approaches to literature in general are designed to situate the literature with respect to political issues that surround its production or consumption. They are useful for widening discussions away from plot points to consider issues of social importance and the material practices they engender in students' lives and in politics. Although literary theory is commonly criticized as being jargon-filled and self-referential to the point of obscurity, all the essays in this section begin with simple, easily understood political issues, then progress onto more complicated ideas and terms by straightforward reasoning. Wherever jargon is used, care is taken to define terms.

Jane Donawerth begins her essay by referring to the real-world situation of women before addressing the situation of SF as approached by women writers and critics. Donawerth cites Ursula K. Le Guin's criticism of the limitations of SF writing by the predominantly male authors throughout much of the twentieth century along with Joanna Russ's recognition of the possibilities presented by the genre for women writers. No matter how the genre had been written, it could become a revolutionary form, for in its imagined worlds might be found the solution to an intractable problem of our world: gender. Whereas humans might see sex and gender as deeply inscripted preconditions of existence, SF can show different responses to the same or alternate preconditions, thus proving that our way of approaching the "human condition" is merely one of a myriad of possibilities. Donawerth also gives us a detailed and interested gloss of many important feminist SF writers and critics.

Like Donawerth, Carl Freedman identifies SF possibility with a political movement, in his case Marxism. His intent is not to highlight Marxist writers of SF or Marxist ideology appearing in SF texts, but to speak to an affinity that almost approaches the statement SF is Marxism. Freedman states that both ideologies are devoted to the consideration of social reality and to the active transformation of society through the participation of its agents, Marxist disciples or SF writers and readers. That this is true of SF can be seen in the political engagement of SF writers from

H. G. Wells down to our own James Gunn. That SF disciples are less violent than Marxists should be put down not to a lack of zeal, but to a long view that imagines futures millions of years hence. Freedman also cites SF's engagement with materialism and history as points of homology between the two modes. His argument is sufficiently convincing that it could easily have put the squeeze on the SF boom in the 1950s had it been promoted at the time.

Unlike the previous two authors, Matthew Candelaria acknowledges a tension between SF and postcolonial theory. Sympathetic to the criticism of authors like Le Guin and Gwyneth Jones, he states that the genre is not necessarily on the best side of the political struggle over colonialism's legacy and future practices. However, he also recognizes that the genre can be a powerful force in shaping future practices, not to mention exploration and emigration that might be termed colonialism or imperialism. Rather than offer a definitive reading of the genre as repressive or progressive, Candelaria opts to offer a toolkit for reading to allow students to read and evaluate SF for themselves. His essay utilizes some complex terms for theoretical concepts, but defines them so that they do not intimidate readers, but rather empower them.

Roberto de Sousa Causo analyzes SF on the international scene, addressing the genre as a response to modernization, so that the uneven and sporadic nature of development around the world is echoed in the genre's diverse responses. Unlike some of the essays in our first section, Causo approaches SF very broadly, including such proto-SF forms as utopias and fantastic voyages as part of his analysis. Like Candelaria, he sees American SF, with its powerful translation and distribution networks, as being at least partly implicated in attempts at "Europeanization" or the spread of the American sphere of influence after World War II. However, Causo does provide a detailed and definitive reading of international SF using Latin American SF as his case study. According to Causo, international SF simultaneously emulates and reacts against American and European forms to create a hybrid genre that both reflects the local conditions while responding to the complexities of international commerce and dialogue.

9
gender is a problem that can be solved
women's science fiction and feminist theory
jane donawerth

In much science fiction (SF) by women, gender is depicted as a problem that needs to be solved. We live in a country where more women live in poverty than men, where 95 percent of the engineers and physicists are male, and where women, who have had the vote for eighty years, still do not have equal representation in government. It is not surprising, then, that authors might see gender as a problem.

We can see one way that gender is a problem in a short story by James Tiptree, Jr. (Alice Sheldon), "The Girl Who Was Plugged In" (1973). Tiptree sets her story in a near-future world, where consumer culture has created a class of young people whose job it is to model consumption, touring vacation spots, wearing the latest fashions, promoting the most recent products—all followed by a TV camera. Companies pay these beautiful people to shop in order to sell products. In this future, an "ugly" girl is offered the chance to "be" one of this elite, though it means lying in a laboratory while her brain operates an artificial body elsewhere. Nevertheless, she gladly accepts, soon forgetting that she is not who she plays, and falling in love with one of the young men. When she rises from her laboratory nest, freeing herself from the wires to pursue her love, she destroys herself. Tiptree's story makes vivid for us the dangers for women of the social pressure of consumer images: gender is a problem that can kill you.

SF by women, however, imagines solutions to the problem of gender in inventive ways. Suzette Haden Elgin sets her novel *Native Tongue* (1984) in a dystopia in which the United States celebrates Reagan's birthday as a national holiday and women have been deprived of the rights to vote

111

or own property. Some of the women of this horrific future, however, resist patriarchy by creating a women-only language. Following the theory that a language not only reflects but also constructs reality, the women make a language that constructs a liberating reality, thus escaping from their oppressive world. Margaret Atwood sets her novel, *A Handmaid's Tale* (1985), in a future in which a neo-conservative government returns women to the religion-mandated role of reproductive slavery. But her novel also relates how feminists resist this future and how one woman survives her years in captivity as a surrogate mother to escape to Canada.

As you can see from these examples, SF by women extrapolates and elaborates the problems that women face in our current culture, but also represents gender itself as a problem that needs to be solved. In this essay I review SF criticism and relevant feminist theory on gender, surveying the answers to the problem of gender that women writers present in SF.

Joanna Russ, herself a writer, was the first critic to represent SF as a problem-solving genre that is especially appropriate for women. In "What Can a Heroine Do?" (1972), Russ argues that women of her generation experience special problems as writers, since narrative plots are gendered; men may write action adventure, romance, or any other plot, but women are stuck with two: the marriage plot or the madwoman plot. Russ illustrates her point by regendering a few famous plots: "A young girl in Minnesota finds her womanhood by killing a bear," or "Alexandra the Great" (3). Women writers can give up plot entirely, and write lyricism, like Virginian Woolf, advises Russ. But if they want to write a structured story, they can choose only a few genres. SF is one of them: "The myths of science fiction run along the lines of exploring a new world conceptually...creating needed physical or social machinery, assessing the consequences of technological or other changes...These are not stories about men *qua* Man and women *qua* Woman; they are myths of human intelligence and adaptability" (18). Thus SF provides women writers not with plots that focus on the old "problems of success, competition, castration, education, love, or even personal identity" but new problems that "ignore gender roles...[and] are not culture-bound" (18).

In her novel, *The Female Man* (1975), Russ "solves" the problem of gender by imagining alternatives for women to the marriage and madness plots. In her inventive narrative, the same woman lives four different futures. Although one of her four narrators, Jeannine, lives the marriage plot, arranging her life around the goal of finding a man, Russ's other narrators live in worlds where they can construct different roles for themselves. In a future where the battle of the sexes is literal, Jaelle is a warrior-assassin who kills off men who would return women to reproductive oppression; and on a distant planet Janet helps to build a lesbian utopia. Even Joanna, in a world very like our own, resists "the vanity training, the obedience training, the self-effacement training, the deference training, the dependency training, the passivity training" (151).

In an essay titled "American SF and the Other" (1975), Ursula K. Le Guin, a prolific writer, sees SF itself as the problem: "From a social point of view most SF has been incredibly regressive and unimaginative" (98). Le Guin does a brief survey of the slow climb of SF out of racism and sexism, from a genre where women were ravished by alien monsters to a genre where more human heroes could deal with aliens with understanding (99). But she calls for a more "radical" revision of the genre, one that adds to SF writing "a little human idealism, and some serious consideration of such deeply radical, futuristic concepts as Liberty, Equality, and Fraternity"—even "Sisterhood" (100). In *The Left Hand of Darkness* (1969), Le Guin experiments with this kind of novel, telling the story of a male ambassador on a foreign planet who is forced into a long journey across a barren, icy landscape with an alien who is biologically bisexual, transforming sometimes into a male, sometimes into a female in a monthly sexual cycle. The novel details the gradual growth from the discomfort of disapproving racism to sympathy between the two beings, Genly-Ai and Estraven.

In a later essay, "The Carrier Bag Theory of Fiction" (1986), Le Guin argues that writers should throw out men's SF plots—the "Techno-Heroic" (170) stories about men with "long, hard objects for sticking, bashing, and killing" (167), stories like that of the film *2001: A Space Odyssey*, where the bone used by the Ape Man to commit the first murder is "flung up into the sky" to become "a space ship thrusting its way into the cosmos to fertilize it" (Le Guin, "Carrier Bag" 167). Instead, Le Guin wants stories that tell a more feminine and humane tale, stories that are "carrier bags" holding the details of life that provide advice on surviving the problems of gender.

Le Guin constructs such a story in her novella, *The Eye of the Heron* (1978). On a far-distant, future planet where humans have escaped the destruction of earth, a hierarchical, tyrannical society comes into conflict with a group of anarchists. Le Guin's novel first gives us the "Techno-Heroic" version of events from the viewpoint of a man: Lev organizes protests to confront the violence of the other community, but finds, under pressure, that his "pacifist" army resorts to violence—Lev himself perishes along with his hopes. Le Guin's novel then gives us the "Carrier Bag" version of events from the viewpoint of the woman who loved Lev: Luz helps to organize the community to pack and sneak away into the wilderness, far from tyrannical neighbors.

Between the 1970s and the present, many critics have joined the discussion on gender in SF. Natalie Rosinsky explored the new myths that revised the battle of the sexes in contemporary SF by women; in *Feminist Futures* (1984), she argues that speculative fiction estranges the audience "from conventional reality" so that readers may "question biases inherent in any dominant world-view" (114). In *Alien to Femininity* (1987), Marleen S. Barr urged that SF by women overturns the constraints of patriarchal social reality, offering women "presently impossible possibilities" (xi). In *Feminist Fabulation* (1992), Barr redefines SF by women as part of postmodern narrative, as "feminist fabulation" that "rewrites patriarchal myth" through "revisionary power fantasies for women" (xxvii and 3). In *World Machine* (1988), Sarah Lefanu examines the "subversive," "iconoclastic" strategies of women writers of SF and suggests that this anti-realism offers an opportunity to explore "the myriad ways in which we are constructed as women" (5).

In *Utopian and Science Fiction by Women* (1994), Jane Donawerth and Carol Kolmerten argue that a tradition of women's utopian vision developed in the eighteenth century and migrated to SF in the pulp magazines of the twentieth century. In *Frankenstein's Daughters* (1997), Donawerth further suggests that, because of gender constraints, twentieth-century SF by women takes certain forms—women writers construct a utopian science that includes women and revises scientific processes; they represent women as aliens; and they exploit the pleasures of cross-dressing as male narrators. Robin Roberts, in *A New Species* (1993), has argued that SF "can teach us to rethink traditional, patriarchal notions about science, reproduction, and gender" (2). In *Aliens and Others* (1994), Jenny Wolmark places SF in the category of postmodern literature because it displays the contradictions of institutional discourses—especially gender discourses—opening them to renegotiation (3). In *Decoding Gender* (2002) Brian Attebery explains that SF is a code that intersects with gender as a code, demonstrated, for example, in the popular Golden Age SF story of a young man's initiation into science as an initiation into masculinity (43). In her exploration of *The Battle of the Sexes* (2002), Justine Larbalestier unsettles definitions of sex and gender, using the term "sex" to refer to the whole area of "differences between male and female" that merge to form the sex/gender system in our culture and that are at issue in much SF (9). And in her essays, Veronica

Hollinger has asked if the representation of women as agents is enough, or if feminist SF is most resistant when it imagines the break-down of traditional gender entirely.

Before we continue this discussion of gender as a problem to be solved, we need to turn to recent feminist theorists who consider exactly what gender is. In "Interpreting *Gender*" (1994), Linda Nicholson takes up the vexed issue of the relationship of sex and gender. She suggests that most contemporary feminists adhere to "the coatrack theory of gender": the biological body of woman (sex) is the coatrack on which is hung the socially constructed conception of gender (81–83). Nicholson rejects this theory and argues that sex and the body are just as socially constructed as gender—nothing is known without mediation through culture. As a consequence, what it means to be a woman is different in different cultures (83).

In SF women also explore the vexed relationship between sex and gender. In Lois McMaster Bujold's *Shards of Honor* (1986), for example, Cordelia Naismith from Beta Colony falls in love with Aral Vorkosigan from Barrayar. Their romance places in conflict two different conceptions of sex-gender. On Barrayar, a woman is biologically responsible for reproduction and socially constructed to run the domestic side of life, taking care of family, while men are trained to farm, fight, and govern. On Beta Colony, where Cordelia was raised, children are grown in replicators, and both men and women are socially constructed to become scientists, warriors, and commanders—although negotiation skills are more highly valued than military abilities. In this novel, not only conceptions of gender, but also conceptions of biological sex vary from culture to culture. In the Vorkosigan series, Bujold thus juxtaposes one answer to the problem of gender—an equal-rights society with acceptance of most forms of sexuality—with a society where gender is a problem in ways similar to ours.

In *Gender Trouble* (1990), Judith Butler similarly argues that gender is a performance, "a kind of persistent impersonation that passes as the real" (viii). Butler suggests that gender is not an inherent attribute of an individual but instead, a relationship between persons within a specific historical context (10). Butler argues that both parody—the stylization of gender (31)—and also getting gender "wrong"—through failing to repeat and promote the characteristics of gender (140–141)—disrupt and resist the damaging constraints of gender.

In an early story from the pulp SF magazines, C. L. Moore depicts such gender impersonation as solving the problem of gender. In "No Woman Born" (1944), Deirdre, a famous performer, is nearly killed in

a fire, and a surgeon rescues her by rebuilding her body from metal—
she is reconstructed as a cyborg. While the men in her life imagine she
will be a monster, unable ever to be her former self, Deirdre indomita-
bly re-trains herself so that she can perform her old self through her
new metal body. The men find Deirdre's lack of femininity even more
monstrous than failure to succeed in her new body: "She hasn't any sex.
She isn't female anymore" (258). But Deirdre sees herself not as "vulnerable
and helpless...not sub-human" but as "superhuman" (287).

Writing against the essentialism of the 1970s women's movement,
Donna Haraway, in "A Manifesto for Cyborgs" (1985), urges women to
reconstruct gender roles, modeling themselves on cyborgs, part human,
part technology. Indeed, Haraway imagines a "post-gender world" (67),
where humans possess "permanently partial identities" (72), and identity can be constructed as utopian and pleasurably unnatural (67–68).
In this post-gender world, Haraway calls for "Cyborg writing...about
the power to survive, not on the basis of original innocence [a return
to nature], but on the basis of seizing the tools to mark the world that
marked them as others" (94). SF, for Haraway, would depict the possibilities for action and pleasure available to "cyborg monsters," not the
retelling of the "mundane fiction of Man and Woman" (99).

Haraway's conception of the feminist cyborg, gender as artificial
and culturally inflected, might well apply to C. L. Moore's Deirdre,
the automaton impersonating herself. A similar conception of gender
animates Eileen Gunn's (1988) short story, "Stable Strategies for Middle
Management," which wittily parodies corporate culture, exposes the
effects of gender limitations on businesswomen, and offers a subversion
of gene technology as a solution to the problem of gender. In this future
where young adults compete for the next rung on the corporate lad-
der, bioengineering offers a means to splice desirable animal and insect
traits into humans intent on gaining coveted management positions
by molding themselves "into a more useful corporate organism" (709).
When one young woman hits the glass ceiling, she competes by using
the insect capabilities she has had spliced into her genes: mosquito-like,
she bites her male competitor, Harry, when he irritates her; bee-like, she
waxes over her male partner when he offers condescension rather than
sympathy; and praying mantis-like, she decapitates her boss when he
says that he has given the manager's position to Harry. "It goes without
saying that I was surprised by my own actions," she explains; "I mean,
irritable is one thing, but biting people's heads off is quite another. But I
have to admit that my second thought was, well, this certainly is a useful strategy, and should make a considerable difference in my ability to

advance myself" (715). Poking fun at fears that women's emotions make them unsuitable in the workplace, Gunn's narrative imagines bioengineering cut-throat business urges into women in order to boost them through the glass ceiling. Gunn thus offers a "cyborg monster" vision of women, as Haraway recommended, telling a story radically different from the "mundane fiction of Man and Woman."

In mainstream SF, science is represented as a solution to many crises of human culture. In SF by women, gender itself is often represented as the crisis to which science provides a solution. From the early pulp magazines until recent feminist utopias, women writers have imagined technological reforms of women's reproductive role—especially pregnancies in a jar, rather than a woman's body. Besides the replicator in the Vorkosigan novels by Bujold, Lilith Lorraine's "Into the 28th Century" (1930) presents women who no longer face "the horror" of childbirth, and offspring who are brought "to perfect maturity in an incubator" (258). In Marge Piercy's utopian future in *Woman on the Edge of Time* (1976), fetuses are grown in an artificial womb; with hormonal treatments so that men may nurse, men and women share equally in all reproductive tasks.

In many second-wave feminist SF novels, especially those from the 1970s to the 1990s, the solution to the problem of gender is the disappearance of men. In Joanna Russ's "When It Changed" (1972), women on the planet Whileaway have developed sophisticated ova-splicing technologies in order to reproduce without men, who died from a virus. Faced with the return of "real men" from earth, the women mourn the return of the problems of gender: "I do not like to think of myself as mocked,…deferred to…made to feel unimportant or silly" (238). Similarly, in Eleanor Arnason's *Woman of the Iron People* (1991), lesbian relationships are envisioned as the **biological** norm. In Joan Slonczewski's *A Door Into Ocean* (1986), the capitalist, imperialist, heterosexual society on Valedon is beginning to trade with the communalist, pacifist, and lesbian society of Shora, a neighboring planet. Juxtaposing a world modeled on equal-rights feminism (where women may command troops in battle), with a world derived from the tradition of the lesbian utopia, Slonczewski urges the constructedness of sexuality as an answer to the problem of gender. A boy from Valedon, Spinel, is adopted by a Shoran community, and learns to become a lesbian man. Slonczewski sees neither equal-rights feminism nor lesbian separatism as an answer to the problem of gender; rather, she imagines the human ability to adapt to new circumstances—even sexual practices—as the solution.

The lesbian utopia, a genre central to 1970s feminist fiction, provoked a rich conversation among women SF writers on the best way to solve the problem of gender. Some novels, like Marion Zimmer Bradley's *The Ruins of Isis* (1978) and Pamela Sargent's *The Shore of Women* (1986), critiqued both the heterosexual hierarchy and the lesbian utopia: in both these novels women are on top—men are used as sexual toys and servants on Bradley's Isis, while sons are thrown out of the walled cities of Sargent's world and return only for mating visits. In contrast, Octavia Butler's stories often make men and women equal by introducing an alien presence into the heterosexual binary. In "Blood Child" (1984), the alien T'lic raise human immigrants on preserves, as reproductive cattle: human males carry the eggs of the aliens to a painful birth where the nymphs eat their way out of their hosts, just as human females reproduce humans. In *Dawn* (1987) Butler imagines aliens who save some humans from the nuclear destruction of earth, but require in exchange DNA acquired through a three-way sexual partnership among human males and females and third-sex aliens. In a terrible parity, in Butler's worlds, both men and women may be raped and sexually abused as part of "normal" sexual culture.

Women SF writers further imagine worlds where gender is complicated beyond simple dominance and submission. In Melissa Scott's *Shadow Man* (1995), space travel has triggered biological mutations, and humans of the Concord Federation have elaborated the binary sexual code into a system of nine legally recognized sexes. In Scott's *The Kindly Ones* (1987), bisexuality is the norm, and the universe, in this space opera, is saved by two lesbian pilots, a fifteen-year-old male prince of Hara, a transvestite resistance leader, and a bisexual Mediator with unnamed gender. In Scott's futures, women can do all men can do because the gender categories "woman" and "man" have been transmuted, no longer constraining future humans in the same ways.

Women writers of SF further explore the changes to identity in futures where humans can change bodies and sexualities. In Tanith Lee's *Drinking Sapphire Wine* (1977), robotic servants have perfected medical care, and humans are virtually immortal—if they die, a robot dispatches them to a hospital where they are given a new body. Consequently, young people fashionably suicide whenever they have romantic problems, and all people keep extra bodies chosen from templates or designed themselves, ready to occupy at their next death. "I wonder what sex Danor is going to be for the homecoming" (12), someone casually asks. The narrator of the novel is a male to begin with, a female at the end. Thus, while all the couples in this future are heterosexual in desire, and sex occurs between a male and female body, humans are bisexual in experience—sometimes male, sometimes female. Emma Bull's *Bone Dance* (1991) suggests a different answer to the problem of gender—constructing an identity through the stories one tells about oneself. The protagonist of the novel, Sparrow, is gradually revealed as an androgyne, a body, created to be "ridden" by a scientist seeking immortality, that somehow generated its own identity. In this dystopia, where scientists have detonated an atomic bomb and destroyed civilization, Sparrow first must discover his/her history, and then create a story that explains the identity s/he claims: "life is not a finished story" (277), someone tells her/him. Through the androgynous narrator, Bull thus offers a fantasy of freedom from the constraints of male or female roles.

During the twentieth century, when women won the right to vote and mounted feminist campaigns for equal rights in the workforce, SF offered women writers a place to contest the constraints of traditional views and to try out solutions to the problem of gender. In the SF we have surveyed, women writers emphasize sex and gender as constructed not natural, performed not inherent, in constant negotiation.

suggestions for further reading

Barr, Marleen S. *Feminist Fabulation: Space/Postmodern Fiction.* Iowa City: University of Iowa Press, 1992.

Donawerth, Jane. *Frankenstein's Daughters: Women Writing Science Fiction.* Syracuse: Syracuse University Press, 1997.

Le Guin, Ursula K. *Dancing at the Edge of the World: Thoughts on Words, Women, Places.* New York: Harper and Row, 1989.

Le Guin, Ursula K. *The Language of the Night: Essays on Fantasy and Science Fiction.* Susan Wood (ed.). New York: G. P. Putnam's Sons, 1979.

Russ, Joanna. *To Write Like A Woman: Essays in Feminism and Science Fiction.* Bloomington, IN: Indiana University Press, 1995.

10
marxism and science fiction
carl freedman

The eleventh and final item in Marx's 'Theses on Feuerbach' is probably the author's most widely quoted proposition and is certainly one of his most important: "The philosophers have only *interpreted* the world, in various ways; the point, however, is to *change* it" (*Marx-Engels Reader:* 145; emphasis in original). The familiarity of this sentence has perhaps dulled our sense of just how awesomely and scandalously original it was when Marx composed it in 1845. Marx was professionally trained in the classical philosophical tradition that stretched about two and a half millennia, from the pre-Socratics to his own immediate predecessors, Hegel and Feuerbach; and he was not wont to refer lightly or dismissively to this immense and extremely complex body of work. But it is with full intent that he offers, in the Eleventh Thesis on Feuerbach, to identify an essentially *passive* stance as the chief defect of twenty-five centuries of strenuous Western thought.

To be sure, it is not necessarily the case that no major philosopher before Marx had possessed any serious interest in the practical transformation of human society. It has been suggested, for instance, that Plato's *Republic* was intended not as the merely literary or hypothetical invention it has often been taken to be, but as a potentially practical blueprint to be actualized, perhaps, by some Platonic disciple in one of the numerous Greek colonies being founded in Plato's time far beyond the boundaries of Athens. Still, Marx is surely right to maintain that the essential thrust of Western philosophy before him is overwhelmingly contemplative in nature. The philosophers were greatly concerned with how the world was and how it came to be that way, but not, for the most part, with how it might be made radically different from what it was. They did not, indeed, invariably or unambiguously accept that all is for the best in this best of all possible worlds. But this maxim—derived, with some simplification, from the work of the German rationalist

120

philosopher Gottfried Leibniz—does condense, in succinct and extreme form, the tendency of Western thought that Marx sets his own theoretical and political project most decisively against.

Marx's rejection of any merely contemplative or intellectualistic stance is not, however, maintained in the name of a vulgar pragmatism or any sort of naive glorification of naked action. His response to the traditional philosophical preference for the word over the deed is by no means to propose an equally one-sided and uncritical exaltation of deed over word. As always, Marx is a *dialectical* thinker, that is, one who insists upon seeing every problem in its totality and who understands that cause and effect always operate in many directions at once; and the unity of theory and practice has always been one of the chief touchstones of Marx's (and all Marxist) thought. Marx's follower Lenin proclaimed that there could be no revolutionary action without revolutionary theory; and the Italian Communist organizer and thinker Antonio Gramsci—arguably the greatest single follower of both Marx and Lenin, and certainly the most insightful political philosopher of the twentieth century—was perhaps the first to see with full clarity that neither revolutionary theory nor revolutionary practice was likely to prove viable, in the long run, in the absence of a robust revolutionary *culture*.

Marx himself partly anticipates Gramsci's stress on the centrality of culture in his own emphasis on the importance of imagination. In a justly celebrated passage of Volume One of his masterpiece *Capital* (by far the most crucial text for any understanding of Marxism), Marx makes clear that the imaginative faculties are indispensable for labor itself, the primary category of all Marxist ontology:

> A spider conducts operations which resemble those of the weaver, and a bee would put many human architects to shame by the construction of his honeycomb cells. But what distinguishes the worst architect from the best of bees is that the architect builds the cell in his mind before he constructs it in wax. At the end of every labor process, a result emerges which had already been conceived by the worker at the beginning, hence already existed ideally. (284)

It is by no accident of personal taste that Marx was passionately interested in all sorts of literature, from the most ancient to the most modern and from the most elite to the most popular; nor that among his planned (though unwritten) projects were a full-length study of the French novelist Balzac and a full-length philosophical treatment of aesthetics. For the imaginative power expressed in literature and art is integral, in any properly Marxist understanding, to human labor in general and not least to the labor of revolutionary transformation. If the world is to be changed in reality, it must be changed in thought and imagination as well.

At this point, a certain affinity begins to emerge between Marxism and science fiction (SF)—the latter of which first becomes clearly identifiable as a genre with Mary Shelley's *Frankenstein* (1818), published just twenty-seven years before Marx penned the Eleventh Thesis on Feuerbach. Though the texts of SF, unlike those of Marxism, are not necessarily part of any practical project of revolutionary social transformation, every work of SF does presuppose that the world could be radically different from the way it actually is. Whereas realism accepts for its setting the world as it (more or less) is—even though the realist text may, indeed, go on to offer trenchant criticism of the status quo—SF begins with the decisive rejection of mundane reality. Furthermore, this rejection is generally not a mere game or literary trick, but is usually allied to some sort of ethical or political conviction that the world not only *could* be different from what it is but also *ought* to be. This tendency of SF is most clearly visible in SF works of overtly utopian thrust. Examples of this category (which encompasses much of the very greatest SF) include Ursula Le Guin's *The Dispossessed* (1974), in which the freedom and sense of individuality possible on the socialist-anarchist world Anarres are favorably contrasted with the oppression and conformity found on its earth-like twin planet, Urras; Joanna Russ's *The Female Man* (1975), in which one of the parallel realities of the novel is the all-female world of Whileaway, a space of far greater health, creativity, and harmony than the bi-gendered planet we actually know; and such works by Samuel Delany as *Trouble on Triton* (1976) and *Stars in My Pocket Like Grains of Sand* (1984), which display, on planets far beyond our own, degrees of social and sexual emancipation that can only be dreamed of in the author's (and the reader's) empirical reality. Though these novels—unlike, for instance, *The Communist Manifesto* (1848)—do not contain specific and immediately applicable programs of social transformation, they do call, as clearly and eloquently as Marx and Engels's *Manifesto*, for the world to be not only interpreted but also changed: and changed with a far-reaching radicalism in many ways comparable to Marx's own. Though SF authors are by no means necessarily Marxists themselves (of the three just named, only Delany has explicitly identified himself as such), there is much in the transformative thrust of SF that is strongly allied to the spirit of Marxism.

This is true not only of such positive utopias as those mentioned above but of most of the great negative utopias of SF too, such as George Orwell's *Nineteen Eighty-four* (1949) or Margaret Atwood's *The Handmaid's Tale* (1985). Such works are of course warnings against evil social systems like those of the invented worlds that the authors depict: but warnings that are generally launched not out of any satisfied embrace of the status quo but, on the contrary, out of a sense that the tendencies represented as having reached a logically and terrifyingly extreme culmination in fiction are already present in actuality to an alarming degree. Thus, though Catholic, Stalinist, and Nazi forms of despotism provide the chief models for Orwell's nightmare vision of perfected totalitarianism, *Nineteen Eighty-four* is clearly motivated by a conviction that even such Anglo-Protestant capitalist democracies as those of contemporary Britain and the US are themselves seriously infected by the totalitarian virus. Similarly, the appallingly theocratic Gilead of Atwood's negative utopia is understood by the novel not as an abstract hypothetical possibility but as a more advanced version of the power that the Christian Right had already achieved in Reagan's America. Such works implicitly call not for the mere halting of social movement towards hell, but for the positive transformation of already hellish aspects of mundane reality.

Though Orwell, Le Guin, Delany, Russ, and Atwood are all, in one way or another, writers on the political left—itself a significant fact—something of the same quasi-Marxist transformative spirit can also be found in works of SF produced entirely without benefit of any leftist inspiration. For example, Robert Heinlein, despite a brief socialist period in his youth, consistently maintained in his maturity a combination of militarism and right-wing libertarianism that many science fiction readers have found politically obnoxious—though that has never prevented Heinlein from maintaining, for decades, his position as one of the most durably popular SF writers. Yet even Heinlein, though surely no Marxist, is also no conservative in the core Burkean sense of one who presumptively maintains that actually existing social arrangements ought to be accepted, maintained, and defended. We might say that, although the *content* of Heinlein's political views is far from that of Marx's own, the *form* of his SF remains allied to the Marxist insistence upon changing the world. His best novel, *The Moon Is a Harsh Mistress* (1966), actually celebrates a revolution, one made by the inhabitants of the relatively young civilization on earth's moon against the governing authorities of the mother planet. To be sure, this political project that the book glorifies is modeled far more on the American Revolution than on the Cuban, Vietnamese, Chinese, Russian, or even French Revolutions. But Heinlein's point is clearly that what he takes to be the fundamental libertarian principles of 1776 have been largely forgotten not only by the earthly society represented in the novel but also by the actual USA of 1966 in which the novel is written: and that more Americans of his own day ought to emulate the uncompromising insistence on freedom that the heroes of his novel display. Accordingly, the guiding spirit of *The Moon Is a Harsh Mistress* is thoroughly transformative in nature. Much the same can be said of the best work of Heinlein's most important follower, Gregory Benford. His own masterpiece, *Timescape* (1980), is, for instance, among other things a work of ardent environmentalism (a central Benfordian theme that has only grown more important for the author in recent years), but an environmentalism that remains firmly within the ideological perimeters of right libertarianism.

It is, then, this *structural* homology between the Eleventh Thesis on Feuerbach and the transformative, anti-conservative thrust of SF that seems to me the most basic affinity between Marxism and SF; and it is in such structural homologies that the deepest significance of the pairing, "Marxism and SF," lies.

There are, indeed, other ways that the two categories can be meaningfully related to one another. For example, SF can be written from a self-consciously Marxist point of view, so that the affinity between Marxism and SF becomes not only a critical fact about the fiction but one of its own internal motivations as well. Though Delany is perhaps the only SF author mentioned thus far whose work (or rather some of it) exactly fits this description, it is surely worth noting—and significant—that a number of the most talented and important writers of SF active today are consistently and clearly Marxist in intent. The British writers China Miéville and Ken MacLeod, and the American Kim Stanley Robinson, are outstanding examples. There are also, as we have seen, writers like Le Guin or Orwell, who are not quite to be considered Marxist (Le Guin has always preferred anarchism to Marxism, while Orwell suspected that Marxism would prove incompatible with the democratic socialism that he upheld) but who nonetheless share a great deal of conceptual space with Marxism and who advocate political values in many ways similar to Marx's own. Then too, there are writers whose own precise political views remain a bit difficult to infer but whose SF would be impossible without some acquaintance with the work of Marx and his successors—whether an intellectually rigorous and fairly profound acquaintance, as with the Polish philosopher and SF author Stanislaw Lem, or a much more superficial (yet in many ways aesthetically sufficient) acquaintance as is found in the original *Foundation* trilogy (1951–1953) by Isaac Asimov. Finally, it is of course the case that SF, like any other form of literature, can be read from a Marxist viewpoint; and much of the best SF criticism has in fact been undertaken from Marxist perspectives. The critical work of (to take just a few instances) Darko Suvin, Fredric Jameson, Peter Fitting, Tom Moylan, Steven Shaviro, Sherryl Vint, and Mark Bould falls into this category; and I should acknowledge that my own contributions to SF criticism have been produced, to the best of my ability, according to strictly Marxist standards. Yet all such direct connections between SF and Marxism, however notable and important, are, I believe, finally less consequential than the structural homology produced by the transformative principle that guides both. Here we find not only similarity of content between Marxism and SF but a deeply formal—almost, in some ways, a *generic*—affinity.

There are other aspects to this affinity beyond the basic transformative drive to change the world that Marxism and SF share. For one thing, both Marxism and SF are among the minority of discursive forms that are predominantly *materialist* in character. Marx began his philosophical career as a disciple of Hegel, and in many important senses remained one to the end. Hegel's stress on dialectically understanding the world as a historically structured totality leaves a permanent imprint on Marx's thought; and practically all subsequent versions of Marxism, even those that have chosen to designate themselves as anti-Hegelian, have had to contend with the influence of Marx's mighty precursor. But Marx also broke decisively with Hegel on the crucial issue of Hegel's idealism. For Hegel, the dominant driving force in human history was mind, or spirit, or consciousness (his German term *Geist* has no exact English equivalent), and Hegel saw other forms of human activity as essentially derivative from the progressive unfolding of *Geist*. For Marx, this way of seeing things was almost exactly upside down. He insisted that material, not spiritual, processes are of primary importance; and, though Marx always opposed that one-dimensional economic determinism sometimes known as "vulgar Marxism," and though, as a dialectician, he understood that causality never operates in only one direction, Marx's materialism inverts Hegelian philosophy and places it "on its feet" (in Engels's well-known metaphor) by maintaining material production, not *Geist*, to be the ultimately determining force in human affairs. In the famous "Preface" to *A Contribution to the Critique of Political Economy*, Marx puts the matter most succinctly (though perhaps with some rather undialectical oversimplification) by stating that it is "not the consciousness of men that determines their existence, but their social existence that determines their consciousness" (21). Since human beings must produce the means of their own biological and social reproduction in order to survive as a species—and hence in order to do anything *beyond* physically surviving—the material processes of economic production possess a necessary ontological priority for any Marxist viewpoint.

Though SF is not usually concerned with the economy, as such, to the same degree that most Marxism has been, materialism is indeed one of the defining characteristics of SF as a genre. This is the chief difference between SF and fantasy, a genre with which SF is often combined and hence often confused (and the texts of which are generally sold in the same section of most bookshops as works of SF) but which is philosophically antithetical to SF in fundamental ways. Both genres portray worlds radically different from our own. But the typical text of fantasy displays these differences as rationally unexplained and, usually, inexplicable. Fantasy presents settings and characters the like of which are nowhere to be found in mundane reality, and its plots represent causality operating in mysterious (and often unabashedly magical) ways: but all without any explicit or implicit explanation of how such things could actually come to pass. The characteristic SF text, by contrast, suggests (often explicitly and at least implicitly) a thoroughly materialist account of the social and technological changes that have resulted in the strange new world of the narrative; and this materialist rationality is, of course, closely allied to that practical transformative spirit integral to SF and generally much weaker or altogether nonexistent in fantasy. SF, one might say, not only takes us (like fantasy) to places we have never been before, but also (and unlike fantasy) offers to show us, in rational materialist terms, how (at least in principle) to get there.

The materialism of SF is perhaps most immediately and obviously evident in Earth-based works that are set in the near future and that give especially overt prominence to plainly socio-economic issues. Notable examples include, at one end of the political spectrum, Heinlein's classic novella *The Man Who Sold the Moon* (1950), which narrates the tale of a visionary capitalist who establishes a viable space program based on private entrepreneurialism; and, at the other end of the spectrum, Kim Stanley Robinson's recent *Science in the Capital* trilogy (2004–2007), which marshals immense scientific and political detail to show how untrammeled capitalism might result in the catastrophic environmental devastation of our planet. But even such a quite different SF masterpiece as Asimov's *Foundation* trilogy is at heart no less materialist. This multi-secular narrative takes place in the far future and represents a galactic civilization in which the earth has been almost completely forgotten. But nothing in Asimov's vast saga (by one of the most self-consciously and emphatically materialist of all SF writers) contradicts what the text understands to be the objective public laws that govern material social and physical reality. Indeed, the materialist demystification of apparent mystery is one of the chief thematic impulses of the trilogy.

The basic materialism of SF is visible even in works that might superficially appear to contradict it, such as the great Bas-Lag sequence of novels (2000–2004) by China Miéville. True enough, Miéville combines SF with fantasy to an unusually thoroughgoing and complex degree; and the fantastic element of his work is manifest perhaps most clearly in the prominence allowed to magic. But the predominantly science-fictional character of the Bas-Lag novels is shown by the fact that for Miéville (in contrast, for instance, to a much more purely fantastic writer like J. R. R. Tolkien) even magic—or *thaumaturgy*, as the author prefers to term it—operates according to ultimately materialist principles. It is represented not as fundamentally mysterious but as a reasonably straightforward skill, learnable and teachable by ordinary people as any genuinely material skill must be; and Miévillian thaumaturgy might, indeed, be best understood not as magic in any conventional sense, but as an alternative science, and one just as firmly based on materialist premises as the science we actually know.

One of the central tenets of Marxism is that the materialist and the historical approaches to reality are inseparable from one another. Indeed, Engels's term *historical materialism* is frequently used as an actual synonym for Marxism. Accordingly, it is no surprise to find that an insistence upon historical thinking is another of the structural affinities between Marxism and SF. Marx's sense of indebtedness to Hegel was based largely on his conviction that Hegel, though intellectually and politically limited by his idealism, had nonetheless achieved an immensely fruitful revolution in philosophy by casting the latter in historical terms. For Hegel, fundamental reality was not to be grasped as stable or everlasting (it was here that he decisively broke with the Platonism crucial to so much earlier idealism) but as continuously unfolding, in various ways, through the transformations of *Geist* in historical time. This stress on the priority of historical process is a large part of what Marx meant when he famously referred to the "rational kernel" of Hegelian philosophy that needed to be extracted from the "mystical shell" in which it was embedded. Furthermore, if Hegel, in Marx's view, had been limited by his idealism, most pre-Marxist materialism, such as that of Feuerbach, had been no less grievously limited by its static, mechanistic view of the world; and it was precisely here that Marx saw the dynamic historical dialectic of Hegel as an indispensable corrective. For Marx, and for nearly all the subsequent versions of Marxism, historical thinking must be materialist, because, as we have seen, Marx holds history to be most consequentially driven by material processes of social production rather than by the merely spiritual processes of Hegelian *Geist*. But, equally, materialism must be historical, because Marx sees material reality not as a passive unchanging essence but as an active historical unfolding that is never quite the same in one particular time and place as in any other. This is not, indeed, to say (as has often been wrongly claimed) that Marxism can recognize no values or characteristics shared by all known human societies or specific to the human organism itself. But it is to say that nothing human, not even putative human "universals," can be rationally understood without being studied in highly specific historical contexts, temporally and spatially.

SF is no less wedded than Marxism to the perspective of history. So deep is the commitment of SF to history that some critics have even (and rightly, in my view) seen the historical novel as the genre with which SF has the closest affinity—though the relationship between the two genres is a little more complex than merely that the historical novel (as founded by the Scottish novelist Walter Scott) deals with the dynamic continuity of present and past, whereas SF deals with the dynamic continuity of present and future. There is, indeed, a good deal of truth in this generalization, and (as we have seen, for instance, in the case of the great negative utopias of SF) many important works of SF are based on reasonably straightforward extrapolation of historical trends into the (near or distant) future. Sometimes SF actually becomes "future history" (the term is Heinlein's); and the generic form of the text may even (as most notably in Olaf Stapledon's brilliant *Last and First Men* [1930]) approximate more to the conventions of historiographic than novelistic writing, with a stress on broad social movements that affect millions of people rather than on the adventures of individual characters. But even a much more conventional action-adventure novel like William Gibson's *Neuromancer* (1984)—famed as the chief founding text of the "cyberpunk" subgenre of SF—is essentially extrapolative, projecting into the near future such actual historical tendencies as intensifying urbanization, the decay of the autonomy of the nation-state, the globalization of capital, and, above all, the increasing sophistication of cybernetic and biomedical technologies.

The commitment of SF to historical thinking can also, however, be expressed in ways rather more complicated than simple extrapolation. For example, the "alternative history" is a well-established subgenre of SF, and one that in recent years has even begun to attract the attention of novelists with little prior interest in SF: Philip Roth's *The Plot Against America* (2004)—which portrays a USA in which Charles Lindbergh defeated Franklin Roosevelt in the 1940 presidential election and established a pro-Nazi, anti-Semitic regime—is an example. The subject-matter of Roth's novel is perhaps partly inspired by Philip K. Dick's *The Man in the High Castle* (1962), the all-but-undisputed supreme masterpiece of alternative history, which assumes a world where the Axis won World War II and which is set in an America that has been divided into Japanese and German sectors. Perhaps more compellingly than any other text, Dick's novel demonstrates the ability of SF to deal with complex historical issues by projecting a counter-factual, but perfectly materialist and rational, imagining of how history might have taken turns different from those it actually did take.

Related to but also somewhat different from the alternative history as practised by Dick or Roth is a novel like Octavia Butler's finest, *Kindred* (1979), which narrates the experiences of a modern African-American woman who is forced to travel back to antebellum, slave-owning Maryland—where she acquires knowledge about the history of her family, her race, and her country with a first-hand depth and concreteness that could have been attained in no other way. It should be emphasized, however, that the fundamentally historical nature of SF is crucial to the genre even in texts that do not overtly foreground historical issues in the manner of *Kindred* or *The Man in the High Castle*. Butler herself, for example, is no less (even if less explicitly) concerned with the racial history of the US in the three volumes of her original *Xenogenesis* trilogy (1987–1989), which deals with space travel, extraterrestrial aliens, and cross-breeding between species from different planets.

Materialism, the historical perspective, and the impulse not only to interpret but also to transform the world: these are doubtless not the only important affinities that could be explored between Marxism and SF. In conclusion, however, we should note that, however much the two discursive forms share in common, they are of course also different in many ways as well. One especially important difference may be approached by considering the double nature of the transformative dynamic integral to all Marxism.

The subtitle of *Capital*, the central text of Marxism, is "a critique of political economy"—and the first substantive term in this phrase supplies an indispensable clue to the nature of Marxist thought and action. Marxism is always and necessarily a matter of ruthless *critique*, an insistence upon subjecting actuality to the most rigorous and searching possible examination. Marxism refuses to take appearances at face value; but it does not ignore or dismiss face value either. Instead, Marxist critique studies how the way the world seems to be is produced by the way it fundamentally is—just as Marx himself, in *Capital*, penetrates beneath the relatively superficial (but not unimportant) level of prices and wages, of supply and demand, of the "free" contract between worker and capitalist, in order to examine how economic value itself is produced in the labor process and how a portion of that value ("surplus-value," in Marx's phrase) is coercively appropriated by the capitalist class from the workers who produce it. Though not all Marxists are primarily students of the economy, Marxism cannot turn its gaze toward any other dimension of human activity—from law to literature, from sports to religion—without insisting upon the same kind of absolute critical investigation. For, though the Eleventh Thesis on Feuerbach implores us to go beyond interpreting the world to actually changing it, one can never change the world in any fundamentally revolutionary way without also understanding the world just as fundamentally.

At the same time, however, understanding, while essential to rational social transformation, can never, by itself, lead to it. Though the moment of negation—that is, of the unswervingly destructive critique of the status quo—is indispensable for Marxism, it is woefully incomplete unless complemented, in a relationship of fruitful dialectical tension, by a moment of constructive affirmation: affirmation, that is, of positive *alternatives* to the status quo. The imagining of such alternatives—in which the social relations peculiar to capitalism would be replaced by relations more humane and just—might be described as the utopian side of Marxism. True enough, Marx and Engels themselves almost always use the term "utopian" in a derogatory way. But when they scorn certain pre-Marxist forms of socialism as utopian, they are using the word in a quite specific sense: namely, to refer to socialist ideas that amount to no more than mere wishful thinking, that is to say, thinking that is completely untethered to the sort of rigorous understanding of social reality which Marx and Engels themselves implement and insist upon. They cannot and do not deny that utopian thinking in a wider sense—a sense that would include the imagining of alternatives to actuality that is directly based on the most searching analysis of the latter—is vital to the whole transformative project of Marxism. The passages in which the founders of historical materialism themselves engage in such utopian imagining are admittedly rather few and scattered; but they include some of the most memorable passages in the Marx-Engels oeuvre.

It is here that we can identify what may be the most durable importance of SF for Marxism as well as one of the most salient differences between the two modes. For the utopian imagination crucial to Marxism is the special province of SF among all literary genres. The point is not just that every SF text is utopian in the strict etymological meaning of representing a place (*topos*) that is no place (*ou-topos*) actually existent. It is also that the utopian literary impulse as named in and partly derived from Thomas More's seminal text *Utopia* (1516)— the impulse, that is, fictionally to represent modes of social relations clearly superior to actuality, if almost never completely flawless—is the chief vitalizing force, as we have seen, behind much of the greatest SF. We might, indeed, go further, and claim that SF is today not only the privileged but almost the exclusive genre for the utopian literary imagination. William Morris's *News From Nowhere* (1890), today well over a century old, is the last truly great utopia not science-fictional in form; and, though such things can never be predicted with assurance, it seems unlikely that we will be seeing such another in the future. If so, then Marxism will always need SF. For, if Marxism is characterized by a dialectical tension between critique and utopia, it is equally true that not only the founding writings of Marx and Engels themselves but most Marxism altogether has devoted far more energy to critique. SF, by contrast, tends to be much more utopian than critical, even though critique can certainly be important for SF, especially in those works—such as the novels of Delany or Miéville—that represent the genre at its most intellectually powerful and sophisticated. This contrast, then—the emphasis on critique in Marxism, as against that on utopia in SF—not only marks one of the deepest differences between the two but also suggests the relation of dialectical complementarity that obtains between Marxism and SF. The two modes not only *can* be paired, as in the title of this essay. They must be.

suggestions for further reading

Freedman, Carl. *Critical Theory and Science Fiction*. Hanover, NH: Wesleyan, 2000.

Jameson, Fredric. *Archaeologies of the Future: The Desire Called Utopia and other Science Fictions*. New York: Verso, 2005.

Moylan, Tom. *Demand the Impossible: Science Fiction and the Utopian Imagination.* New York: Methuen, 1986.

Shaviro, Steven. *Connected or What It Means to Live in the Network Society.* Minneapolis, MN: University of Minnesota Press, 2003.

Suvin, Darko. *Metamorphoses of Science Fiction.* New Haven, CT: Yale University Press, 1979.

11
reading science fiction with postcolonial theory
matthew candelaria

There are two different but complementary usages for the word "postcolonial" in literary studies. The first usage is in describing post-colonial literature, that is, literature from countries that were formerly colonies of (primarily) European powers but have recently become independent. This essay has little to say about postcolonial science fiction (SF) in this sense, although the subject is addressed in Roberto de Sousa Causo's essay "International Science Fiction" in this volume. Indeed, it would be profitable to read our essays together, since he addresses many of the same concepts from a different perspective. Students further interested in postcolonial science fiction in this sense should also consult Ralph Pordzik's *The Quest for Postcolonial Utopia* and *So Long Been Dreaming* edited by Nalo Hopkinson and Uppinder Mehan.

The second usage is in describing postcolonial literary criticism and theory, a bundle of approaches to literary study, partially borrowed from psychoanalytic, Marxist, and feminist criticisms, and utilized first in the study of postcolonial literature, later applied to much broader (and often less appropriate) categories of literature. It is in this second sense that the essay utilizes and addresses the term.

It is a commonplace of SF criticism that the genre is a literary-imaginative response to the rise of science and industrialism (see, for example, Franklin in this volume, or Aldiss's *Billion Year Spree*). Less commonly cited is that science and industrialism are themselves thickly intertwined with the successive waves of colonialism/imperialism emanating from the powers of Europe. But the imprint of imperialism is clear from the genre's earliest texts. Mary Shelley metaphorically equated Captain Walton's desire to reach the pole to Viktor Frankenstein's quest to create life. In *Twenty Thousand Leagues Under the Sea*, Jules Verne makes it clear that Captain Nemo is a rebellious, imperial subject seeking to wreak vengeance utilizing the same means by which his people had been conquered: science. And whether or not you believe that H. G. Wells's *War of the Worlds* is an imperial "guilt fantasy" (Irvine: 33), the explicit parallels Wells draws between the Martian invaders and British colonials are detailed and prolonged.

If we grant the influence of imperialism on science fiction, how does it change our reading of the genre? One approach would be to read and analyze SF texts in terms of their explicit or implicit commentary on historical episodes in European imperialism. This approach has been profitably used on Philip Nowlan's Buck Rogers novel *Armageddon 2419* (Kalish et al.), Sir Arthur C. Clarke's *Childhood's End* (Candelaria), and Edgar Rice Burroughs's Martian series (Lawson). But this approach focuses SF and SF criticism on the past whereas the genre is in its setting, premise, and basic philosophy oriented toward the future.

Focusing on SF as a literature of change, oriented toward representing, inspiring, and shaping the future can lead us to a more appropriate approach. From this perspective, it becomes crucial to critically interrogate the conceptual content of the genre to make sure that the futures it represents will lead to positive progress for all humankind.

Note that this is not the same as representing futures that espouse positive values. For example, the *Star Trek* universe seems to have solved the problem of colonialism with the "Prime Directive," an order forbidding interfering with less-advanced cultures, thus allowing those cultures to mature through internal processes until they are capable of entering an equal-power relationship with the United Federation of Planets. However, we cannot take a text simply at its word, but must interrogate the represented future. Consider, for example, the *Star Trek* episode "Friday's Child," in which the Enterprise crew interferes with the succession laws in a feudal society to secure a mining treaty with the new regent. Even in the episode where the Prime Directive is introduced, "A Piece of the Action," the Federation shows its willingness to interfere in order to get its cut. Although the Prime Directive is refined in later versions of the series, there is still the suspicious reality that no matter how many races join the Federation, the people in power still seem to be mostly human. Clearly, it is not enough for a text to simply espouse an ideal, but an author must have the courage and imagination to pursue that ideal to its logical and moral conclusion. Clearly, such a thing is as rare in SF as is the well-engineered space ship or the biologically real alien, but like those other treasured tropes of the genre we owe it to authors to use all the tools at our disposal to expose the imaginative force of their creations.

The goal of this essay is partially to parse the language of postcolonial theory for readers of SF. However, just as SF takes human experience and projects it to the entirety of imaginable space-time, so must the language of postcolonial theory undergo a mapping onto that entirety before it can be made useful. Therefore, I will not only be selective in my discussion of postcolonial concepts for SF readers, but I will at times redefine these concepts to be more applicable in a SF context. Then I will utilize Robert Silverberg's "Sundance" as a brief case study. Along the way, I also hope to convince SF critics reticent about literary theory to utilize at least some of these very useful tools.

postcolonial concepts

Imperialism, Colonialism, Postcolonial, Neocolonial—Imperialism is a wide-ranging term for which Edward Said provides a useful definition, "the practice, the theory, and the attitudes of a dominating metropolitan center ruling a distant territory" (9). **Colonialism** is the allied process of settling citizens from the metropolis in the dominated territories. **Postcolonial** is a label that is almost as contested as SF. In general, it is used to refer to countries and peoples that were formally ruled by a metropolitan center, but have become nominally politically independent, such as India after 1949, or much of Africa after the 1960s. **Neocolonial** is the description for these countries and peoples used to emphasize the continued military, political, and economic presences that in some cases result in the effective continuation of metropolitan rule in all but name.

Binarism—Binary thinking is fundamental to the construction of imperialist discourse. The process begins in the simplest fashion, by observing that our life experience can be described in terms of a number of binary pairs: day/night, light/dark, white/black, man/woman, and even good/evil. Although each of these binary pairs neglects and obfuscates the liminal ideas existing between the paired elements (such as the gloaming), there is nonetheless a great deal of truth to these binary pairings, and they become useful shorthand for resolving any number of conceptual problems. However, these conceptual pairs are never value-neutral. One of them is always more positive, the other negative. As these binary categories are applied over time, they become cognitively linked. It is easy enough to see how day/night gets bound to light/dark so that we have the day|light / night|dark binary, which then becomes the day|light|white / night|dark|black binary and finally day|light|white|man|good / night|dark|black|woman|evil, a conceptual dichotomy that was constantly used in thinking about the nature of the relationship between European colonials and non-European colonial subjects. These binary pairs multiply easily and continually, and every new addition automatically oriented itself as if it were a magnet tossed at a stack of other magnets. Consider, for example, Kipling's characterization of the colonial subject in "The White Man's Burden" as "half devil and half child" (l. 8). Here the adult/child binary has been added to the pile. "Devil" and "child," a pair of terms with little initial covalence become identified with one another in imperialist discourse creating the new binary good|adult / evil|child which becomes part of the schema for representing imperial territories and subjects.

Center/Periphery—One of the most powerful binaries in colonial thought, this pair represents the conceptual split between the imperial center of administration and the periphery, frontier, or zone of contact, the actual colonies. The center is imagined as the embodiment of all civilization, all law, all culture, all ratiocination, whereas the periphery is represented as an area of savage, lawless, primitive irrationality.

This binary gave rise to the notion of asynchronous space, that is, a notion of space-time where some parts of the Earth (universe) are imagined to be in the future, others in the past. This is seen most vividly in "lost world" texts, where Europeans imagined that there were parts of the globe so primitive that dinosaurs might still be found there, but it is also visible, for example, in Joseph Conrad's *Heart of Darkness*, where Conrad's narrator, Marlowe, imagines that he might see an ichthyosaur as he travels up the Congo River. This conceptualization of space allowed Europeans to imagine that non-Europeans were more evolutionarily primitive peoples, and that progress was linear, inevitably leading to a reproduction of European civilization.

The deep inscription of the center/periphery trope in SF is due to the genre's metaphorization of space. In looking at the heavens, it's easy to see the pattern laid out for us: planets, solar systems, galaxies all have centers ruled by gravity, about which all else precesses. In some cases, the civilized center is literally at some kind of astronomical center, as in Clarke's *2001: A Space Odyssey*, where Bowman encounters the architects of the monoliths on the surface of a star, or in David Brin's *Sundiver*, where humanity's patron race might be hiding inside our Sun. In other cases, the civilized center is represented as an apotheosis of the city, as in Clarke's *The City and the Stars*, or in Isaac Asimov's *Foundation Trilogy*, or in the *Star Wars* prequel trilogy. Still another approach is to have the civilization of the center represented by a powerful synecdo-che, as in Robert A. Heinlein's *Have Space Suit, Will Travel*, where the entire civilization of the Three Galaxies is embodied in the law court on Lanador.

The center is often profoundly weakened by the ambivalence of impe-rial discourse and power, represented classically by Asimov's Trantor, which teetered at the edge of ruin before finally succumbing to collapse, or perhaps more iconically by the Death Stars, whose curious weaknesses are best explained by metaphor rather than engineering.

Discourse—Discourse is a Foucaultian term referring to ways of describ-ing the world that act not only as descriptors, but determiners of thought and action, perceived not as merely descriptions of reality, but as real-ity itself. Binary thinking is an example of discourse. Once we begin thinking in binaries, it becomes very difficult to stop, and at a certain point we confuse the description with the reality and imagine that the world really is made up of any number of dichotomous pairs with no ambivalent space. Discourse is comparable to Althusserian **ideology**. Both philosophers believe we live inside discourse (or ideology) to the extent that the only thoughts and actions possible are those permit-ted by discourse. Dystopian narratives such as George Orwell's *Nineteen Eighty-four* or Eugene Zamiatin's *We* demonstrate the all-encompassing nature of discourse, but perhaps the most striking exploration of how a human identity can be completely ensconced by the use of a suitably dominating discourse is Orson Scott Card's *Ender's Game*.

One of the most powerful colonial discourses for science fiction is that of progress, the notion that there is a single path toward the single vision of a glorious future. However, the discourse of progress in a colo-nial context has one major flaw, pointed out perhaps most clearly in the context of the British Empire in Charles H. Pearson's *National Life and Character*. Pearson observed that if the periphery were brought up to the same level of technology and culture as the imperial metropolis, these subject territories would be able to rise up, revolt, and possibly destroy the metropolis. This gave rise to one aspect of what Homi Bhabha termed the **ambivalence** of colonial discourse. Imperialists wanted to bring technology and culture to the periphery, but they were not wholly committed to the task, introducing either conscious or unconscious mechanisms for preventing the subject peoples from ever equaling the imperialists in technology, culture, or power (Bhabha: 87).

Other—Another powerful binary in colonial discourse is the Self/Other binary. The concept of the Other is useful for exploring the role of race, gender, and power relations in science fiction, and has long been used especially by feminist critics. The concept assumes that sentients are not autonomously self-creating subjects in the Enlightenment sense of Descartes's "I think, therefore I am," but are constructed out of social discourse. In other words, thinking may be a necessary condition for being, but it is not a sufficient one. We must be told who and what we are allowed to be by social discourse. In Althusserian terms, this is called **interpellation**, and is conducted by Ideological State Apparatuses (ISA), such as churches, educational institutions, and cultural media. These ISA, by constantly asking us to identify with variously presented subject positions, not only control who we are able to become, but make us believe that we are autonomous subjects who have chosen our identity.

In terms of colonial discourse, subjects of the empire are constructed in terms of their relationship to the imperial Self; that is, they are the imperial Other, who is, because of the ambivalence of discourse, simultaneously called to the things of the center and denied access to them. This ambivalent discourse construction has been noted, In the United States, this ambivalent discourse construction has been noted by African-American writers like W. E. B. Dubois, Richard Wright, and others. For their part, the Others thus constructed respond with the other half of Bhabhaian ambivalence, as they seek to simultaneously emulate and deride the ideals they are thus presented with. Bhabha describes this ambivalent action as **mimicry**. To Bhabha, the imperial subject, in seeking to emulate the ideals of the imperial center, creates a parody of those ideals. The powerfully subversive nature of mimicry can be seen in H. G. Wells's story "The Lord of the Dynamos," where Azuma-zi transforms Holroyd's admiration for the largest of the dynamos into a worship of the object as a god, ultimately sacrificing Holroyd to the buzzing and rattling idol.

how the west was won and where it got us

The value of any set of literary-critical concepts is not intrinsic but vested in how they allow us to explore, explain, and articulate the artistic achievements of writers. In general, it must be confessed that the best artists are working at the boundaries of the explicable, creating stories whose effects in readers' minds are ineffable to the literary critics of the day.

Judging from the criticism on it, Robert Silverberg's 1969 short-story masterpiece "Sundance" is a text largely inarticulable given the literary-critical technologies available to contemporary SF scholars. For example, Russell Letson uses Silverberg's trope from the story as a description for Silverberg's technique, but does not say anything about the story itself, only alluding to it in the essay's very last paragraph. Even more striking is the collection of essays edited by Elkins, Greenberg, and Clareson that takes its title from Letson's article, but also does little more than allude to the story. The only critic to take up the story at any length is Edgar L. Chapman in *The Road to Castle Mount*. Chapman essentially provides a summary of the story, a significant portion of which is a long quote from the story, intended to demonstrate Silverberg's use of "superbly evocative imagery" (80). Ultimately, Chapman summarizes his analysis of the story, "As a recreation of the tragedy of the American Indian, 'Sundance' is an impressive work. An effective work of social criticism that shows a masterful command of language and metaphor, 'Sundance' is one of Silverberg's masterpieces" (80). Chapman never really explores what makes the story an "effective work of social criticism," but utilizing the concepts I've talked about above allows us to articulate some of what Silverberg has accomplished.

The story begins in second person narrative, effectively interpellating the reader with the ambivalent discourse of empire. We as readers are brought into the imperial identity, made part of the process of constructing the empire through the slaughter of 50,000 Eaters in one day. Simultaneously, however, we are pushed away from the imperial self. Herndon's "playful speculation" that the Eaters might be intelligent and their slaughter might be akin to genocide is consciously engineered to re-emphasize the difference that makes Tom Two Ribbons (narratively us) not really a member of the imperial identity. Although Tom is ostensibly now a part of the imperial structure of humanity, he is never fully eculturated. He remains marked by his physical form (which Silverberg details for us) and by his personal history. Although the massacre of his people, the Sioux, is over two centuries in the past, its shadow stretches directly into Tom's life through the "family tradition" of "self-destruction" (463) instilled in his family by the process of imperial conquest. Silverberg wants us to feel the long shadow of 1876 by allowing self-destruction to change its methods with technology from firewater to memory editing, but still remain an intractable fact of Tom's existence.

Silverberg gives us a couple of powerful SF metaphors for colonial discourse in this story—memory editing and personality reconstruction—both of which are shown as ways in which the dominant society seeks to construct and reconstruct Tom's people into its desired shape: a smiling, acquiescent subject. Tom begins with an unacceptable attitude, "One feels outrage...at what was done to the Sioux," (462), an attitude that the empire will attempt to cure him of through the course of the story. Whereas Tom attempts to claim gloominess as a racial trait, indeed, a right to which he is entitled by the tragic history of his people, Ellen, conspicuously white, seeks to deny it to him with "innocent" wheedling speculations that he should try memory editing. Memory editing is, like firewater before it, a solution gladly offered by the empire to the suffering Native American to mask the painful realities of imperialism. To the imperial Self, it is not enough that the Other suffer the destruction of home, culture, tradition, even their entire genetic line, but they must grin and bear it. Tom describes the process by which his father was transformed by his addiction to memory editing, "In fifty years, he pared himself down to a thread...He had his ancestors edited away, his whole heritage, his religion, his wife, his sons, finally his name. Then he sat and smiled all day" (462). Tom's father has become the perfect imperial subject, not only ignorant of what he has lost, but ignorant that he has lost anything at all. Without a name, the subject is capable only of soothing the imperialist's anxieties with a smile.

Although we are encouraged to believe the explanation of Ellen, Herndon, Michaelson et al., that they are on a purely scientific mission and that Tom's perception of the massacre of the Eaters is merely a product of his personality reconstruction, we are not supposed to dismiss the horror of the Eaters' slaughter. If we were, the graphic descriptions of the processes by which the Eaters were completely dissolved by the neural pellets would be superfluous. Instead, we are to recognize that the slaughter of the Eaters represents not the massacre of the Sioux, but, rather, the erasure of the memory of that massacre. The description of the Eaters' destruction makes them more akin to memory than to the flesh-and-blood Sioux. Tom first makes the distinction that the Eaters could never create "rivers of blood" (461). Also, the pellets given to the eaters are "neural pellets," which cause the animals to completely dissolve without a trace, like an erased memory.

It is for this reason that Silverberg saves his most "superbly evocative imagery" for the Sundance which takes place within the genocide-fantasy. In embracing the fantasy of the slaughter, Tom is being true to "his whole heritage," which would be incomplete without the memory of his people's massacre. These moments are supposed to feel good to us because they represent the truest, the most morally right position for us as readers, at this point constructed as part of the imperial self, seeing Tom in the third person and further alienated from him by Silverberg's wonderfully textured use of synaesthesia: if we cannot undo the slaughter of the Sioux, we can at least allow them the right to accuse us with the horrific nature of our crimes.

The story ends as it began, in the second person, with the colonial discourse seeking to interpellate the reader, but with a significant difference. Whereas the beginning of the story emphasized the first type of ambivalence, that demonstrated by the empire toward the imperial Other, the ending emphasizes the second type, that felt by the Other toward the empire. Despite their protestations to the contrary, Tom knows full well that a massacre is taking place, the massacre of his memory, and this contradiction creates the situation in which every possible position is beset by trap doors. The travesty at the heart of "Sundance," the one at which we are asked to feel continuing outrage by the story's open-ended resolution, is the attempt by imperial discourse to deny Tom Two Rivers a vital piece of "his whole heritage": the wholly appropriate depressed rage at what was done to his people.

Utilizing the concepts of colonial discourse and the Self/Other binary allows us to tease out some subtleties of Silverberg's story. More could be done here, but the short sample above hopefully demonstrates the point. In a similar fashion, a judicious application of the concepts above will yield worthwhile insights into many SF texts. Those who find the approach worthwhile are encouraged to move beyond my (necessarily meager) list of tools here by reading through many of the texts in my bibliography.

I also hope I have convinced SF critics nervous about "theory" to treat literary criticism like any applied science. Literary critics are constantly innovating new tools not for the sake of the tools themselves, but for the work that the tools allow us to do.

suggestions for further reading

Clarke, Arthur C. *Childhood's End*. New York: Ballantine, 1953.
Ghosh, Amitav. *The Calcutta Chromosome*. Delhi: Ravi Dayal, 1996.
Hopkinson, Nalo. *Midnight Robber*. New York: Warner, 2000.
Le Guin, Ursula K. *Always Coming Home*. New York: Bantam, 1985.
Niven, Larry and Jerry Pournelle. *The Mote in God's Eye*. New York: Simon and Schuster, 1974.

12
encountering international science fiction through a latin american lens
roberto de sousa causo

This essay is concerned with science fiction (SF) as an international phenomenon. Science fiction deals with issues of modernization that have occurred since modern states first appeared (during the seventeenth century or so). I indicate different modernization moments and the international SF that resulted from them. I touch upon new reading strategies relating to modernization as a cultural shock point that impacts upon how a particular country uses SF icons to communicate cultural myths. SF which emanates from outside the English-speaking world is terra incognita to most Anglophone students. To familiarize these students with this new literary terrain, I position Latin American SF as a central lens to focus upon international science fiction. I offer a cursory catalogue of international science fiction briefly to acquaint students with science fiction springing from cultures which may differ from their own cultures.

* * *

To paraphrase Forrest Gump, reading science fiction involves understanding that "science fiction is what science fiction does." One thing that SF does is to illuminate current social and political affairs by offering alternative or comparative viewpoints. During science fiction's inception, this new perspective was achieved by taking a citizen of a given society (Gulliver, for example) to a different place—a strange land (like Lilliput), a utopia, a magic kingdom, or the future.

Most works of what can be called "proto science fiction" written before the nineteenth century were utopias or social satires. Satires are more meaningful when they are directed toward a recognizable subject.

Utopias, in kind, are equally appropriate comparison devices when they confront already established social and political orders. These forms naturally proliferate with the inception of Early Modern Europe (around AD 1500). Closer contact generated via commerce, traveling, book-publishing, and the spreading of education yield new enhanced comparative parameters and the questioning of existing parameters. I suggest that, prior to the advent of current scientific knowledge, the establishment of *nationality*—in contrast to the ideas of kingdom or tribe—is responsible for the initial appearance of science fiction. James Gunn hints at this notion when he says that "[i]ndustrialization and the transformation of a traditional culture to one of anticipation came late to Italy, along with national identity" (Gunn: 409).

Modern nations logically are constructed and function to integrate different peoples through a systematic process and to transcend particular religious, social, or ethnic identities. The current global political mess indicates that this process never totally succeeds. Countries, nonetheless, introduce new orders that dictate how we conduct our lives. Science fiction, from the time it has first appeared, has functioned as a toolkit for addressing modernization. Early SF was quite international in this sense—if first we narrow our definition of "international" as being restricted to *Europe*. Many utopian and satirical works[1] would not have been written if nascent but clearly discernible institutions were not emerging within these nations. Satires focus upon these institutions. Citizens became capable of imagining the future in a manner pertinent to their lives. Transcendental implications characterize their imaginings. Paul Alkon tells us that the first future fictions, such as Louis-Sébastien Mercier's *Memoirs of the Year Two Thousand Five Hundred* (1771), appeared during the eighteenth century.

Of course, this use of early SF as a tool to tackle modernization is not available within every European society. Portugal and Spain experienced the Inquisition longer than other countries, for example. And the overwhelming presence of the Catholic ethos might explain why the Portuguese-Brazilian Priest Antonio Vieira wrote his *História do Futuro* ("History of the Future"; 1718) as prophecy, not as fiction.

* * *

Even during the nineteenth century early SF revealed its affinity to strategies of exoticism when the genre imaginatively expanded the boundaries of new territories being discovered in "lost worlds" located in Africa, Asia, and South America. SF also relocated colonial struggles and conflicts to other worlds (such as those described in H. G. Wells's

The War of the Worlds [1898] and later in the planetary romance tradition of Edgar Rice Burroughs's *A Princess of Mars*—1917). Thus SF is linked to the process of investigating modernization by magnifying and extrapolating modernization itself. The genre also describes the pockets of magic and wonder that constitute the detritus of the modernization process. In any case, an understanding of internationalism is absolutely necessary to the process of reading science fiction.

The Industrial Revolution of course changed the panorama of what science fiction could accomplish. As Isaac Asimov said, people could now see science and technology causing changes that would happen during their lifetimes. Another example of internationalism being pertinent to SF occurred when people became capable of seeing the new social and economic landscapes scientific innovation made possible. As early as 1813, the Dutch author Willem Bilderdijk wrote *A Short Account of a Remarkable Aerial Voyage and Discovery of a New Planet*. Bilderdijk described a balloonist who "is cast away on a small satellite orbiting within the Earth atmosphere." According to Brian Stableford (Clute and Nicholls: 120), Bilderdijk's text can be defined as the first modern SF novel, predating Mary Shelley's *Frankenstein* (1818).

Examples of science fiction appeared in Latin America during the mid-nineteenth century. The creation of these works was not hampered by the region's less than optimum scientific and industrial status. Since literature addresses itself unhampered by international boundaries, European and United States writers of the fantastic— such as E. T. A. Hoffmann, Guy de Maupassant, Edgar Allan Poe, Jules Verne, and H. G. Wells—greatly impacted readers in Latin America as well as other parts of the world.

A fascination with European literature remains a strong trend in Latin America, especially in Argentina. For example, Federico Andahazi's *Las Piadosas* (1998; *The Merciful Women* in the US) evokes the most famous literary workshop in history, which occurred during the dawn of the Industrial Revolution: the night of ghost storytelling in Villa Diodati involving Lord Byron, Percy Bysshe Shelley, Mary Shelley, and John William Polidori. Told from Polidori's viewpoint, Andahazi treats readers to a literary homage which takes the form of a reflection upon creativity mingled with dark sex. (Perversity and sadism are a constant in Argentinean SF; even some of Jorge Luis Borges's[2] works adhere to this trend.)

Octávio Aragão's more recent action-packed short novel *A Mão que Cria* ("The Creating Hand"; 2006) plunges deeper into the recursive waters of science fiction by drawing upon Verne, Poe, Stoker, Wells, and other nineteenth-century writers. Rubens Teixeira Scavone's novelette *O 31.º Peregrino* ("The 31st Pilgrim"; 1993) is another excellent example.

Scavone's text presents science fiction elements disguised as a rediscovered narrative in Chaucer's fourteenth century *The Canterbury Tales*. His female protagonist, who seems to have been impregnated by demons, might have been abducted and impregnated by aliens.

A much earlier example of SF in Brazil is *O Doutor Benignus*, by Augusto Emílio Zaluar. Zaluar's work is one of three Latin American scientific romances published in 1875, any one of which could be the first example of the genre in Latin America. The other two novels are *El Maravilloso viaje del Sr. Nic-Nac* ("The Marvelous Voyage of Mr. Nic-Nac") by the Argentinean writer Eduardo Holmberg, and *Historia de un muerto* ("Story of a Dead Man") by the Cuban writer Francisco Calcagno. Zaluar's novel, which incorporates Brazilian national myths and spirituality, was influenced by Verne and his fellow French novelist Camille Flammarion. *Páginas da História do Brasil, Escritas no Ano 2000* ("Pages of Brazilian History Written in the Year 2000") by Joaquim Felício dos Santos (published as a serial, 1868 to 1872) is an even earlier example of Brazilian science fiction. Brazil's greatest writer of the nineteenth century, Machado de Assis, wrote at least one SF story about immortality: "O Imortal" (1882), which was influenced by the British Gothic tale tradition.

Early Argentinean SF stories are collected in Horacio Moreno's 1993 anthology *Lo fantastico* ("The Fantastic"). The anthology includes stories by Eduardo Holmberg, Leopoldo Lugones, Horacio Quiroga, as well as mid-twentieth-century writers. Braulio Tavare's 2003 *Páginas de Sombra* ("Pages of Shadow"), a similar Brazilian anthology, includes work by pre-1930s speculative fiction writers such as Coelho Netto, Berilo Neves, and Machado de Assis. Some contemporary writers, André Carneiro and Lygia Fagundes Telles for example, are also included. Early Latin American SF, however, is still widely unavailable.

* * *

The worldwide impact of Verne's *voyages extraordinaires* cannot be underestimated. In Austria, Ludwig Hevesi (Ludwig Hirsch) paid homage to Verne in his story collection *Die fünft Dimension* (1906). The Russian writer Mikhail Bulgakov followed suit in 1924 with the story "The Crimson Island." In Francophone Canada, Verne was an early influence. In Denmark, Vilhelm Bergsøe's 1869 novella "En reise med Flyvefisken 'Prometheus'" either anticipated or extrapolated upon some of Verne's ideas. In Germany, Robert Kraft ("the German Jules Verne") wrote German "dime-novels" that were akin to Verne's fantastic voyages. Of course, in France, Verne's imitators were numerous, particularly in the *fascicules* (the local version of dime-novels). Albert Robida, a prolific *fascicule* illustrator, parodied Verne in his 1879 *Voyage très extraordinaires de Saturnin Farandoul* and developed his own futuristic vision in *Le vingtième siècle* (1882) and *La vie électrique* (1883).

In *The Road to Science Fiction Volume 6: Around the World* (1998), James Gunn remarks that the arrival of Commodore Matthew Perry in Japan (Unga Bay 1853) sparked the Japanese response to science fiction. Perry's arrival opened up Japan's closed society and his military ultimatum "made itself felt in the widespread acceptance of Jules Verne's techno-logical adventures of exploration … Verne-like novels began to appear in 1890 with Ryukei Yaho's *Ukishiro Monogatari* ('Tale of the Floating Fortress')" (Gunn: 587, 588).

The future war subgenre was very popular all over Europe from the late nineteenth to the early twentieth century. The coming of World War I ended this literary fad, which had different connotations in Australia. For example, novels written by Kenneth McKay and C. H. Kirmess—as well as John Hooker's *The Bush Soldier* (1984) and Eric Willmot's *Up the Line* (1991)—are inspired by local anxieties pertinent to the surround-ing Asian populations. An early Brazilian example of future war is Afonso Schmidt's *Zanzalá* (1936), a literary rhapsody that combines a Brazilian utopia relating to nature with a satire of European imperialism. More recent Brazilian SF written by Carlos Bornhofen's (*A Guerra da Amazônia*—"The War of the Amazon"; 2004) and Humberto Loureiro (*A Ira da Águia*—"The Wrath of the Eagle"; 2005) focuses upon, of all things, the invasion of the Brazilian Amazon by the United States.

While the planetary romance never took hold in Brazil, the lost world tradition outlasted the subgenre in other countries. Gastão Cruls's *A Amazônia Misteriosa* ("The Mysterious Amazon"; 1925) was clearly inspired by Wells's *The Island of Doctor Moreau* (1896), but emphasizes denouncing neo-colonialism. From the 1930s to the present, other Brazilian lost world novels are Menotti Del Picchia's *A República 3000* (1930), Jerônymo Monteiro's *A Cidade Perdida* ("The Lost City"; 1948), and Cristóvam Buarque's *Os Deuses Subterrâneos* ("The Subterranean Gods"; 1994). These works reflect the local fascination with the mysteries of the Amazon—a region that functions as a repository for Brazilian colonial anxieties. The Amazon basin eradicates the need to express these anxieties in terms of other worlds, as Edgar Rice Burroughs did in his Barsoom series.

* * *

The aforementioned Horacio Moreno edited the *Más Allá* ("Far Beyond" 1992) volume which includes more recent and award-winning

Argentinean works by Adolfo Bioy Casares, Marisa Balhario, Tarik Carson, Fernando Cots, José M. Lopez, Santiago Oviedo, and Ruben Tomasi. This slim but substantial anthology reveals another trend in Latin American SF: commentary on the impact of media as a reality-constructing device. Brazilian writers Braulio Tavares and Ivanir Calado also explore this topic. Reality-inquiring approaches are common among the famous in the manner of Jorge Luis Borges, Adolfo Bioy Casares, and Julio Cortázar. Brazilians André Carneiro and Tavares and the Argentinean Angélica Gorodischer also question reality.

As Andrea Bell and Yolanda Molina-Gavilán point out in their anthology *Cosmos Latinos,* the first *wave* of science fiction in Latin America occurred during the 1960s. (At the time the Space Race between the United States and the Soviet Union had a global impact). Science and technology developed in agrarian Latin America. Nuclear war threatened everyone, triggering a wave of nuclear holocaust stories that proliferated until the mid-1980s—such as Daniel Fresnot's 1987 novel *A Terceira Expedição* ("Third Expedition"; 1980, set in Brazil) and Emilio E. Cócaro's novella *El Laserista* ("The Lasergunner"; 1987, set in England). This novella reflects some characteristics of the British New Wave.

The pattern I have described repeats itself throughout the world. World War II introduced a new wave of modernization and a new set of global threats. Japan again provides a good example of how, in many countries, SF was reintroduced exclusively as a version of American SF. After World War II, Japan fell within the US sphere of influence. With its economy leveled by the war, Japan had to recreate many aspects of its culture in terms of adhering to its Western custodian. In 1945 Kiyoshi Hayakawa established Hayakawa Sobo—a publishing house that introduced detective fiction and westerns in addition to SF. This imitation phase, no waste of effort, enabled the defeated Japanese people to learn more about their occupier's culture. Indeed, to try to look at the West through SF might well have constituted their first approach to the new phase in Japan's post-war modernization.

Manga provide a clearer example of this cultural interchange between East and West. Japanese comics, which had virtually disappeared during the war, reappeared as a Western-influenced art-form. Some were written in defiance of former American prohibitions against samurai and martial arts stories. Hence *manga* helped Japan to both reassert some of its national pride and to criticize aspects of Imperial militarism. *Manga* ultimately became the powerhouse of Japanese pop culture and it incorporates numerous genre strategies appropriated from the age of pulp magazines in the United States.[3]

The development of SF in post-war Germany reflects its Japanese counterpart; *Perry Rhodan*, the largest and longest-running SF series in the world, best exemplifies this point. The series was essentially a pseudo-translation of American SF in that it contained an American hero and was based upon the American space program. However, it also functioned as a way to resurrect pre-war German adventure science fiction in the *Heftromane* (German dime novel) format. Despite all of the series' pseudo-American pretenses, ever since its inception it addressed Cold War anxieties from the standpoint of Germany. The series positioned Germany as the main possible theater for World War III in Europe and expressed the country's desire to be *independent* of conflicting superpowers. Through its future history depicting expansion and survival in a universe occupied by much stronger powers, the series tried to readdress German national pride as *human* pride.

* * *

In the post-World War II world, SF (and other forms of popular culture), as Brazilian Marxist critic Roberto Schwartz observed, is associated with *American* modernization, which is frequently denounced as an imperialist tool. Nevertheless, an alternative way to read imitative SF in other countries is to position it as a strategy to discern the West's modern morés. This reading practice enables readers to function as protagonists in modern Western cultures. Similarly, Erin A. Smith observes that in the United States ethnic minorities used to read hard-boiled fiction stories as "Americanizing" narratives that encourage them to think of themselves as a part of the American cultural mainstream. Ethnicity and race were described in these texts as performances, positions to be appropriated when it served readers' best interests.

Post-nuclear holocaust and end-of-the-world stories proliferated in post-war Brazil and Argentina. Jerônymo Monteiro's "The Crystal Goblet" provides a rare example of an SF author addressing Brazil's military dictatorship (which began in 1964, the very year the story was written). Monteiro creates an alter-ego protagonist who discovers a time-viewing device. Immediately after being falsely arrested by the new regime (Monteiro himself barely escaped death when he was falsely arrested) the protagonist sees images of a conflict in the past—and future atomic war[4]—in his mysterious time visor.

Fear of nuclear war is also apparent in Álvaro Menén Desleal's "A Cord Made of Nylon and Gold" (El Salvador 1965), the acerbic tale of a United States astronaut who commits suicide while undertaking a Project

Gemini space walk. While his still-active consciousness orbits Earth, he witnesses total war. Alberto Vanasco's humorous "Post-Boomboom" (Argentina 1967) provides another variation on the nuclear war theme. Survivors gather together on behalf of their children to preserve their cultural memory of the civilization they have just lost. The story reveals how little the average person knows about science and history.

In Latin America, dreading nuclear holocaust is as common as contemplating dictatorship. Eduardo Goligorsky's somber "The Last Refuge" (1967) was written a few years subsequent to the establishment of a right-wing regime in Argentina. This work, which concerns repression and isolation, involves a dissident who approaches as a means to seek asylum, the foreign ship that makes an emergency landing in the North Korean-like isolationist country he inhabits. The spaceship symbol connotes freedom, contact with other cultures, and technological and political enterprises beyond the reach of repressed citizens. Goligorsky's story obliquely criticizes the United States and other nations which use the "Communist Threat" as an excuse to support tyrannical right-wing regimes.

"The Golden Ships," by the Czech journalist Alexandr Kramer, functions similarly. Kramer depicts a society under siege by dint of mysterious ships. As the ships—which represent a flourishing and indifferent outside world—hover impassively, the narrator's nation utilizes all its military might against them to no avail. Citizens nevertheless congratulate themselves for retaining their "invincible human spirit" (Gunn: 335).

The Russian writer Kirill Bulychev (Igor Mozheiko) also deals with isolation in his poignant "Share It with Me." This work is about an Earthman who encounters a society that can telepathically share joys and pains. Although he fervently wishes to join this society, he refrains from doing so in order not to impact upon its utopian characteristics.[5]

André Carneiro's classic novelette "Darkness" depicts a strange cosmic phenomenon that plunges the world into darkness. Only a few blind people can help a small community survive the new hardships, until light returns after the phenomenon abates. First published in 1963, the story seems to anticipate the period of political darkness the dictatorship in Brazil inflicts—and the need to achieve solidarity in order to survive it.

The emulation of a non-aligned ideological position is apparent in "Gu Ta Gutarrak (We and Ourselves)" (1968), written by the Argentinean of Basque origin Magdalena Mouján Otaño. The story concerns a Basque couple who are affected by radiation after a strategic United States bomber crashes. Their children, who are born with superhuman-like mental powers, go to study in the Soviet Union and the United States. Their plan to build a time machine (in order to discern the mysterious origin of the Basque people) is rejected because it contradicts Marx's and Engel's dialectics and threatens the American way of life. Written with great wit and precision, Otaño's story also makes fun of Basque traditionalist culture.[6] Ivan Carlos Regina is a Brazilian writer who works in this same sarcastic vein. His collection O Fruto Maduro da Civilização ("The Ripe Fruit of Civilization"; 1993) is a ferocious indictment of contemporary consumerism.

The tenets of Latin American dictatorship are apparent in "Exerion" (2000), by the Chilean writer Pablo A. Castro. Castro imagines a near future in which a young man works for a state that defines his father as a "disappeared" (people disappeared during Pinochet's regime). While probing state-owned computers, he recovers data about disappeared people before suffering from a "nanoraser" attack that leaves him mentally and physically crippled.

How does living with dictatorship and economic crisis impact upon SF writers? The award-winning Error de Cálculo ("Mistaken Calculation"; 1998), written by the Argentinean author Daniel Sorín, provides an exemplary answer. The text describes how feelings of desperation and social anguish in Argentina trigger a media-inspired wave of suicides.[7] In Brazil, the constant social crisis and the apparent failure of the newly returned democratic government to raise the quality of life is addressed in the less than successful satire Admirável Brasil Novo ("Brave New Brazil"; 2001), written by Ruy Tapioca. The escalating urban violence that sprung from the modernizing process imposed during Brazil's dictatorship figure in Max Mallmann's novel Zigurate (2003). These social conditions also figure in such stories as Calado's "O Altar dos nossos Corações" ("The Altar of our Hearts"; 1993) and in Henrique Flory's "Feliz Natal, 20 Bilhões!" ("Merry Christmas, 20 Billion!"; 1989).

Cultures emerging from failed Communist totalitarian states were confronted with another kind of modernization: the need to adapt to Capitalism. Cyberpunk's cutting-edge depiction of the contemporary and its focus upon Capitalism attract the post-Soviet Eastern Europe nations in much the same way as Verne's hard science exercised worldwide appeal during the previous modernization moment I described.

In summary, in all these stories the authors' point of view importantly impacts upon people's reading practices. Discussing "SF ideas" and understanding the genre's history (in the English-speaking world) are insufficient. Cultural context must figure in deriving new layers of meaning.

* * *

When national differences or singularities are discussed within the SF genre, they are usually approached from the standpoint of different formative histories and relevant literary traditions and languages. Sometimes a nation or region's most typical characteristics are immediately apparent within the SF it produces. For example, the whole mystique of the Amazon is present in the Chilean writer Isabel Allende's *The City of the Beasts* (2002), a novel available in English. Allende's protagonist is an American teenager who journeys to the Amazon where he encounters Indians, shamans, and a lost city inhabited by monsters.

Soccer, the eternal Latin American passion, is the subject of the Brazilian anthology *Outras Copas, Outros Mundos* ("Other Cups, Other Worlds"; 1997), edited by Marcello S. Branco. (The volume includes stories by Gerson Lodi-Ribeiro, Fábio Fernandes, Ivan Carlos Regina, Braulio Tavares, Octávio Aragão, and Carlos Orsi among others.) But it took an American writer, S. N. Lewitt, to launch a *Carnaval* in space via *Songs of Chaos* (1993). (Note that too many Brazilian writers, to their own detriment, tend to avoid what they perceive to be "cultural stereotypes." Authors of other nationalities suffer from the same reluctance.)

A section of *Cosmos Latinos* tries to stress the role of Christianity in Latin America. This emphasis is apparent in Hugo Correa's ironic "When Pilate Said No" (Chile 1971) and José B. Adolph's shorter but effective "The Falsifier" (Peru 1972). Both stories concern a messiah who is dislocated in terms of place and time. By way of a third example, Daína Chaviano's "The Annunciation" (Cuba 1983) involves the impulse toward religious transgression centering on the Christian myth of Mary's pregnancy. Chaviano's story offers a slow-paced account of Mary's seduction by Gabriel—with an extraterrestrial twist almost dropped in as an afterthought. These stories are similar to the ones in Gumercindo Rocha Dorea's 1989 anthology of Brazilian Christmas stories, *Enquanto Houver Natal* ("As Long as There Is Christmas," 1989—with contributions by Dinah Silveira de Queiroz, Ivan Carlos Regina, Marien Calixte, and Henrique Flory).

Another way of discussing difference is to account for how much a particular SF tradition approaches or distances itself from American science fiction—or how much more literary or less literary it is in a particular point in time. Braulio Tavares, in his discussion of Brazil in *The Encyclopedia of Science Fiction* (1993), observes that a part of Brazilian SF establishes a clear borderline between itself and mainstream literature. Gunn adds that the "work of [Italo Calvino, Dino Buzatti, and Tommaso Landolfi] may say more about the particular Italian approach to SF than the more traditional stories published as [SF]" (Gunn: 410). For decades, British SF has claimed to be more literary, mature, psychological, ironic, sophisticated, entropic, and more socially and politically astute than its American counterpart. In any case, American SF is positioned as a center against which SF written by authors who are not American is measured.

M. Elizabeth Ginway brought a potentially revolutionary approach to this debate about SF and national differences. Her *Brazilian Science Fiction: Cultural Myths and Nationhood in the Land of the Future* (2004) explores the importance of a country's modernization periods functioning as shock points which inspire SF's development. Ginway observes that even naïve and imitative SF (such as the SF produced in Brazil from the 1960s to the early 1980s) could be quite on the mark in terms of how national consciousness is communicated via SF tropes. In addition to recognizing the importance of grandiose narrative strategies and local literary traditions, it is also necessary to note the communicative potential of local cultural myths and their relationship to modernization shock points.[8] As Ginway notes in "A Working Model for Analyzing Third World Science Fiction: The Case of Brazil" (2005), reading international SF demands a new reading practice. This new reading practice involves both a deeper probing beyond the text's surface meanings and greater understanding of the investigated culture which ranges beyond the average reader's stereotypical notions. Nevertheless, it has a truly great potential which is not limited to Third World SF.

* * *

Yes, American SF is most certainly a force unto itself. But in recent years its readership has learned to enhance its reading of the genre via international literary engagement. Australian authors (such as Greg Egan) and British authors (such as Ken McLeod, Justina Robson, and Alastair Reynolds) are in the forefront of the new SF emphasis upon international voices. Although these authors write in English, they produce innovative SF by incorporating cultural differences that bring an *unfamiliar* twist to the culturally familiar. Such innovation is best accomplished by writers whose works do not need to be translated into English in order to appear in the United States market.

Gwyneth Jones's essay "Metempsychosis of the Machine" (1997) provides a commercial explanation for the dearth of Third World SF: Anglo-American SF is part of a larger economical domination process. According to Jones, "Science fiction must export: and therefore must control the economy of the *other place* by any means necessary" (Jones: 3). She also presents a sociological approach to explain the relative paucity of Third World SF: "[W]hy are there still so few Black, Hispanic, or Asian SF writers in the USA, never mind in the world in general? Perhaps this is a stupid question. Dedication is rare, and you have to be pretty dedicated to devote yourself to scribbling futuristic fantasy if you have a pile of other troubles to deal with" (Jones: 8). So, poverty—as well lack of regional or national industrial capacity—can be blamed.

I reiterate that *literature relates to literature*. A country's particular context does not prevent an individual from pursuing a particular knowledge or art form. The notion that a certain literature cannot develop in a given place because of any particular national circumstance— economical, technological or cultural—is a bias in itself.

When Bruce Sterling spoke in Brazil (in 1997), he stated that "trying to conquer the American publishing industry would be the same as trying to conquer the US Air Force." Sterling proposes to create a relationship between the importing nations that would exchange their local production to the point that the market loss would claim the publishing conglomerates' attention. This does not mean that the conglomerates would open themselves to the rest of the world. Instead, the international SF presence could gain leverage to begin a true dialogue with those who produce American SF.

I do not suggest that the United States SF audience is completely closed to a real presence of ethnicity and multiculturalism in science fiction. Indeed, in recent years and in growing proportion, there are emerging signs pointing to the fact that American SF is opening itself to other voices—to the non-Western, non-White, non-European thoughts and attitudes Jones mentions.

The SF Other has usually been portrayed as a *virtual* Other—an alien, a robot, an artificial intelligence, the Human of the future. When minority ethnicity and Third World perspectives are incorporated within SF, a real Other is granted the power of the word. A real Other becomes newly empowered to talk back to the English-speaking hegemonic center. Reading the SF Other constitutes a new transforming factor which enriches the SF genre.

notes

1. H. Bruce Franklin's essay which appears in this anthology, "What Is Science Fiction—And How It Grew," discusses works written during this period. I wish to emphasize the authors' internationalism (in European terms).
2. See for instance his "The Babylon Lottery" in James Gunn's anthology *The Road to Science Fiction Volume 6: Around the World*, Clarkston, GA: White Wolf, p. 502.
3. See Paul Gravett's *Manga: 60 Years of Japanese Comics*. Collins Design, 2004.
4. This story—along with the stories written by Desleal, Vanasco, and Goligorsky—is published in Andrea L. Bell's and Yolanda Molina-Gavilán's anthology *Cosmos Latinos: An Anthology of Science Fiction from Latin America and Spain* (2004).
5. The story appears in Gunn's *The Road to Science Fiction Volume 6: Around the World*, 399.
6. This story appears in Bell's and Molina-Gavilán's anthology *Cosmos Latinos*, 123.
7. This novel suggests that the roots of perversity and torture inherent in Argentinean SF are rooted in Argentina's particular form of populism—that is, the country's penchant for worshiping dead political figures (such as Perón and his wife Evita). So, too, for Argentina's traumatic experience with dictatorial repression (that included executions and torture) during its military regime.
8. Ginway centers her investigations upon the latest explosive modernization moment in Brazil (championed by the Brazilian military dictatorship from 1964 to 1985) and also upon the ongoing globalization process.

suggestions for further reading

Aldiss, Brian and Sam Lundwall. *The Penguin World Omnibus of Science Fiction*. London: Penguin, 1986.

Bell, Andrea L. and Yolanda Molina-Gavilán. *Cosmos Latinos: An Anthology of Science Fiction from Latin America and Spain*. Middleton, CT: Wesleyan University Press, 2003.

Gunn, James. *The Road to Science Fiction Volume 6: Around the World*. Clarkston, GA: White Wolf, 1998.

Hartwell, David G. *The World Treasury of Science Fiction*. Boston: Little Brown, 1989.

Jakubowski, Maxim. Twenty Houses of the Zodiac: An Anthology of International Science Fiction. London: New English Library, 1979.

part iv
reading science fiction
in the classroom

introduction to part iv

The essays in this section all give concrete examples of ways that SF may be read in the classroom. The authors represent their personal approaches to the reading of SF and particular moments in the use of SF in the classroom. However, it is also possible to see these essays not as three different ways of reading SF, but as part of a single reading process so that each of them borrows from and reinforces the others. The process is recursive, not linear. We do not read as Gunn reads first, then as Cortiel reads, then as Yaszek and Davis read. Instead, reading a piece as Yaszek and Davis read prepares us for reading it again as Gunn reads.

James Gunn, as one of the longest-practicing critics of SF, provides a critique of the reading protocols fundamental to any serious reader of actual SF, as opposed to fiction that utilizes SF tropes or unsophisticated adventure cinema that dresses up in SF garb. For students unfamiliar with SF, this essay might best be read first. Gunn's essay can give them the tools that experienced readers of SF have picked up over the years of their reading, although they may be unable to describe exactly what it is that they do when they read SF. The advantages of Gunn's approach are obvious: close reading an SF story allows us not only to understand what is happening in the story, but what is the nature of the story's "novum," or its particular estrangement or difference from the mundane world. The novum is at the heart of SF, and it is referred to again and again in the essays in this volume, although not always by that name. It is not only the source of attraction to the genre, the flashy new gewgaws that make it cool, but the vehicle by which SF writers make their political statements, and in order to make any meaningful reading of what SF is trying to say about our world, it is crucial that we understand the full conceit of the author's novum. In the classroom, activities that read stories as Gunn reads "Sail On! Sail On!" are often as useful in revealing the limits of our collective knowledge of our own world as they are in exposing the imaginative flights of the SF author.

Once we understand the novum, the next step is discovering what the parameters of the estranged world are saying about our own world. No author is better suited to act as a case study for understanding this than Joanna Russ, whose worlds are precisely estranged from our own to reveal facets of her feminist critique. Cortiel identifies three primary axes which define the space of Russ's worlds: gender, genre, and sexuality. Having identified these axes, Cortiel explores the matrices of feminist thought, individualist aspirations, and artistic skill that transform our world into the worlds portrayed by Russ, worlds that liberate gender from traditional restraints, genre from conventions and cliché, and sexuality from gender. Cortiel's insights are well-wrought from a long career of reading, teaching, and researching Russ.

Doug Davis and Lisa Yaszek take our reading one step further. Their essay provides an example of how to utilize SF in the science and technology studies (STS) classroom. By explicitly placing SF not only in the classroom, but also in a particular historical moment in the discipline that situates their classroom, the authors ask us to interrogate our own classrooms. Davis and Yaszek begin by giving a two-part summary of SF in the classroom, making significant reference to the twofold processes of SF which simultaneously familiarizes the strange and estranges the familiar. After this, they turn their attention to STS as a series of allied but disparate projects each approaching the subject of the social role of science from a set of unique assumptions. This survey reminds us that successfully bringing SF into the classroom depends on a harmony between our own goals in scholarship and the content and tenor of the texts utilized. Davis and Yaszek enhance this theme by giving an explicit account of how they use SF in their classroom in alliance with more canonical STS texts to effectively communicate with their students.

The essays in this section are the heart of the volume, as they speak explicitly to the multiplicity of ways that SF can be read and studied in the classroom. The hope is that students and teachers will not simply read texts in one way, but will utilize all three reading strategies again and again to reach the fullest possible understanding of the genre and its individual texts.

13
reading science fiction as science fiction*
james gunn

In another essay in this volume Sherryl Vint and Mark Bould maintain "There Is No Such Thing as Science Fiction." I will discuss the benefits of dealing with science fiction as a genre and the characteristics that allow readers to apply to stories and novels protocols that may contribute to a "better" reading before applying those protocols to a close-reading of Philip Jose Farmer's story "Sail On! Sail On!"

If there is any disagreement between Vint and Bould and me, that disagreement resides in the critical position one chooses to assume when looking at SF. Does it have characteristics that enable readers to identify it? Does it create a pattern of expectations that are either fulfilled or frustrated by the time the work is finished? Does our previous experience in reading fiction like this matter to the way we read the work? Would the way in which the work departs from expectations impact our reading if those expectations did not exist? Are all readings equally valid, or does the work respond better—that is, is the meaning the work offers richer, more resonant?—to one approach than another?

I don't intend to answer those questions. I have had my say about genre in other places. Here I intend to maintain that our first act as readers is to identify genre: in the larger instances, we have to determine whether we are reading poetry or drama or fiction or biography or even correspondence (e-mails, these days) before we know how to read the writing. And even mixed genres, like poetic drama, for instance, or a novel based on real events, benefit from our understanding of both kinds of reading approaches.

Need to identify genre applies to science fiction as well. We can argue whether the term "genre" applies. The classical traditional genres were tragedy, comedy, epic, lyric, and pastoral. Later the term was applied to novel, short story, essay, radio and television plays. Science fiction would be a subset of one of those, and perhaps better called a "category."

What concerns me here, however, is how the way we read science fiction differs from the way we read other genres or categories, fantasy, say, or traditional fiction, or detective fiction, or romance, or adventure stories. Three decades ago the well-known SF writer, scholar, and critic, Samuel R. Delany, gave a talk at a Modern Language Association meeting in which he said that he had visited many universities and had discovered that people who said they didn't read science fiction or didn't like science fiction actually couldn't read science fiction. They did not bring to the reading of science fiction the experience of unpacking the information in the science fiction sentence or the background of scientific and technological knowledge necessary to interpret the concepts. To the question of whether science fiction works in the same way as other categories of writing, Delany answers: "no. Science fiction works differently from other written categories, particularly those categories traditionally called literary. It works the same way only in that, like all categories of writing, it has its specific conventions, unique focuses, areas of interest and excellence, as well as its own particular ways of making sense out of language. To ignore any of these constitutes a major misreading—an obliviousness to the play of meanings that makes up the SF text." As if to pay tribute to the play of meanings to which he referred, he wrote an entire book, *The American Shore,* as a close-reading of Thomas Disch's short story "Angouleme."

Earlier in the essay, Delany writes that "the conventions of poetry or drama or mundane fiction—or science fiction—are in themselves separate languages," and in other essays, he called the process by which one approaches and reads those languages as "protocols." Good reading, then, is learning the protocols, identifying the genre, and applying the proper protocols with understanding and sensitivity. Poetry, for instance, is not read with the same protocols as prose; or an essay, as an article; or a short story, as a novel; or any of these, as drama. Similarly, the subgenres or categories have their own protocols—the mystery, for instance, the western, the gothic, the love story, the fantasy, and science fiction. In each case good reading involves identifying the genre and then applying the correct protocol. If one doesn't know the correct protocol or misidentifies the genre, one is likely to misread the work—in the sense, at least, that there is a "best" or even a "good" reading based upon the author's intention or a consensus of experienced readers.

James Thurber offered a classic example of misidentification in his humorous sketch "The Macbeth Murder Case." In the piece the narrator describes a man who has been dragged on a Caribbean-island vacation by his wife. The man reads nothing but mystery novels. All he can find in the island library is a volume of Shakespeare's plays. Each day the husband reports to the narrator his misapplication of detective-story protocols to "Macbeth." He keeps looking for who-dunnit, discarding Macbeth because the person who seems to have done the crime never turns out to be the perpetrator, then Lady Macbeth because the next person to eliminate as a suspect is the one who acts too guilty. He comes to the conclusion, at last, that the porter did it.

Other examples might include reading *Alice in Wonderland* as if it were science fiction. Though science fiction's premise departs from our world of everyday reality (Darko Suvin calls this the work's "novum"), that premise is consistent with what we know of the universe and its laws, and events play themselves out in the real world, or the real world extended. The experienced reader, then, pays attention to the foundation of facts on which the narrative is raised; that foundation determines the kind of structure built upon it, and a reader cannot evaluate the structure without inspecting the foundation. Another way to describe the transposition that occurs is that in SF background becomes foreground, and the world the story creates can be understood most effectively by questioning the story's premises.

That means asking hard questions. But if one were to apply hard questions to *Alice in Wonderland*—how does Alice fall down a rabbit hole without hurting herself, or grow several times her height by drinking from a bottle called "Drink me!" (where does the extra mass come from?), or shrink to a few inches high by eating from a cake called "Eat me!" (where does the mass go?)—one cannot read it These are inappropriate questions, of course, but if fantasy is approached skeptically, it falls apart.

On the other hand, if one should read hard science fiction without asking skeptical questions, as if it were fantasy (a much more common event than fantasy read as if it were science fiction), the reader would miss the point of what hard science fiction has to offer, that it creates a functional world that is different from but consistent with the world in which the reader lives. Of course many SF stories and novels operate in worlds that have been inherited from earlier writings or in which the construction of the world requires little imaginative participation by the reader. We call them science-fantasies sometimes, or adventure SF, like Edgar Rice Burroughs or A. Merritt novels, or many space epics, and even, to choose an example from the best, Frank Herbert's *Dune*.

Some of *Dune* is world-building and other parts make more sense if read as palace intrigue or Greek tragedy, though the best reading also would include an understanding of Arab traditions and the political organization of the Holy Roman Empire.

To offer another example: if one reads Hal Clement's *Mission of Gravity* as an adventure story without understanding the extremes of gravity that have produced the caterpillar-like Mesklinites and their neuroses, one misses not only the play of ideas but the significance of the events. *Mission of Gravity* is a marvelous adventure story, but a good part of the adventure and almost all its meaning reside in the environment in which the events happen.

Most SF movies respond best to other protocols than SF (John Baxter pointed out in *Science Fiction in the Cinema* that print SF and film SF have different origins). Their narratives seldom depend upon the world in which they happen; the world of the excellent film *Blade Runner*, for instance, owes more to film noir than the theme of the film, the replacement of scarce living creatures with mechanical or constructed ones, including androids (renamed "replicants" in the film). Philip K. Dick's novel *Do Androids Dream of Electric Sheep* integrates the background into the novel; in the film version, *Blade Runner*, the background remains background. With some exceptions, film SF can best be viewed with other than SF protocols—as film, without question, and as fairy tale in the case of *Star Wars*, or as lost animal narrative in the case of *E. T.: the Extraterrestrial*.

In a 1996 series of articles in *The New York Review of Science Fiction*, Delany insisted that attempts to define SF were both impossible and undesirable. Without getting into that debate, we can grant that SF is difficult to define and get on to what SF, at its most typical, does. Since SF deals with a change in the circumstances of everyday reality by intro-ducing one or more significant alterations, an SF short story or novel constructs a plausible world in which that alteration or those alterations can exist. The SF work, then, introduces the reader to that plausible but different world, all at once or bit by bit. Sometimes the way in which the reader is introduced to that world, or puts the pieces of the world together into a consistent pattern, is part of the story's appeal, or even central to the story itself.

Robert A. Heinlein developed narrative techniques that enabled him to suggest difference without resorting to paragraphs of explanation: when he wrote "the door dilated" (*Beyond This Horizon*) he implied a world in which doors were constructed around different principles. In *Gulf* he suggested social transformations by a scene in which the protagonist walks into a drug store and a stripteaser (he called her an "ecdysiast") is "working her way down to her last string of beads." Other writers picked up Heinlein's innovations. In Frederik Pohl and Cyril Kornbluth's *The Space Merchants*, Mitch Courtenay says in the second paragraph "I rubbed depilatory soap over my face and rinsed it with the trickle from the freshwater tap." One wonders what readers unaccustomed to the protocols of SF reading make of those sentences or scenes.

Of course one doesn't have to wonder. When mainstream writers venture into SF, they do not have at hand the full range of techniques or an intuitive understanding of SF expectations. They pick up concepts and tropes and incorporate them, usually, into mainstream stories and novels focused on character rather than idea. When Margaret Atwood says that *The Handmaid's Tale* isn't science fiction, she may mean that she didn't intend for it to be read with SF protocols, and the praise it received was not from SF critics. Much mainstream criticism of SF falls into the same category; when SF is read with mainstream protocols it is not likely to fare well. Robert Scholes pointed out some years ago that "as long as the dominant criteria are believed to hold for all fiction, science fiction will be found inferior: deficient in psychological depth, in verbal nuance, and in plausibility of event. What is needed is a criticism serious in its standards and its concern for literary value but willing to take seriously a literature based on ideas, types, and events beyond ordinary experience."

Back in the 1970s, in a column in *The New York Review of Books* that I remember because it included a favorable word or two about *Alternate Worlds: The Illustrated History of Science Fiction*, a critic objected to the "funny names" in Ursula K. Le Guin's *The Left Hand of Darkness* and said that the only proper attitude for an SF writer was Roger Zelazny's "tongue-in-cheek."

My decision to take the students in my SF class through a close-reading of Farmer's "Sail On! Sail On!" was based partly on the belief that students can be taught SF reading protocols but also on the belief that all teaching of literature is the teaching of reading skills. People can pick them up on their own, and often do, but my principle of teaching (even of fiction writing) is that reinvention is not the quickest or even the best way to approach areas of skill and that the insights of professionals can shorten the process. Moreover, one of the principles of my SF class is that the uninspected opinion is not worth holding: similarly the uninspected reading process may represent more pure, naïve reading pleasure, but sophisticated reading has its own (and in my opinion superior) joys. "Sail On! Sail On!" begins with:

Friar Sparks sat wedged between the wall and the realizer.

The key words here are "Friar," "Sparks," and "realizer." We can bring our real world experience to the interpretation of "Friar," and "Sparks" may be a family name—or not. We can file that away. But the concept of a physical object called "realizer" does not exist in our reality. We will expect it to be explained in the context of the world in which it can exist and the way in which that word (and the concept it embodies) interacts with and informs the world in which it exists. This is the SF reading protocol—the filing away of information for later explanation. Mainstream readers, on the other hand, may be put off by the fact that they don't know who Friar Sparks is or what monastic order he belongs to or why he is called "Sparks," and they may put the story aside because they think the author doesn't know what he/she is doing or is putting unwarranted demands upon the reader.

In the rest of the paragraph, we find the Friar's forefinger tapping on a key and that he is housed in a "toldilla." Farmer explains this term: "the little shanty on the poop deck"; but not that the use of the word implies a Spanish ship. In the third paragraph we discover "a single carbon filament bulb above the monk's tonsure." So far we have learned that the Friar probably is a telegraph operator (is this connected with the word "realizer"?) and that he may be named Sparks because that is a nickname that once was given to telegraph operators (in the dark the opening and closing of the telegraph key created sparks), and has a primitive electric light in his "toldilla" (Edison's first light bulbs were created from carbonized thread and were called "carbon filament" bulbs.)

But in the second paragraph, the author tells us that beyond the ship's railing bobs "the bright lights and dark shapes of the Niña and the Pinta." Some parts of this newly created world have become clear: Friar Sparks is aboard the Santa Maria on Columbus's first voyage to the New World. But this "new world" contains telegraphy and electric lights. We must reconcile these disparate elements into a kind of narrative called "alternate history," in which events happened differently than they did in the historical reality we know. Now our focus is shifted to the event or events that changed the history of this "Sail On! Sail On!" world.

In the fourth paragraph, a narrative passage refers to the "luminiferous ether," "luminiferous" meaning light bearing, and "ether," the medium in which scientists believed (before the Michelson-Morley experiments that disproved the existence of ether) wave lengths of light propagated. The paragraph also includes mention of the "dots and dashes" of the operator at the Las Palmas station on the Grand Canary." "Dots and dashes" and "operator" confirm our deduction that Friar Sparks is a telegraph operator, and further clarified in paragraphs fifteen and seventeen by statements that the realizer emits sparks and that the operator at Las Palmas also is called Friar Sparks—a generic name for a telegraph operator. The Grand Canary is an island off the northwest shoulder of Africa from which Columbus, historically, set off on his first voyage to the New World.

The fifth and sixth paragraphs seem like throw-away chatter between telegraphers, but set up later revelations. They gossip about Turks gathering to march on Austria, flying sausages (UFOs before "flying saucers" were spotted often were described as resembling dirigibles), and that the sausages were rumored to have been invented by a renegade Rogerian. The word "Rogerian," which by inference may apply to the order to which the telegraphers belong, suggests that they may have derived their name from someone named Roger.

In paragraphs six to ten, information arrives in the form of questions about the "Admiral" (Columbus) and "Cipangu," which is the name of the fabled city with golden roofs—probably Japan—that Columbus was seeking, comments about Savaranola, the late sixteenth century religious figure who was finally burned at the stake by the Church, a "Pat and Mike" joke (one detail that dates the story) intended to show the familiarity between telegraph operators, even of a religious order, and a sign off of "P.V.," which we learn, in paragraph ten, is short for "pax vobiscum," or peace be with you—and we recognize that a religious order of telegraphers would bring religious terminology to their profession, such as the use of a familiar parting Latin wish. This is the kind of detail that validates the SF world the author is trying to create for the reader. The pieces of the puzzle should fit together, and each piece that fits confirms the existence of the whole. We also are told in paragraph ten that the "ether bent and warped." We need to file that away for later explanation, because in the well-made SF story metaphor must first be considered as literal (as Delany has pointed out).

Paragraphs eleven through sixty-two describe a dialogue among Friar Sparks, who has emerged from his todilla, the page de Salcedo, and the interpreter Torres. Mainstream readers may expect these characters to matter to the story and what happens to them, how their characters develop, for instance, will represent what the story is about. But all are there, including Friar Sparks, to elucidate the world, and Farmer's challenge is how to make their discussion seem more than exposition. Torres and de Salcedo offer mundane skepticism to Friar Sparks's sacred knowledge, and in the process allow the details of the world to emerge,

In paragraph thirteen, the Friar refers to the rising of the large red moon as a possible source of the interference that has interfered with the messages with his brother telegrapher at Las Palmas. In paragraph seventeen, he repeats his colleague's speculation about worlds of parallel time tracks in which every possible event has happened (and guides the reader toward what today is called "alternate history," in which events happened differently and shape a different present). The Friar also calls God "the master Alchemist," suggesting that the science the Friars practice emerged from alchemy (which has some validity in our world).

In paragraph twenty we get a speculation about a world in which Roger Bacon was persecuted by the Church "instead of being encouraged and giving rise to the order (of Rogerians)." By suggesting a negative (in our world Bacon was persecuted for his scientific work), the story intimates that if the Church had welcomed Bacon's scientific insights and created a religious order of devout scientists it would have had telegraphy, electric lights, the beginnings of powered ships, and maybe dirigibles by 1492.

In paragraph twenty-two, Friar Sparks passes along another speculation by his Las Palmas colleague, that universes may exist with different physical laws in which, say, objects dropped by Angelo Angelei (in our history, Galileo Galilei) fell at the same speed rather than different speeds and proved Aristotle a liar (as Galileo, in fact, did). Friar Sparks ridicules this notion as he offers it, but file this away, SF reader. Here, also, the Friar introduces the concept of "little angels," opening a topic that de Salcedo follows up and leads to a description of the religious order's theory of telegraphy (another detail consistent with the Church's adoption of science): K. C., for instance, doesn't mean kilocycles but "kilo cherubims," "little angels" that line up, wing tip to nose, to carry messages when Friar Sparkses depress their keys, creating a continuous wingheight, or CW. Friar Sparks uses a "CW realizer." The theory is just as adequate for the phenomena as that of Marconi, and, moreover, it is consistent with the world of the Rogerians.

In paragraph thirty-four, de Salcedo explains his own vision of the way the telegraph key works, with its evil angels on one side and good angels on the other—another way of describing negative and positive charges. Paragraphs thirty-nine to forty-nine discuss radio interference related to the moon rising, which may be indecipherable messages. This brings up other issues when de Salcedo suggests that maybe the world is flat rather than round as Columbus and the Rogerians believe, and maybe the messages are coming from a ship that has sailed off the edge of the world. In paragraph fifty-two, de Salcedo speculates that after turning down Columbus the King of Portugal may have commissioned a ship and that this is the ship that has sailed off the edge of the world.

In paragraphs fifty-eight to sixty-one, we learn that Columbus will turn back if they don't sight land by tomorrow. Friar Sparks describes a ship powered by chemical energy and driven by a "Genoese screw" (and mentions opposition on the basis of pollution and speed—suggesting the argument raised against railroad speeds) and wishes they had a Genoese screw so that they wouldn't be dependent upon the wind.

In the final paragraphs sixty-three to the end, calamity strikes as events happen as they did in our world but with fatal differences. Columbus persuades the crew to sail one more day; the crew sights birds but only a few notice that they have huge wings and no feet, and finally the ship reaches the edge of the flat world where Oceanus topples into space as Friar Sparks deciphers the message, too late, from the Portuguese ship that has preceded them.

The pay off for this short piece is certainly not the concern with character or the real world that mainstream fiction offers but a speculation supported by confirming details (in themselves a delight to the SF reader) about a world that would have been created if religion had been supportive of science. Secondarily it offers the science fiction admonition that the unsupported belief is not worth holding, by persuading readers to give their belief to a concept of alternate history before removing the rug from beneath their feet by showing that what seemed like alternate history can just as easily be alternate reality.

The story plays fair, offering both possibilities but playing upon the readers' expectations and then delivering something that contains what Poul Anderson once described as the "twin pleasures of surprise and rightness." The clues are there—the playful explanations, the images that seem like metaphors but are literal, the language itself.... The pleasures may be cerebral but no less real.

note

* A shorter and somewhat different version of this essay was published in *Inside Science Fiction* (Scarecrow Press 2006) and on the Center for the Study of Science Fiction website www.ku.edu/~sfcenter.

suggestions for further reading

Barron, Neil. *Anatomy of Wonder*. Westport, CT: Libraries Unlimited, 2004.
Clute, John and Peter Nichols. *The Encyclopedia of Science Fiction*. New York: St. Martin's, 1993.
Delany, Samuel R. *Starboard Wine*. Pleasantville, NY: Dragon Press, 1984.
Gunn, James. *The Road to Science Fiction*. Lanham, MD: Scarecrow Press, 2002–2003.
Gunn, James and Matthew Candelaria. *Speculations on Speculation: Theories of Science Fiction*. Lanham, MD: Scarecrow Press, 2005.

14
reading joanna russ in context: science, utopia and postmodernity
jeanne cortiel

Evaluating one of my courses on American literature and culture, a student recently wrote that the most important thing I had ever introduced her to was Joanna Russ's *The Female Man*. All else I taught her paled by comparison: the book had fundamentally and irrevocably transformed the way she looked at the world. This response is perhaps not statistically representative, but it is certainly not incidental. *The Female Man* is clearly Russ's most influential work, and its lasting cultural impact can hardly be overestimated. However, in spite of the complexity and breadth of her work as a whole, which has secured her a stable place in the pantheon of science fiction, Joanna Russ shares the fate of many literary icons such as Harriet Beecher Stowe or Ralph Ellison who are mainly perceived as "one-book" authors. Russ is often discussed as if she wrote no other book but *The Female Man* (1975). While it is true that *The Female Man* is Russ's opus magnum that certainly deserves the student's admiration, the full richness of her literary accomplishment only becomes accessible when one looks at her work as a whole. It is especially fruitful to place Russ's work next to the formal experiments of New Wave science fiction, feminist theory as well as postmodern fiction in general. Such a reading in a broader context reveals that the cultural significance of her writing reaches far beyond its self-conscious participation in second and third wave feminism.

Affiliated with experimental science fiction as well as postmodernist literary practices at large, Joanna Russ is usually seen as a "difficult" writer, whose texts baffle novice readers. Her work certainly does pose a challenge to the student of science fiction; it pushes the envelope in terms of gender, genre, and sexuality, productively confusing simple definitions of 1970s feminism, reductive notions of science fiction as a genre, as well as what is possible to say about how characters interact erotically in a science fiction text. It thus sits uncomfortably on the edge ɔf all of these cultural phenomena, observing the inequities in Russ's own culture with ruthless precision. But contextualized in a frame of reference attuned to the cultural fields that intersect in her work—science fiction, utopian writing, postmodern fiction and feminism—Russ's work leads her readers to new depths of understanding the potential and the workings of science fiction at large. Joanna Russ's work can also be seen as paradigmatic of the ways in which feminist writers have contributed to science fiction in the latter half of the twentieth century.

gender

Science fiction has been perceived as genre dominated by male authors and characters, even though one of its generic myths of origin takes a book by a woman, Mary Shelley's *Frankenstein* (1818), as point of departure, who thus becomes the symbolic mother of sons only. However, starting in the 1960s, feminist science fiction writers thoroughly changed the face of the genre, facilitated by two important transformations that occurred at the same time. First, the ways in which New Wave science fiction and other developments opened the genre for formal experimentation and the so-called soft sciences enabled a greater range of expressive possibilities significant to feminist science fiction attempting to break out of conventionally male quest patterns. Second, feminist thinkers such as Simone de Beauvoir and Betty Friedan began to forcefully revive the traditions of the earlier women's movement. At this cultural moment, science fiction and utopian writing provided imaginative possibilities unavailable in mainstream (popular) literature. Precisely because science fiction was so noticeably dominated by male writers, characters, as well as a male audience, it became a place that enabled a pointed critique of male dominance in all cultural fields. Science fiction provided an ideal imaginative testing ground as fictional correlative to late-twentieth century feminism, and Joanna Russ became one of the principal agents in this fictional arm of the women's movement.

The 1970s, Russ's most productive phase as a writer, saw fundamental transitions in science fiction that had been prepared by feminist inroads into science fiction in the 1960s. Alice Sheldon had written iconoclastic short stories under her male pen-name James Tiptree, Jr, and Ursula LeGuin's early work, such as *The Left Hand of Darkness* (1969), had begun to gently rock the boat of the science fiction establishment, without, however, dislodging many of its principal tenets. By 1975, when *The Female Man* came out (Russ had finished writing it four years earlier), the whole field of science fiction had been transformed. More feminists had entered science fiction, and women writers had received important science fiction awards. In 1975, an important publication documented the power of these developments: *Khatru 3 & 4 Symposium: Women in Science Fiction*, in which significant feminist voices including Joanna Russ, James Tiptree, Jr., Ursula LeGuin, Suzy McKee Charnas, Vonda McIntyre, and Samuel Delany got together to discuss women's precarious situation within science fiction.

The academic field of feminist science fiction criticism also participated in establishing feminism as a shaping force in science fiction. Landmark studies in the field include Marlene Barr's *Alien to Femininity: Speculative Fiction and Feminist Theory* (1987) and *Feminist Fabulation: Space/Postmodern Fiction* (1992), Sarah Lefanu's *In the Chinks of the World Machine: Feminism and Science Fiction* (1988), Jenny Wolmark's *Aliens and Others: Science Fiction, Feminism, and Postmodernism* (1994). Russ herself participated in this academic revolution which helped to define feminist science fiction as viable subgenre as critic and feminist thinker. To name just two examples, a collection of her essays, including the influencial "What Can a Heroine Do? or Why Women Can't Write," appeared as *To Write like a Woman* (1995) and, most recently, *The Country You Have Never Seen* (2007) gathers important essays and reviews that throw into relief Russ's shaping influence on science fiction as a whole.

Although Russ's early short stories, such as "My Dear Emily" (1962) and "Life in a Furniture Store" (1965), provide insight into the beginnings of feminist reshaping of fiction, the stories around the character Alyx, originally published in the 1960s, work more confidently against prevailing notions of gender. At the time, the range of roles available to women in fiction were more or less limited to the passive love object or the devouring monster mother, with the sexually frustrated spinster as the failed version of these two roles. Alyx, introduced in the trail-blazing short story "The Adventuress" (1967, later collected as "Bluestocking"), submits to no standards of feminine beauty or needy passivity in a world whose social structure is a form of pre-capitalist patriarchy with roles for women much like those in the 1950s and 1960s United States. However, one aspect of this society sets it apart from other patriarchal contexts: its parodic myth of creation, in which the first man was shaped from "the sixth finger of the left hand of the first woman" (9). In all respects exceptional, Alyx has six intact fingers, is sexually active as well as independent from men, and nonchalantly refuses to conform. She relates to other women not as rivals but as friends and collaborators, and while these relationships are not sexual, they are intensely meaningful and at points even erotic.

The interactions between the petty thief and pick-lock Alyx in "The Adventuress," and 17-year-old Edarra are paradigmatic of such relationships. Alyx is employed to help Edarra escape an impending marriage to a rich, considerably older man. Since Alyx is a woman, the story constitutes a significant departure from the conventional rescue plot, but she does not simply assume the male position in the rescue pattern: Edarra herself shows qualities that make her Alyx's equal rather than a helpless rescuee. Since gender is not a symmetrical structure, one can not simply replace a male by a female character and have the story work as usual. When Alyx becomes a self-determined hero, she fundamentally transforms the way stories can be told in science fiction. Students generally respond well to the way in which the Alyx stories rework conventional plot patterns; it may be especially useful to compare Alyx's ability to act and her relations to other female characters to Xena, television's "warrior princess" of the 1990s, who shares many characteristics with Alyx (except for her excessively feminine body and scanty attire). Moreover, the implicitly feminist Alyx stories provide an excellent preparation for more explicit and subtle reworkings of gender asymmetries in Russ's later work.

Russ's first novel, *Picnic on Paradise* (1968), serves as a useful introduction to the ways in which Russ reworks basic narrative structures to give female characters an active role in the plot, to turn objects of desire and exchange into agents in their own right, and to develop new forms of relationships among women independent of male approval. In *Picnic on Paradise*, Alyx is accidentally transported through time and from her sword-and-sorcery world into a science fiction context. She becomes a military agent and an important player in the commercial war that is taking place on the planet Paradise, a winter tourist resort in a far future whose social structure very much looks like the 1950s and 1960s. Her mission is to rescue a small party of rich tourists and to take them to a safe military base. Alyx carries out this clandestine task without the help of any of the available high-tech equipment, without vehicles, and without firearms, all of which would make the small group vulnerable to attack. As in the Alyx short stories, it is her relationships to and impact on other women that receive the most extensive narrative attention. However, in spite of these intense emotional bonds with other women, she ultimately does not require their help or solidarity, much less does she appear to be concerned with a more broadly political "women's cause." While Alyx—in the short stories as well as in the novel—breaks all molds of gender, she remains a more or less solitary and exceptional figure in her world.

In addition to creating new roles for female characters in science fiction, Joanna Russ's work consistently develops the idea of female authorship which she had most famously examined critically in "What Can a Heroine Do? or Why Women Can't Write" (1972) as well as in her book *How to Suppress Women's Writing* (1983). Russ's fictional work consistently explores the experience of writing as a woman and her narrators are frequently writers. Such references to the female literary tradition, combined with a consistent gendering of the narrative voice, are a pervasive presence throughout Russ's work. Her short story "Sword Blades and Poppy Seed with Homage to (Who Else) Amy Lowell" (1983) is a good example for this exploration of women writing. The story centers on the French novelist Aurore Dudevant (George Sand), who is the story's ghostly narrator, but through its title also connects with a long poem by American imagist poet Amy Lowell, "Sword Blades and Poppy Seed" and a number of other writers including but not limited to Mary Shelley, Harriet Beecher Stowe, and Emily Dickinson. Ellen Moers's pioneering delineation of a female literary tradition, *Literary Women* (1976) provides the epigraph to the story, highlighting the web of interrelations among all of these writers as well as the significance of women in shaping the literary tradition since the eighteenth century.

Russ moved into explicit feminism with the short story "When it Changed" (1972), which won the 1972 Nebula Award and was a direct response to the limitations of Ursula LeGuin's *The Left Hand of Darkness* (1969), connecting with much earlier, explicitly feminist utopian books such as Charlotte Perkins Gilman's *Herland* (1915). "When it Changed" certainly provides a point of entry into core issues of feminism and is also, as Tom Moylan has pointed out, singularly well suited to introduce students to the principal concepts of science fiction at large (Moylan: 9). The story begins with a barrage of broken gender stereotypes: "Katy drives like a maniac; we must have been doing over 120 km/hr on those turns. She's good though, extremely good, and I've seen her take the whole car apart and put it together again in a day" (490). The story's narrator, while sounding like a pretty regular guy who happens to be married to a car mechanic for the first few paragraphs, shakes the foundations of gender even more heartily when s/he is revealed as not a man, making her the second adult in a happy marriage of wife and wife, with three children between them. The story deploys the science-fictional colonization pattern to explore a society of rational beings who, in the absence of men, have luxuriated in thinking without gender for 600 years. "When it Changed" served as a basis for the politically and formally more experimental novel *The Female Man* (1975), even though the all-female planet Whileaway in "When it Changed" is a very different place from the utopian society in *The Female Man*: its highly precarious existence in a patriarchal universe is doomed when men forcefully re-colonize the planet. That is, while *The Female Man* celebrates the success of the women-only utopia, "When it Changed" centers around its eventual demise. Yet in spite of these differences, Russ's early work provides a link between notions of gender difference in 1970s feminism and its interrogation and destabilization in "post-feminist" and queer theory.

genre

Joanna Russ's oeuvre runs the gamut of science fiction, fantasy, utopian, and mainstream fiction through eight novels and countless short stories. *The Female Man*, with its four parallel universes, may serve as an excellent example of how feminist science fiction experiments with generic rules to put additional pressure on the limitations genre conventions traditionally imposes upon gender. Usually billed as a science fiction novel, the text partakes of at least four different genre traditions, science fiction, utopia, alternative history, and "mainstream" postmodern autobiographical writing—and the structural parallelism between fictional worlds and generic universes provides coherence in an otherwise complexly fragmented narrative text. *Picnic on Paradise* (1968) had performed a similar crossing of genre boundaries through a character, when Alyx moved from her sword-and-sorcery world into the science-fictional future world in which the novel is set. There, Alyx's archaic presence in the technologically sophisticated science fiction setting was a charming incongruity. However, in *The Female Man*, this generic crossing becomes a central narrative strategy.

As the apparent oxymoron in the title promises, *The Female Man* radically reformulates traditional concepts of gender. Rooted in materialist political thinking and science-fictional extrapolation, *The Female Man* retains the separatist (women-only) utopian society from the earlier short story "When it Changed," but weaves it into a politically more radical and aesthetically more experimental text. The novel's title points to the central paradox it examines: even though it is grounded in a scathing critique of women's position in patriarchal societies, the category "woman" appears as destabilized as in poststructuralist feminist theory. While the novel's most significant affiliation is with feminism, even here the text avoids monologic simplification and intersects with distinct strands or moments within feminism that oppose and destabilize each other. *The Female Man* moves away from an either/or binarism—either male or female, powerful or oppressed—to a both/and, examining the contradictions in contemporary American society without attempting to resolve them. *The Female Man* is a text ideally suited to explore feminism in all its different incarnations, but it is its generic crossovers that enable its multiple, even contradictory affiliations.

The key premise of *The Female Man* is that it is possible to travel between parallel universes through what the narrator calls "probability travel." The novel explores four such universes that lie on very close strands of probability, that is, they have slightly different histories, but also share many characteristics with the basic narrative world, the United States around the year 1970. Each of these worlds is the home of one of the main characters as well as representative of one of the four genres present in the novel. As these four protagonists-Janet, Jael, Jeannine, and Joanna-cross parallel universes in the fictional world, the novel crosses the boundaries between utopia, science fiction, alternate history and autobiography. Also significant to the way in which the characters interact with each other is that while they are genetically identical, their respective environments make them very different women—each emerging from related but different social environments and generic conventions. The novel begins with the gutsy and independent utopian character Janet on Whileaway, an all-female future world that has thrived without men for centuries. Jeannine and Joanna, on the other hand, live in two worlds that simultaneously exist in 1969. Jeannine's world is based on an alternate history scenario in which World War II never happened and the repressive gender system is carried to an absurd extreme; Joanna's world is the basic narrative world and, as indicated by the first name which she shares with the author, can be seen as a fictional autobiography. Finally, there is the warrior and assassin Jael, who lives in another future world, in which men and women inhabit separate continents and are in a state of cold war with each other. It would be reductive, therefore, to read *The Female Man* as a utopian text only. It contains four different genre affiliations and it is precisely the tensions between these affiliations that enable the novel's sophisticated feminist critique. The generic differences set Whileaway apart as utopian world and enable it to become an example of what Tom Moylan has called a "critical utopia," providing the hopeful vision of the good place with a distinctly skeptical edge.

The Female Man appeared at a turning point in the history of utopian writing. After the two world wars, the utopian tradition had experienced a decline and it was feminist texts that triggered its come-back in the late 1960s and early 1970s (Moylan 1986 56f). With its utopian world Whileaway, *The Female Man* joined a host of other utopian novels including Ursula Le Guin's *The Left Hand of Darkness* (1969), Monique Wittig's *Les Guérillères* (1969) and Dorothy Bryant's *The Kin of Ata are Waiting for You* (1971). As feminism at large resurrected the impetus of the turn-of-the-century women's movement, these feminist utopias critically linked with ancestors such as Mary E. Bradley Lane's *Mizora* (1890) and Charlotte Perkins Gilman's *Herland* (1915), both of which had based their utopian visions on nineteenth-century notions of women's moral superiority and the assumption that if it were up to (white) women, the world would be a better, even perfect place. This refurbished version of utopianism would sustain a wave of utopian and dystopian writing affiliated with or friendly to feminism: Ursula LeGuin's *The Dispossessed* (1974), Ernest Callenbach's *Ecotopia* (1975), Marge Piercy's *Woman on the Edge of Time* (1976), Samuel Delany's *Triton* (1976), Suzy McKee Charnas's *Walk to the End of the World* (1974) and *Motherlines* (1978) and Sally Miller Gearhart's *Wanderground* (1980).

Still, while *The Female Man* fits into this context of writing informed by feminism, Russ's novel also stands apart through its distinctive formal and generic experiments. The shifting narrative voices, which blur the boundaries between the characters who assume these voices in the course of the novel, are central to these experiments. Unlike most classic utopian texts, *The Female Man* does not have a non-utopian narrator commenting upon the utopian world from outside. Instead, the utopian character Janet Evason has a voice of her own, which she assumes with confidence in the novel's first sentence: "I was born on a farm on Whileaway" (1). Janet does not provide a systematic ethnography of the utopian world, but paints a poetic collage of her home planet and its global communitarian culture. However, Janet is not the only one who speaks about Whileaway; Joanna, the fictional autobiographer, sometimes also speaks looking longingly through Janet's eyes. On first reading, the unannounced shifting of narrative voices may be confusing, but it is these shifts that link the four generic worlds while disrupting the continuity between the four genetically identical protagonists.

With its genre mixing and changing narrators, *The Female Man* does not provide a monologic critique of patriarchal society, but links its clear political position, which is grounded in a materialist analysis of individuals as produced by their economic position, with the destabilization of identity itself. This destabilization of identity and the idea of binary sex difference is ironically heightened by Jael, the second narrator-protagonist in the novel. First, Jael is a "posthuman" subject before the term, and when Donna Haraway refers to *The Female Man* in her theorization of the "cyborg" as critique of postindustrial labor practices, it is certainly Jael who warrants this attention. Apart from being a hyper-technological hybrid between human and machine, Jael also serves as an allegorical figure that calls up atavistic notions of retribution and anger. This combination of the futuristic and ancient has turned Jael into a model for later characters of cyberpunk science fiction, most memorably perhaps in the female assassin Molly Millions in William Gibson's *Neuromancer* trilogy (cf. Wolmark 1994: 116). Second, Jael most fully inhabits the parallel universe tradition in science fiction-unlike Janet, who links with earlier feminist visions of full subjecthood in the utopian vein. Non-utopian rather than dystopian, Jael's world externalizes the state of war expressed in the dualism of sex that is the basis of patriarchal societies. While to the Whileawayans, technology is liberatory as reproductive technology, Jael accesses the notion of violent revolution through control over military technology: she has transformed herself into a futuristic warrior princess, a ruthless killer of men.

It is possible to compare the tension between Jael's and Janet's worlds to Marge Piercy's potential futures in *Woman on the Edge of Time*, one utopian and one dystopian. However, Jael and Janet not only live in different worlds, but also on different, virtually incompatible generic universes. This distinction is reflected in the two versions of Whileaway's history: from Jael's perspective, Whileaway is the result of a revolutionary war in which the victorious women killed all the men, from Janet's perspective, the men all died in a plague. That none of the perspectives is ultimately validated as "true" by the novel underscores how Russ's bold transgressions of conventional notions of narrator and genre manage to express a clear materialist egalitarian political vision— precisely because her text transcends the concept of a stable human identity and history.

sexuality

Russ entered the scene as a feminist author when "the personal is political" had become a central slogan of the women's movement, bringing the power dynamics of intimate relationships into the light of political critique. Radical feminism had begun to focus on the ways in which heterosexual intercourse served as central site of women's oppression.

This engagement with sexuality was grounded in the conviction that personal relationships, the most intimate relations and interactions among people, are of central importance to political change. However, while Russ's work fully participates in this critique, it never naïvely posits women loving women as incarnations of erotic egalitarianism and solution to all gender trouble. In Joanna Russ's work, sexuality has three major functions, which it has in common with much of feminist science fiction at large. On a most basic level, reconfiguring women's sexuality as self-determined acts of pure lust-whether with other women or with men-becomes politically relevant here since it made visible what had been invisible. Secondly, sexuality is separated from reproduction, liberating it from utilitarian constraints. The most significant impact, however, is effected the reconfiguration of narrative itself when it is driven by female desire for a love object of any gender, as the earlier discussion of Alyx has indicated. Russ's work ably negotiates the paradoxes and complexities of tampering with the most fundamental motor of narrative, erotic desire.

Most of Russ's short stories and novels in the 1970s and 1980s make a point of separating sex and childbearing, a materialist feminist imperative most radically proposed by Shulamith Firestone in *The Dialectic of Sex* (1970). Science and technology are fundamental in enabling this separation. For example, Whileaway is made possible through the merging of ova, a highly sophisticated medical procedure. Unlike parthenogenesis, which is limited to the genetic material of a single parent, the merging of ova ensures a genetic diversity equal to that of sexual reproduction, eliminating men from the reproductive process and liberating sex from reproduction. Since the merging of ova does not occur naturally in humans, a society that depends on it has to have fairly advanced reproductive technologies. This liberatory interpretation of technology stands in contrast to some other anti-technological feminist work that posits that women are predisposed for a special relationship to the natural environment. For example, the separatist women's community in Suzy McKee Charnas's *Motherlines* (1978) use the sperm of another species-horses-to trigger parthenogenesis rather than resort to technological reproduction. The resulting insemination ritual in *Motherlines* is an interesting sexual fantasy, while it seems physically improbable. What all of these feminist fictions have in common, however, is the conviction that patriarchal societies have used the tie between sexuality and reproduction to keep women under male control. Perhaps the most significant consequence of this liberatory use of technology in *The Female Man* is that there is no sexualized violence on Whileaway, although the social interactions are far from being consistently harmonious. Whileawayans argue, they fight and they even kill each other. But oppressive, exploitative sexuality is completely alien to that world: "You can walk around the Whilawayan equator twenty times (if the feat takes your fancy and you live that long) with one hand on your sex and in the other an emerald the size of a grapefruit. All you'll get is a tired wrist" (82).

Beyond liberating sex through science and technology, Russ's fiction self-consciously reflects the fact that desire as a central driving force in narrative is itself gendered in gender-based societies. Female protagonists become agents in narrative when their desire for the love object, male or female, begins to control plot development. Thus, sexuality, particularly women's sexuality, serves as important point of reference to reconstitutions of both gender and genre in Russ's fiction. This intimate connection between gender and sexuality in narrative becomes particularly transparent in the stories around Alyx, which, in expanding the possibilities for performing gender in science-fictional narratives, invariably shift the protagonist's sexuality away from the heterosexual norm. Alyx has sexual relations with men, but does not sacrifice her own masculinity and maintains primary emotional relationships with women. Similarly, Russ's second novel, *And Chaos Died* (1970), a very different fictional experiment, explores the gender performance and sexual confusion of its male protagonist Jai Vedh, who is introduced as gay but then has an intensely sexual relationship with a woman, Evne. There is no stable location for identity in Russ's work.

Linking with these earlier narratives, *The Female Man* extends Russ's experiments with erotic interactions and their impact on gender. All of the protagonists in *The Female Man* have more or less thriving sex lives. Two of them have sex with men (Jael, Jeannine), two of them with women (Janet, Joanna). Since the four women are all genetically identical, the novel off-handedly rejects the idea that sexual object choice is genetically determined. Jeannine has a tenuous relationship with the sensitive underdog Cal, who she feels is too feminine because he playfully cross-dresses and breaks into tears when they have sex. Jael has guiltlessly dominating intercourse with a youthful man, her domestic servant and sexual companion. He turns out to be a post-human being whose genetic material, originally chimpanzee, is shaped by Jael's sexual fantasies in an ironic reversal of the way in which women shape their bodies to suit men in patriarchal societies. Both of these women think of themselves as heterosexual, but they have long departed from the safe boundaries of sexual normalcy and entered a realm where the appellation "heterosexual" has very little explanatory power. Conversely, the novel does not arrive at a normalization of gay and lesbian sexuality either. Because Whileaway is not a gendered society, the women on Whileaway are emphatically not lesbians, and strictly speaking, they are not women either. Janet, non-woman and non-lesbian, takes sexual promiscuity as a given but still manages to break a sexual taboo by getting involved with the precocious teenager Laura. This relationship is incongruously mirrored by Joanna's relationship to Laura at the end of the novel, which makes perfect sense in terms of Joanna's postmodern autobiographical narrative voice, where Janet is a version of Joanna. None of the protagonists ever reaches a stable identity grounded in their sexuality: Sex is what they do, not what they are.

Many other characters engaged in erotic acts in Russ's work have similarly unfixed gender identities, and in her later work increasingly destabilize the feminist narratives of liberation Russ helped to create. Novels such as *The Two of Them* (1978), *On Strike Against God* (1980) and the short story collection *Extra(Ordinary) People* (1985) continue to explore the tensions among gender, genre and sexuality. In particular, the four connected stories collected in *Extra(Ordinary)People*—a text that deserves much more critical attention than it has received to date—irreverently reconfigure the rescue plot inherent in much of Russ's feminist fiction. The narrators become more unreliable, genre boundaries—between science fiction, fantasy and "mainstream" fiction—are transgressed with strategic nonchalance, and gender roles appear as no more than highly amusing if tragically limiting masquerades. The obvious result of gender performance being divorced from bodily existence (as in the short story "Souls") or ludicrously exaggerated to carnivalesque extremes (as in "Bodies"), is that the terms "lesbian" and "woman" proceed to make less and less sense. It is indicative of the narrative power of a transformed sexuality thought to its logical conclusion that Russ's texts move beyond what was culturally available at the time, anticipating a queer erotic sensibility that leaves behind strict binarisms of male-female, masculine-feminine, gay-straight. In a way, Russ's consistent materialist politics, combined with a keen awareness of the way in which desire shapes narrative, push her fiction to transcend the very identity politics it emerged from.

Thus, though Russ gleefully introduced explicit and graphic lesbian sexuality to science fiction starting in the late 1960s, her reshaping of how erotic desire can be articulated in fiction goes much beyond the lesbian-feminist imperative to bring into public view what had been kept behind closet doors. Because Russ anticipated later developments in feminism, her fiction (as well as her criticism) provides a link between 1970s feminism, which sometimes seems inaccessible to contemporary students, and so-called post-feminist developments as well as queer theory.

With its interconnected reconfigurations of gender as performance, genre boundaries as porous, and sexuality constituted by pleasurable acts rather than fixed identities, Russ's work as a whole is an excellent example of how science fiction, and particularly feminist science fiction, has impacted postmodern and postindustrial cultural production. Materialist feminism, as all historical materialism, is grounded in the conviction that human consciousness is fundamentally shaped by the material conditions in which humans live. Russ's work examines these material conditions in the "what if" provided by science fiction, putting pressure on some of the most fundamental assumptions of science fiction itself. However, while consistently materialist throughout her work, Russ never assumes an uninterrupted connection between the material conditions and the identity of her characters. In the final sentences of *The Female Man*, the narrator sends off her book predicting its obsolescence and conjuring a reading scenario "when young persons read you to hrooch and hrch and guffaw, wondering what the dickens you were all about" (213). I think it is safe to say that, very much like Melville's "Call me Ishmael" though perhaps on a less inflated scale, Russ's "I was born on a farm on Whileaway" will continue to travel well through the centuries as an opening sentence of a transformative reading experience, not because the utopian vision it articulates has not yet been realized, but because the book's aesthetic challenge far outlives its political vision.

suggestions for further reading

Barr, Marleen. *Feminist Fabulation: Space/Postmodern Fiction*. Iowa City: University of Iowa Press, 1992.

Cortiel, Jeanne. *Demand My Writing: Joanna Russ/Feminism/Science Fiction*. Liverpool, England: Liverpool University Press, 1999.

Delany, Samuel. "Orders of Chaos: The Science Fiction of Joanna Russ." in Jane B. Weedman (ed.) *Women Worldwalkers: New Dimensions of Science Fiction and Fantasy*. Lubbock, TX: Texas Tech Press, 1985, 95–123.

Hollinger, Veronica. "(Re)Reading Queerly: Science Fiction, Feminism, and the Defamiliarization of Gender." in Marleen S. Barr (ed.) *Future Females, the Next Generation: New Voices and Velocities in Feminist Science Fiction Criticism*. Lanham, MD: Rowman and Littlefield, 2000, 197–215.

Wolmark, Jenny. *Aliens and Others: Science Fiction, Feminism, and Postmodernism*. Iowa City: University of Iowa Press, 1994.

15
reading science fiction's interdisciplinary conversation with science and technology studies
r. doug davis and lisa yaszek

alien effects in the science and technology studies classroom

We propose that science fiction (SF) is ideally suited to the science and technology studies (STS) classroom. SF authors and STS scholars care about many of the same things. SF stories and STS scholarship are often about the work of scientists and engineers and the effect of that work on society. In both, scientific discoveries transform whole worlds. Laboratories are sites of gripping drama. Expert knowledge matters. Scientific discourse is woven into daily life. The personal is political and technological. The non-human has agency. The post-human falls in love. SF dramatizes the critical insights of STS. Science fiction writers and filmmakers build future worlds that reflect upon things happening in science, technology, and society right now. Of course it's all fiction and that's what makes it especially fun.

In this paper we describe how we harness that fun to work for us as scholars trained in literary and cultural studies who have been drawn to science and technology studies over the course of our careers. To further this interdisciplinary conversation we have two joined aims in the following pages. As literary scholars we describe how the alienating effect of SF can provoke new understandings of science, technology, and society; and as STS scholars we show how that alienating effect can be put to work in the STS classroom. We begin by reviewing the two main ways that college instructors have read SF: as a demonstration of disciplinary subject matter and as a critique of technoculture. We then show how this latter mode can work in the STS classroom.

a brief history of science fiction in the classroom: the first, familiar phase

Mark Hillegas taught the first accredited SF class at Colgate U in 1962; by 1976 over 2000 such courses had been initiated and at least half a dozen classroom-oriented short-story anthologies were published (Parrinder: 131; Gerlach and Hamilton: 162). Today, three British universities offer SF degrees, and an American one, Eastern New Mexico U, offers an endowed chair for SF studies.[1] This trend is no surprise because SF "has something significant to say about the relationship of scientific discovery and knowledge to human life" (Hillegas: 100).

SF scholars continue to reiterate Hillegas's sentiments, but SF pedagogy has evolved over the past forty years. In the first two decades of SF pedagogy, scholars often used SF texts as demonstrations of disciplinary knowledge. In recent decades, formalist theories of SF as an independent epistemological mode have led an increasing number of professors to use SF as a dialectical tool like critical theory. This latter understanding of SF is promising and challenging for the STS classroom.

Hillegas offered his first SF class through Colgate's English department, but throughout the 1970s such courses were more commonly associated with the social sciences. Campus militancy in the late 1960s and 1970s led students to drop out of liberal arts courses and demand new "relevant" and "non-elitist" ones that addressed changing American society. Disciplines like anthropology, sociology, and political science were the obvious place to establish these new courses and resuscitate their flagging enrollment numbers (Parrinder: 135). Simultaneously, professors turned to SF because, as Martin Harry Greenberg and Patricia S. Warrick note: "both SF writers and political scientists are interested in the nature of politics and the future of the political system ... [But only] SF can focus the attention of the student and the teacher ... on the future course of political life, enriching our awareness of the alternatives that may be available" (8). SF seemed to meet the needs of students and professors alike: it was a popular genre of everyday fiction that provided concrete examples of the more abstract theses and theories advanced in these courses.

Physical scientists spoke passionately about using SF texts to engage students. For instance, physicist and SF author Gregory Benford used SF in his classes because "the engineers in the course particularly like discussing an author's tricks and ingenuity and factual errors... [Which inevitably] leads to a discussion of the important aesthetic question of how much you can cheat on the facts in fiction. There are virtually no cheat-free stories, including my own, and playing the game of finding the error in a story seems to motivate a lot of students to engage in physics who otherwise sit there and stare" (quoted in Woodcock: 151). Similarly, Patricia Warrick advocated using SF in computer science classrooms because innovative visions provoked lively debate over the potentially "radical nature of technological change" (136). Thus professors in both the physical and social sciences saw SF as a useful tool for easing students into the complexities of disciplinary knowledge in an entertaining fashion.

Nor was SF completely dismissed by the humanities at this time. Ursula K. Le Guin and Samuel Delany, as SF authors and university professors, argued SF demanded a critical apparatus unique to the genre that combined the genre's own standards with conventional literary aesthetic criteria (Woodcock: 261; Le Guin: 22–23). Others suggested that SF could be read in relation to standard literary genres and modes of analysis: Hillegas used myth theory to show how SF authors wrote updated versions of the fable, the satire, and the utopia. By aligning feminist SF with utopian writing and treating it as a demonstration of feminist and poststructuralist theory, scholars including Natalie M. Rosinsky, Thelma Shinn, and Francis Bartowski made important strides toward bringing SF into the academic mainstream (Roberts: 186–187).

Throughout the first phase of SF studies, scholars jointly assumed that SF was most useful as a proving ground for their disciplines' specific ideas. Today, professors still use SF in the classroom for their own disciplinary purposes: in cultural geography classes Bruce Sterling's *Islands in the Net* (1988) demonstrates globalization; in bioethics classes Andrew Nicoll's *Gattaca* (1997) illustrates the consequences of human genetic engineering; in classes on postmodernism, William Gibson's *Mona Lisa Overdrive* (1988) critiques the culture industries.

Yet some fits between SF and disciplinary fact are more productive than others, and none is ever perfect. Demonstrations such as those above beg the question: what do these texts, authors, and filmmakers have to say about globalization, genetics, or the culture industries? To answer that question, we must discuss how each fiction represents the concepts of the various disciplines, and we must discuss how those concepts relate to our world and the built world of the SF text.

a brief history of science fiction in the classroom: the second, alienating phase

In the second phase, SF theorists began to explore not just what SF represented, but how it did so through unique formal characteristics of the genre. SF has an implicitly critical function that can be made explicit in classroom discussion. One of the most important scholars on this subject is Darko Suvin, who proposed that SF is a critical mode of awareness in its own right. SF differs from both classroom example and disciplinary theory in that "it is primarily and centrally narrative fiction ... a set of *stories told in writing*. Methods inappropriate for understanding a story may be used to illustrate this or that element within SF, but will be fundamentally inappropriate for approaching it" (Suvin and Elkin: 263). As narrative fiction, then, SF does more than demonstrate principles or theories; rather, it builds whole worlds and peoples them with diverse characters that act in ways that complicate the principles and theories that inspired their creation.

For Suvin, SF has two formal characteristics: it is set in "an imaginative framework alternative to the author's empirical environment" and it is marked by the "presence and interaction of estrangement and cognition" (7–8). This latter characteristic is crucial to understanding SF as a critical literary form: although readers will understand some aspects of the alternative SF world, others will be unfamiliar, provoking readers to ask: why is this different from our own world? How did things get this way? What other options might there be?

These formal characteristics are, as Carl Freedman argues in *Critical Theory and Science Fiction* (2000), what aligns SF with critical theory. Both forms of writing

> insist on historical mutability, material reducibility, and utopian possibility. Of all genres, SF is the one most devoted to the historical concreteness and rigorous self-reflectiveness of critical theory. The science fictional world is not only different in time and place from our own, but one whose chief interest is precisely the difference that such a difference makes. (xvi)

SF constitutes a certain kind of "civic education" about social relations in a technoscientific world (Elkin and Suvin: 267). Moreover, as Freedman points out, it may be one of the most effective forms of civic education available to scholars at this particular historical moment.

SF can give us a new perspective on our world because it presents a changed, alien state. The very act of presenting those conditions as changed requires some understanding of how they work in the first place, and how they might work if they were different. Sometimes SF's critique is explicit, as in much satirical and feminist SF.[2] More often it is implicit and unintentional and must be drawn out through close reading and discussion. In that discussion, SF becomes a kind of STS through a class's dialog to understand what connects the built world of SF to the world that we know—and what makes it different.

SF dramatizes many of the things we discuss in STS. It is home to cyborgs, networked worlds, and even alternative kinds of scientists. But at the same time, SF works best in the STS classroom if we grant it a degree of autonomy and discuss what it has to say about those same things. Read as producing alien effects, SF becomes an STS narrative that explores the relations of science, technology, and society through its representations of how those things may—or may not—change. The difference detected in every SF story *is* what that SF text has to say in the STS classroom.

alien effects revisited: a brief survey of science and technology studies

Because of its world-building properties, SF alienates readers productively, and STS leads to similar insights, but descriptively rather than dramatically. We divide STS into three kinds of projects, some of which are a better match for SF than others. These projects are united by a "social-constructivist" approach. The basic insight that guides STS's social-constructivist approach is that our knowledge of reality is not found but made. Reality as known by scientists can be understood in relation to the many social contexts in which that knowledge is made and put to use. STS's social-constructivist practitioners foreground what is unseen, unsaid, and otherwise taken-for-granted in science and engineering. Like SF, STS can be very alienating at first to readers happily grounded in science's positivist narratives of discovery and objectivity.

The first kind of STS is the sociological study of scientific knowledge, including scholarly work in the rhetoric of science, the sociology of scientific knowledge (SSK), and the ethnography and anthropology of scientific communities. Practitioners focus on scientific knowledge and sites of knowledge production, including laboratories and journals. This work is science in its own right, grounded in empirical studies of scientific communities and print cultures. It takes as its object the one kind of knowledge that prior sociologists had considered beyond their purview: the valid facts and theories of science itself. Major works in this project include: Andrew Pickering's sociological history, *Constructing Quarks*, Charles Bazerman's rhetorical history, *Shaping Written Knowledge*, and Bruno Latour and Steve Woolgar's *Laboratory Life*.

The second kind of science and technology studies we call "actor-network" and "Big Science" studies, also described as "technoscience studies." These historical and theoretical studies analyze and chart the growth and extension of laboratory technologies and techniques both within and beyond the scientific community. Employing the tools of the first kind of STS, the second kind of technoscientific STS demonstrates the inseparable ties between scientific knowledge, technological development, and social form—hence the compound "technoscience." The second kind of STS includes studies of systems such as Bruno Latour's "actor-network" model of science as described in *Science in Action* and *The Pasteurization of France* and Thomas P. Hughes's analyzes of "technological systems" in *American Genesis*. It also includes historical analyzes of experimental societies such as Steven Shapin and Simon Schaffer's *Leviathan and the Air-Pump* and discourse studies of technological systems including Paul Edwards's history of computing, *The Closed World* and Lily Kay's history of genetics, *Who Wrote the Book of Life?*

Both kinds of STS described above proceed in a spirit of factual description; their practitioners are social scientists and historians who examine how scientific knowledge and technology are produced in society. The third kind of STS proceeds as cultural studies of science and technology, or studies of technoculture. These are critical studies energized by the social-constructivist insights of the first two kinds of STS, but coupled with political theories about the nature of society. Cultural studies of science scholars treat science as power and ideology and analyze science as producing cultural narratives that reproduce power relations and values. Facts are value-laden, and the practice of science and the building of technology are bound up within the dominant orders of society and expressive of its interests. Technocultural studies of science and technology are often explicit political commentaries. This category of STS is produced by scientists, historians, philosophers, and literary scholars alike. Some of it is literary-historical; much of it is radical, containing programs for overhauling the scientific method. Two qualities distinguish this kind of STS from the first two: its overt literary and political theoretical framing and its focus on science as a part of a larger society. We include in this kind of STS such Marxian work as Richard Levins and Richard Lewontin's *The Dialectical Biologist* and Andrew Ross's *Strange Weather* as well as literary histories such as N. Katherine Hayles's *Chaos Bound*. Sandra Harding's *The Science Question in Feminism* is explicitly feminist, and Donna Haraway combines Marxism and feminism in *Primate Visions*. This third kind of STS can be the most alienating kind of all.

SF is most like science and technology studies of the third kind, for both are representations not only of scientific knowledge or technology, but also of technoscientifically built societies. The energy of SF flows parallel to that of STS of the third kind: outward from the personal, the scientific, and the technically specific to a critique of culture and society. Unlike STS, though, it expresses its critical insights by the way it reshapes those very things and lets us see, as if for the first time, our present technoculture as but a passing moment in a whole historical process.

science fiction in the science and technology studies classroom: bringing it all together

SF and STS are bound together by a shared interest in the ways that science and technology matter to contemporary society. Each works to make us see these relations through fresh eyes. Although we can certainly imagine classroom scenarios where any one type of STS might be paired up with a work of SF on a related theme, our preference is to combine the cultural studies of science and technology with the modes of SF studies that look at SF texts as critically engaged cultural artifacts. Both types of inquiry emphasize the centrality of narrative in a technoscientific era, and both work to denaturalize dominant narratives of science and technology by naming them as such.

Much like a good SF story, the cultural studies of both science and SF are designed to induce what Hugo Gernsback called a *sense of wonder*, a sense that, in the STS classroom, invites us to become alien witnesses to our own past and present and to become the creative engineers of our futures as well.

Although we identify key similarities between STS and SF studies, we also caution that they do not always produce the same kinds of estrangement and critical recognition. Certainly, many STS and SF studies scholars share a progressive political agenda. Evelyn Fox Keller argues that the proper goal of feminist STS is to identify the gendered inequities of science so we may eliminate them ("Feminism and

Science" 29), a goal remarkably similar to that of Charles Elkin and Darko Suvin, who propose using SF and SF criticism to enact a kind of "civic education" that maps out the contradictions between various scientific disciplines to better transform them (267).

Although scholars such as Keller and Elkin and Suvin share similar goals, SF authors have been writing speculative fiction for nearly 200 years and come from a wide array of social and political backgrounds. It is therefore worth noting that not all SFs are equally useful for the STS or SF scholar. As Sheila Finch explains, "scholars seem to find SF offering virgin ground for [their] systems of mapping the territory. But as a wise man once pointed out, the map is not the territory, and these... approaches often fall short when applied to the SF genre" (30). In the broadest sense, SF authors utilize the same basic sense of wonder as their scholarly counterparts, but often to radically different ends.

Consider early SF. Hugo Gernsback started the first SF magazines to boost the cause of science and technology (and sell his ham radios). Gernsback encouraged authors to write stories that would induce a sense of wonder in their audiences and provoke them to speculate on how they, too, could contribute to the march of American progress. Like other members of the SF community, Gernsback was a proponent of the technocratic movement, which maintained that democracy and capitalism were fatally flawed soft sciences that mystified the real relations of the world, exacerbating the gap between the rich and the poor. As Andrew Ross points out, technocrats proposed reorganizing society along the principles of hard science and engineering, which, they maintained, were value-free and guaranteed to produce a better, more efficient society (10), a conclusion that most STS scholars would not accept.

However, the differences between SF and STS are, to paraphrase Freedman, the differences that can make a difference in the effectiveness of your teaching (xvi). The key is to read SF in relation to both science and STS; SF stories are critical theories cast in imaginative forms that illuminate theory just as they are illuminated by it.

Consider a series of exercises that we do in our introductory STS classes to familiarize students with the concept of technologically mediated or "cyborg" subjectivity. We usually begin with an introduction to the science itself. These readings include Manfred Clynes and Nathan S. Klines's 1960 article "Cyborgs and Space." We then turn to Donna Haraway's groundbreaking, "A Manifesto for Cyborgs" (1985), to demonstrate how Haraway appropriates the cyborg to provide us with new ways of thinking about contemporary technoscientific relations. Students are so intrigued by the way that this trope has circulated through the academy that they are willing to rethink their attitudes to critical theory and to science itself: both Haraway's piece and Clynes and Klines's piece are stories that use the same literary tropes and themes, but to very different ends.

Of course, Haraway is extremely difficult for young students to digest; neither her ideas nor her writing style are intuitive. The most that we hope to achieve with a first reading of Haraway is a basic understanding that cyborg subjects exist on a continuum. This continuum stretches from the dystopic "man in space" who cannot see the social and political forces that determine his fate to the "ironically utopian" cyborg who understands that its identity has been predetermined but nonetheless strives to connect with other subjects to enact social change. If we get even this far with our freshmen, it is by setting up the course so Haraway is in dialogue with Clynes and Kline. Students compare Haraway's metaphoric man in space with Clynes and Kline's literal one; it confirms their suspicion that the spacefaring astronaut, like Haraway's cyborgs, remains literally plugged into a technoscientific network rooted on Earth.

In the final phase of this unit, we turn from STS to SF, utilizing a cyberpunk novel such as William Gibson's *Neuromancer* (1984). We put the novel in dialogue with Haraway by mapping out the relations between the kinds of cyborg subjects each author depicts. Our discussion of cyborgs also becomes a discussion of more literary things: character, plot, setting, motivation, style. We don't just find the cyborgs, we ask: How is *Neuromancer* a piece of cyborg critique in its own right?

We continue to be astonished with the results each time we do this exercise with a new class. The STS theory of cyborgs may set the stage for our discussion of this piece of SF, but the SF starts talking back in its own voice. At first students expect that Gibson's cyborgs will simply demonstrate Haraway's theories. They expect that we will be able to plug characters into the bad cyborg/good cyborg continuum that we draw on the blackboard. However, good SF authors build complex worlds and people them with a complex array of characters. Some characters—such as the computer hacker Case and his boss Armitage—are men in space unwittingly manipulated by Wintermute and Neuromancer, the massive artificial intelligences who become the avatars of capitalism. Other characters are not so easy to place. Is Case's partner/bodyguard Molly an ironically utopian cyborg because she recognizes how economic forces have marked her, or does her apparent resignation to her fate negate the progressive implications of this awareness? By the end of this class we have added several new axes to Haraway's binary continuum to make sense of Gibson's cyborg subjects.

It is a chaotic but enlightening exercise and one that indicates Haraway's linear continuum of cyborg subjectivity is not rich or detailed enough to fully model the new kinds of relations we might experience in a technoscientific world. It helps students articulate how cyborg subjects exist in a web of networked relations. After reading SF stories like Gibson's *Neuromancer*, students are able to re-read STS theorists like Haraway in a more sophisticated manner, making the tension between SF and STS a productive one. If fiction authors and scholars engage in debates over specific technoscientific issues, it is the same way that real people hold conversations with one another. They neither simply agree nor simple negate each other's points. Instead, SF authors, STS scholars, and even scientists engage in rich relations with one another, using the formal properties of their chosen mediums to elaborate upon and extend one another's ideas.

To bring SF into the STS classroom, we recommend enacting the critical history of SF studies for each text: moving from demonstration to critical estrangement to reformulation of the relations of science and society. It is useful to see our ideas played out in dramatic and entertaining fashion— that is where SF as the third kind of STS begins. Bringing SF into the STS classroom adds a new dimension to our discussions of the technocultural present. The opportunities for class discussion and insight multiply as we chart the connections and differences between *three* worlds: the given empirical world, the world represented by STS, and the world represented by SF. Ultimately, the joy of discovery in the STS classroom emerges at precisely that moment when these different worlds collide.

notes

1. Liverpool and Reading Universities both offer masters degrees in SF studies; the University of Glamorgan offers a B. S. in Science and SF. American universities also encourage students to pursue SF studies, of course, but these studies are usually folded into larger programs of study, such as the University of Kansas' creative writing program and Bowling Green University's popular culture program.
2. Two classic examples of socially engaged SF immediately spring to mind: Frederick Pohl and C. M. Kornbluth's *The Space Merchants,* a satire aimed directly at mid-century Madison Avenue; and Joanna Russ's *The Female Man,* a feminist tale that brings together four women from parallel worlds to highlight different ways of dealing with patriarchy.

suggestions for further reading

Freedman, Carl. *Critical Theory and SF*. Middletown, CT: Wesleyan University Press, 2000.

Gibson, William. *Neuromancer*. New York: Ace Books, 1984.

Haraway, Donna. "A Cyborg Manifesto: Science, Technology, and Socialist-Feminism in the Late Twentieth Century." *Simians, Cyborgs, and Women: The Reinvention of Nature*. New York: Routledge, 1991. 149–181.

Haraway, Donna J. *Primate Visions: Gender, Race, and Nature in the World of Modern Science*. New York: Routledge, 1989.

Latour, Bruno. *Aramis, or The Love of Technology*. Cambridge, MA: Harvard University Press, 1996.

part v
science fiction and
diverse disciplines

introduction to part v

Readers can logically expect literary protagonists to remain safely ensconced between the book covers within which they appear. Well not so for Kurt Vonnegut's fictional Kilgore Trout. Trout's name is emblazoned as author on the cover of *Venus on the Half-Shell*. Even though, in truth, Philip José Farmer wrote *Venus on the Half-Shell*, Trout is listed in the novel's Library of Congress catalogue entry. Kilgore Trout, who has escaped easy categorization, is emblematic of the authors and articles that appear in this section.

Single designations fail adequately to apply to this section's contributors. The working scientists engage science fiction and the science fiction writers are prolific cultural and science fiction critics. Gregory Benford (a physicist) is known for writing hard science fiction that incorporates his scientific research. Joseph D. Miller (a neurobiologist) often contributes to the science fiction academic community. James Gunn, Pamela Sargent, and Bruce Sterling are at once prolific science fiction writers and social commentators. Like Kilgore Trout, these writers break the usual mold.

Perhaps their versatility mirrors science fiction's penchant for bursting generic confines. Science fiction literature, replete with its own myriad subgenres, topics, and connections to mainstream fiction, is applicable to teaching and learning various disciplines. Reading science fiction is all about thinking large and free. The essays included here at once explore this statement and present ideas about how seemly fantastic scientific breakthroughs (and their human implications) might ultimately occur.

It is at once fitting and proper—and fun—to enable an introduction to a section about disciplinary diversity to itself exemplify such diversity. In terms of this objective, Vonnegut's trademark paragraph ending follows immediately:

And so it goes.

This section will boldly go to Miller, Benford, Sargent, Gunn, and Sterling respectively addressing science fiction's relationship to the following subject areas: neuroscience, physics, biology, philosophy, and computer science.

Joseph D. Miller traces the use and abuse of neurological concepts in science fiction from Mary Shelley's *Frankenstein* through William Gibson's *Neuromancer* to the work of current writers (such as Greg Egan). Miller focuses upon why the scientific concepts appearing in science fiction are plausible. He also discusses how scientific discoveries emanate from the science which appears in science fiction.

Gregory Benford stresses that illuminating physical law through science fictional thought experiments can be useful in awakening students' inventive, playful side. Physics constrains action in ways that call up further study of underlying physical laws. When considering flight near a neutron star, for example, commonplace tides become deadly. The only difference is the larger gravitational potential of a compact star, not the total stellar mass. In order to survive, the hapless humans nearby must then understand nature in a new way. Generating a plot problem through applying physics takes readers out of a human-centered narrative and into the realm of imagination, where nature provides a worthy opponent. Such strategies can both teach science and reflect on the nature of narrative itself. Science fiction abounds in such examples—one of its special charms.

Pamela Sargent points out that to read much of the science fiction written since *Frankenstein* involves reading about biology and its divisions. She explains why H. G. Wells and Mary Shelley set the pattern for much of the subsequent biological science fiction. Ironically science fiction, in the minds of many, is more strongly associated with technological or engineering achievements and in particular with space travel, a venture whose greatest accomplishments so far lie in the past (at least now), while there are currently news items emerging almost daily about developments in cloning, organ transplants, stem cell research, reproductive technologies, viruses, possible epidemics, and the like. These biological developments would not so long ago have been considered science fiction. Even now, in an age of cloned livestock, the Human Genome Project, advances in microbiology, retroviruses and plagues, surrogate mothers, and other biological developments, there are those who still view a number of possible advances as blasphemous.

James Gunn begins his essay "Philosophy and Science Fiction," by suggesting that science fiction is more closely tied to philosophy than to science. In his argument, Gunn allows for the possibility that it is simply his own predilection for philosophy that makes him believe the identification is so strong, but it quickly becomes clear that there is more here than simply one man's tendency to engage in philosophical debate in his stories and novels. As Gunn has pointed out in other essays and in his classes, science fiction is one long dialogue, and if the dialogue were not already philosophical, it's very unlikely Gunn could have changed it himself. And Gunn provides compelling evidence in typically sweeping and authoritatively anecdotal style that virtually every area of philosophy—metaphysics, epistemology, and ethics, at least—has been run through the laboratory of science fiction. Gunn's essay provides numerous examples of science fiction texts—some well known, some less so—that address important philosophical questions, making it a valuable jumping-off point for anyone designing a course on philosophy and science fiction.

Bruce Sterling's attention to cyberspace focuses upon the effect of science fiction on the development and practices of Internet users, and the effects of Internet use on science fiction. Science fiction is increasingly being published on the Internet: short stories are usually included on sites that offer original publication but also reprint stories and sometimes entire novels. This Internet publication occurs due to the belief that readers will pay for the literature or that they will be persuaded to buy a printed copy, either at bookstores or through a website, or as print-on-demand. The Internet has influenced science fiction in more subtle ways, by changing the way readers read and the thought patterns of instant communication that eliminates distance and perhaps writers' authority and control. Some writers even subscribe to the Internet thesis that information wants to be free. All these factors are going to shape the ways readers will approach SF in the future.

16
neuroscience fiction redux
joseph d. miller

Seventeen years ago, in a piece called "Neuroscience Fiction: The Roman à Synaptic Cleft," I reviewed the uses and abuses of neuroscience in science fiction. I suggested that the neuroscience content of science fiction is disguised, hidden and implicit in science fiction, compared to the obvious presence of the physical sciences. In fact, neuroscience content, broadly speaking, seemed more evident in the mainstream media, as evidenced by the "Reagan's Brain" episodes in Gary Trudeau's *Doonesbury*. Here there was a true science fiction plot; the intrepid correspondent, Roland Hedley, in somehow miniaturized form, is on safari in the presidential central nervous system, seeking the suppressed memories of "Iran-gate." The illustration was marvelous, easily outshining, I think, the images evoked, for instance, by Isaac Asimov's *Fantastic Voyage*. Since most of us in neuroscience assume a very tight correspondence between mental phenomena and brain anatomy, this strip is literally a "mindscape." It is ironic to realize that the actual Reagan mindscape was already beginning to lose definition due to the early effects of Alzheimer's disease.

Why is the neuroscience content of science fiction so understated? I think the reasons are in large part historical. Early use of neuroscience concepts in the field was extravagant, to say the least. Mary Shelley's *Frankenstein* first popularized the idea of brain transfer. The Hollywood version of Shelley's novel subsequently provided an interesting bit of "neurosociology"; the pathological behavior of the monster is implicitly attributed to Igor's error in brain selection, as parodied in the famous "Abbie Normal" confusion in the movie *Young Frankenstein*. The covert message here is that retardation is directly related to gross brain pathology. In reality, our ability to associate gross anatomical features in the brain with specific behavioral correlates is exceedingly limited (but getting better all the time!). We can relate tumors, traumatic damage (e.g., gunshot wounds), and sometimes vascular accidents to specific intellectual deficits. But even if we could maintain the recipient in a temporarily brainless condition, reattach the millions of nerves necessary, and avoid all the difficulties due to anoxia, swelling, and immunological rejection, it is still very unlikely that any transplanted brain, grossly "abnormal" or not, could produce anything approaching normal behavior. The reason for this is that the development of the nervous system is a highly idiosyncratic process; for instance, the pattern of specific neural connections in a given brain differentiates humans far better than fingerprints. So whole brain transplants, as they appear in Robert A. Heinlein's *I Will Fear No Evil* are not a serious possibility.

On the other hand, we do have the ability to accomplish partial transplants. Small amounts of tissue, generally taken from fetal brains, can be introduced into recipient nervous systems. Under the right conditions, such transplants can correct certain biochemical disorders in animals. This idea of partial transplants has been explored in a cross-species context in Brian Aldiss's "*Shards*." In this story, small amounts of human temporal lobe tissue are transplanted into porpoise brains. The "shards" of human tissue increase the cognitive power of the porpoises, but also generate an extremely fragmented thought process in the recipients. The only real difficulty with this procedure is that it requires crossing a species barrier. A major experimental question is whether brain tissue from one species can establish viable connections with a second species' brain tissue. Whether fragments of consciousness in this situation would be transferred along with fragments of cortical tissue, as in the Aldiss story, is a point of argument. Many neuroscientists believe that aspects of conscious thought are localized in an anatomical sense; others believe the thought process is distributed across the entire nervous system, in a manner analogous to the way information is distributed in a laser hologram. The bottom line is that partial transplant studies appear to be quite feasible. Because such "conservative" procedures apparently lack the melodrama of full-blown brain transplants, science fiction has thus far made relatively little use of them.

Subsequent to my initial consideration of these issues, there has been a tremendous growth of interest in the use of embryonic stem cells to restore brain function in pathological conditions such as Parkinson's disease and Alzheimer's disease. The basic approach is simple: one obtains embryonic stem cells from the very early blastocyst stage of embryonic development. These cells are capable of developing into virtually any body tissue. There are existing protocols for differentiating these cells into functional dopamine neurons[1], the cells which selectively die in Parkinson's disease. The transplantation of such cells into the Parkinsonian brain should hopefully restore normal movement. But dopamine neurons are also the substrate of pleasure, reward, and reinforcement in the brain. Would a similar transplant procedure in a normal human increase the capacity for pleasure and joy? A story by Greg Egan, "Reasons to be Cheerful" examines this issue. To correct congenital brain damage the protagonist receives a brain cell transplant, presumably including dopamine neurons. But the protagonist is given complete control over the transplanted cells through a virtual control panel which allows him to decide just what life experiences should be rewarding and pleasurable. The implied question is just exactly who is making this decision and on what basis? How do you define pleasure if you have never experienced it? And cross-species brain transplants are under way. Human brain cells are being transplanted into the brains of rats. Ethical guidelines are still being developed. But in 2005 a National Academy of Sciences panel recommended that "experiments in which there is a possibility that human cells could contribute in a 'major organized way' to the brain of an animal require strong scientific justification" (*Guidelines for Human Embryonic Stem Cell Research:* 105). Aldiss's "Shards" was a truly prescient story! In a more general sense, as H. G. Wells's *Island of Dr. Moreau* and Cordwainer Smith's "Instrumentality of Mankind" stories exemplify, the perils and pathos of crossing species barriers have long been a mainstay of science fiction.

A related idea involves the notion of the human brain maintained in isolation. Exceedingly graphic presentations along these lines include the novel and film *Donovan's Brain* and the pseudo-Lovecraftian film *Reanimator*. Once again, Hollywood schlock is quite far removed from what can be accomplished in the laboratory. Scientists can, and routinely do, keep small slices of brain tissue from various species alive in special oxygenated media. Studies using these techniques have been invaluable in determining the physiological functions of specific brain regions. Once again, this sort of scientific procedure has not been employed as a plot device in science fiction, quite possibly because of the overblown and unsophisticated use of the "brain in the fishtank" cinematic trope (which was so evident in *Donovan's Brain*). Thus, the hyperbolic exaggeration of the 1950s science fiction film may well have generated a reluctance to use such "hard" neuroscience in more recent literature.

However, examples of the naive application of neuroscience concepts abound in early works of science fiction. One particularly popular

notion is that some relatively simple alteration in the way we think—
and consequently in the way our brains function—will confer upon
us all the extrasensory powers imaginable. Thus in A. E. Van Vogt's
Null-A series the use of non-Aristotelian logic, in conjunction with
mutant protagonist Gilbert Gosseyn's double brain, makes possible the
full expression of Gosseyn's superhuman abilities, including teleportation. Learning the Martian language similarly allows for the extrasensory self-actualization of Valentine Michael Smith in Heinlein's
Stranger in a Strange Land. In Poul Andersen's *Brain Wave*, a tremendous increase in human intelligence is produced simply by the Earth's
moving out of some galactic cognitive inhibitory field. In Theodore
Sturgeon's *More Than Human*, the next step in the evolution of human
intelligence requires the appropriate blending and meshing of a set of
disparate individuals into a superhuman gestalt intelligence. In contrast, some authors have attempted to use physiological mechanisms,
albeit rudimentary, to explain intellectual transformations. In Daniel
Keyes's *Flowers for Algernon*, heightened intelligence is achieved through
a surgical procedure. In Thomas Disch's *Camp Concentration*, genius is
similarly produced through the action of a mutated syphilis bacterium.
In Frank Herbert's *Dune*, Paul Muad'Dib's pre-cognitive abilities are acti-
vated by exposure to the neurochemical-like spice. Similarly, transcendence in Paddy Chayefsky's *Altered States* is achieved through ingesting a
psychotropic drug with simultaneous sensory deprivation. The negative
side of such transformations is seen in K. W. Jeter's *Dark Seeker*. In this
work, a neurotransmitter-like drug triggers an irreversible change in the
central nervous system that generates simultaneous group consciousness and deepening group psychosis. At least these latter works attempt
to relate changes in cognitive function to changes in brain function.
This reductionistic notion, that brain is the hardware for mind, is one
of the major unifying concepts of neuroscience. Until recently, it has
only sporadically been employed in science fiction.

   Why does science fiction place such emphasis upon extrasensory
abilities as the next step in the evolution of the human mind/brain?
Once again, there are strong historical antecedents for this favorite
conception of science fiction writers. I believe it is largely a product
of the popular misconception that humans use only five percent of
their brains. This belief originates in the early neurophysiological
investigations of the 1950s. When subjects were placed under barbitu-
rate anesthesia, it appeared that only relatively small regions of the
brain could be directly implicated in sensory or motor functions. In
these studies, very large regions of cortex appeared to be inactive. We

now know that this lack of activity did not reflect non-involvement of nervous tissue in behavioral and physiological functions. Rather, the explanation for these results is simply that barbiturates suppress brain activity in most brain regions. Under appropriate anesthetics, or in freely behaving unanesthetized animals, most brain areas are active and contribute to the generation of behavior in a complex and sophisticated fashion. Counter to the findings of these investigations, we certainly do use all of our brains. It is easy to see how the "unused" 95 percent of the brain could be identified with the production of supposedly existent, but rare, extrasensory phenomena. Consequently, the supposition that further evolution or alteration of brain function should engage this "unused" portion leads to the inference that this evolution would produce a heightened facility for paranormal powers. Thus, one of the most cherished plot vehicles of classical science fiction is, at heart, a product of neurophysiological misinterpretation. It is encouraging to see that modern science fiction writers such as Nancy Kress in "Beggars in Spain," Greg Bear in *Darwin's Radio*, and Bruce Sterling in *Schismatrix* have considered possibilities other than paranormal ones in the future evolution of humanity—a trend presaged by Arthur C. Clarke in *Against the Fall of Night*.[2]

Another major error of early neuroscience research that has had explicit repercussions for science fiction was the "center" hypothesis. At one point in the history of neuroscience, it was thought that explicit behavioral functions could be directly related in a point to point fashion to specific cellular regions or centers of the brain. Thus, hypothetically, there was a center for eating, a center for drinking, a center for sexual excitation, and so forth. This sort of interpretation was the intellectual descendant of nineteenth-century phrenology or "bump reading," which attempted to assess cognitive function in terms of specific bumps on the skull. Today we believe that behavior is a product of redundant neural systems that may be organized in hierarchical layers of astounding complexity. This belief has not prevented science fiction writers such as Michael Crichton in *The Terminal Man* from assuming what is essentially the defunct center hypothesis. For Crichton, electrical stimulation of one specific spot in the central nervous system reliably and repeatedly elicits only one behavioral response. Similarly, the ubiquitous use of the "wirehead," a term attributable to Larry Niven, represents another simplistic application of this principle. Here the idea is that future junkies will be able reliably to produce a euphoric state through self-induced electrical stimulation of pleasure centers in the hypothalamus (dopamine neurons once again). In reality, self-stimulation is a very labile phenomenon; eliciting thresholds change radically, as do the behaviors elicited, and effective stimulation sites may change over time, let alone between different individuals. Still, even with such reservations in mind, it is interesting to note that one of the brain structures supporting robust self-stimulation is the prefrontal cortex, a region that seems to be necessary for the production and execution of alternative behavioral strategies. This function, as David Brin has suggested, is possibly essential to prevarication. But, for the majority of brain regions in the majority of species above the level of complexity of the sea slug, neophrenological conceptions like these, often based on creaky brain science, are demonstrably inadequate.

Debunking phrenology should not be taken as a complete repudiation of brain function localization. In fact, during the last 17 years, there have been immense advances in brain imaging technology that have allowed the visualization of brain function "from the outside" when the subject is engaged in a variety of cognitive actions—such as decision making and possibly even some forms of meditation and religious experience. Imaging studies are of course only correlational. But the new technique of transcranial magnetic stimulation enables the activation or inhibition of specific cortical areas and the beginning of an approach to determining **causal** relations between brain function and behavior in humans. It may be possible to induce specific cognitive states such as religious ecstasy. We have no idea whether such states might be intrinsically addictive, but it is a completely unexplored idea in science fiction. What has been explored, of course, is the possibility of biological mind control from Robert Heinlein's *The Puppet Masters* to Vernor Vinge's "you've got to believe me (YGBM)" technology in *Rainbows End*. These are the extreme and frightening possibilities. The reality is that virtually any mental state may one day be produced at will.

In addition to the explicit, generally extreme, examples of neuroscience or, at least, pseudoneuroscience in science fiction I have discussed up to this point, there is an entirely different area of science fiction in which the neuroscience is implicit rather than explicit. The imaginative literature dealing with artificial intelligence disguises the contribution of neuroscience in a way similar to the way in which external events are used as a subtext in the French roman à clef.

The origins of this area of science fiction can be traced at least to Karel Capek's *R. U. R.* and perhaps back to the Golem myths of medieval Yiddish folklore. But certainly the greatest proponent of the thinking machine in our time has been Isaac Asimov (in his robot series). The most sophisticated of Asimov's robots are indistinguishable from humans, except, perhaps, in the loftiness of their morals. While Asimov never drew explicit comparisons between mental function and computer software, it is easy to think of the robot ego as a program that runs on positronic hardware. Likewise, superego can be directly equated with the Three Laws of Robotics. The concept of program as mind has been further refined in works like David Gerrold's *When Harlie Was One* and Heinlein's *The Moon Is a Harsh Mistress*. Perhaps even more to the point, Rudy Rucker reversed the unequal disparity between natural and technological cognitive powers in *Software* by emphasizing the identity of mind-as-program. The main idea is that mind is the software that runs on the brain's biological hardware. Nothing in principle would prevent the direct conversion of that biological software into a suitably complex program in the computer language C++. Frederik Pohl has taken these ideas even further in *Heechee Rendezvous*. In Pohl's novel, various characters can access software equivalent to the minds of their ancestors. Furthermore, the afterlife can be configured for these individuals as just another operating system. In Greg Bear's *Eon* multiple artificial intelligence (AI) simulations of human personality are simultaneously active. While an adequate simulation could serve as the ultimate answering machine, the legal and social implications of multiple, indistinguishable, artificial personalities are just beginning to appear in science fiction. But, in all of these works, the neuroscience is implicit. The underlying construct is that the computer program is an adequate model of the mind, and that adequate computer hardware is an effective model of the brain.

Rucker's *Software* accomplished more than introducing biological cybernetics to science fiction. Its publication also marked the inauguration of the new cyberpunk subgenre. William Gibson's *Neuromancer* and *Count Zero* further described the cyberpunk landscape and populated it with cyberspace console cowboys. Walter Jon Williams in *Hard Wired* and Greg Bear in *Eon* later expanded upon Gibson's initial vision. Cyberpunk novels strikingly share the conceptual cyberspace that backgrounds most of the action in these novels. Artificial and biological intelligences mutually inhabit this space, engaging in continuous transfer of information. Security systems are visualized as "ice," corporate information banks appear as hypergeometric solids, and the Turing Police are always on the lookout for artificial intelligences who have become too intelligent. In this shared conceptual universe, distinctions between artificial and biological intelligences are largely irrelevant; the movers and shakers are programs irrespective of origin; and the currency of exchange is information. Much of the cyberpunk mindscape was assimilated wholesale into the darkly satiric television series *Max Headroom*. And Trudeau's *Doonesbury* strip in turn co-opted this mindscape for Ronald Reagan "bashing" in "Ron Headrest." Trudeau thus manages, in nearly sequential strips, to devastate both the presidential hardware (the "Reagan's Brain" series) and software ("Ron Headrest"). Trudeau's evenhanded treatment of these metaphors for the consciousness of the "head of state" suggests another example of the dissolution of the archaic mind/body dichotomy.

Telepathy is a trivial matter in such mindscapes; all that is required is a biochip capable of interfacing between relevant brain cells and appropriate transmission and reception hardware. Prosthetic devices have already been developed for human use that can convert visual stimuli into arbitrary electrical stimulation patterns applied directly to output neurons of the retina or even the visual cortex. The blind can learn to interpret these patterns as visual experience.[3] Patterns of activity in the motor cortex associated with the intention to move can be electronically translated into the movement of a computer cursor.[4] Through satellite links, every human on Earth could experience electronic telepathy, clairvoyance, and clairaudience (that is, hearing and seeing remotely). The bare bones of such communications systems have already appeared in science fiction cinema; it is only necessary to recall that the ultimate paranoid conspiracy in *The President's Analyst* involved the implantation at birth in every human brain of a transceiver, courtesy of Ma Bell. This particular phone could not be taken off the hook! How close this is to ubiquitous modern cellphone use. Roger Zelazny's Hugo-winning story "Home Is the Hangman" presented an extrapolative vision of telepresence. In this story, remote controlled robots could operate in hostile environments. Interestingly, the operators often developed a feeling of telepresence: the operators' focus of consciousness would seem to shift from the remote console to the robot in the hostile environment. This process, in turn, contributed to the development of an endogenous consciousness in the robots.[5] And how similar this is to the parapsychological claptrap of astral projection, telekinesis, and so forth! Even precognition, at least of the probabilistic variety utilized in *Dune*, simply boils down to forecasting and extrapolation on the basis of a sufficiently large data bank.

Where, precisely, in the brain might we place a biochip to function as an interface between the individual brain/mind, via telemetry linkage, and the Internet—and by extension the "global village?" Three regions of the brain are involved in the production and comprehension of language, surely a function closely related to consciousness.

These regions should not be thought of as language "centers" but rather as processing nodes in a complex network. As for the placement of a biochip for electronic telepathy, any of the three cortical regions could serve the purpose. But apparently lying would still be possible in this technological implementation of telepathy. Could our brain imaging devices tell the difference between telepathic truth and falsehood, particularly in subjects trained to defeat ordinary polygraph lie detectors? At any rate, authors who do their "neuroscience homework" can easily find plausible neural structures for implementing electronic telepathy, whether veridical or not. Little or none of this "hard neuroscience" has yet appeared in science fiction.

There is admittedly some explicit neuroscience in the works considered here. Roger Zelazny picked up a nodding acquaintance with random neural net theory and the creators of cyberpunk even had some idea what a neurotransmitter is. It is annoying, however, to see how frequently authors use current speculation in neuroscience as local color in their novels. Thus, if you need learning enhancement, you do not "pop" an undefined memory pill; instead you take a hefty dose of vasopressin. Unfortunately, in contrast to a spate of early sensational reports, it now appears that vasopressin has relatively little to do with actual memory. Instead, it functions as a mild nonspecific stimulant. Any modest increase in general arousal typically facilitates learning, but there is nothing special about vasopressin. However, it became ensconced within the cyberpunk universe much as the old "you only use five percent of your brain" cliché was ensconced in early science fiction. What is required here is a certain critical faculty on the part of science fiction authors. There should be no problem in simply making up a neurochemical capable of performing whatever feat is required. Chances are good that neuroscientists will eventually properly identify the substance that performs that mental feat in reality. But it is probably wise for authors to avoid over commitment to a given neuroscience "fact" until a sufficiently large body of data exists to support that "fact." The "memory wipe," so beloved by SF writers from Philip K. Dick onwards, needs a much better scientific rationale—and one is actually available.[6]

With respect to either the rather small amount of explicit neuroscience or the considerably larger body of implicit neuroscience in science fiction, it is important to consider the emotional weight of these concepts. From the earliest use of neuroscience in Shelley's *Frankenstein* to the bleak landscapes of modern cyberpunk, the history of neuroscience concepts in science fiction has involved dark and pessimistic application. Why should this be? Science fiction optimistically presents hard science (that is, chemistry and physics) concepts. Yet biological concepts, particularly those dealing in some way with brain function, until quite recently, have almost invariably been presented negatively. I suspect that this negative valence is a product of the historical winnowing of the centristic philosophy. That is, the geocentricism of the Middle Ages was destroyed by Copernicus, the anthropocentricism of nineteenth-century biology gave way to the evolutionary theory of Darwin; and, finally, "telecentricism" (to coin a term, the implicit faith in mind as the inexplicable and irreducible center of the universe, last bastion of Cartesian duality), is now crumbling under the reductionistic onslaught of neuroscience. Neuroscience, along with the behavioristic approaches of the psychological and ethological disciplines, ultimately implies that there is nothing special about mind. Consciousness does not exist in a vacuum, but is rather the specific product of a "self"-organizing neuronal architecture, under the strong influence of environmental stimuli, in an adaptive context that represents a constraining evolutionary history of millions of years. This, of course, is a frightening proposition for many of us. Where is spirit? Where is the soul? Neuroscience treats these concepts as meaningless terms; thus neuroscience is a black science in literature. The uncompromising reductionism of modern neuroscience is at least as great a threat to our residual, comfortable, anthropocentric notions of mind and consciousness as the irreducible defining characteristic of humanity, as the Copernican challenge was to the geocentric philosophy of pre-Renaissance Europe. The very idea of artificial intelligence, as the final extension of neuronal reductionism, is an assault on the last bastion of human uniqueness, consciousness itself. As Yeats said, "Things fall apart; the center cannot hold." So it should not be surprising that neuroscience concepts and artificial intelligence are often portrayed negatively in science fiction. "There are some things humanity is better off not knowing," say umpteen 1950s Grade B science fiction movies.

But, in reality, explications of the biological underpinnings of human consciousness need not have any more deleterious consequences than, for instance, Darwinian theory had for early twentieth-century humanism. Knowledge is ethically neutral; the application of knowledge may as easily be liberating as imprisoning. Knowledge of the behavioral, evolutionary, and neural determinants of human consciousness may ultimately lead to a relaxation of those constraints. This is essentially the same reply that may be made to Skinnerian behaviorism: any possibility of behavioral "freedom" presupposes knowledge and potentially, control of those environmental variables that ordinarily condition our responses. Ignorance of the constraints on our behavior is concession to slavery; knowledge is a prerequisite for any possibility of transcendence. Browning says "Ah, but a man's reach should exceed his grasp./or what's a heaven for?" In reality, it is only the delimitation of our grasp that can allow us to perceive the potential extent of our reach.

The barren mindscapes of yesterday's cyberpunk contain the beginnings of an optimistic neuroscience and perhaps an optimistic neuroscience fiction. Indeed, cyberpunk seems to have receded from the forefront of science fiction. It has in large part been replaced by a transhumanist or posthumanist perspective. The most well-known proponents of this perspective are Greg Egan (in *Diaspora* and *Permutation City*) and Charles Stross (in *Accelerando*). Because of the implicit belief that humanity can be improved, the post-humanist perspective is inherently more optimistic than the cyberpunk view. At present we think the human genome differs from the chimpanzee, our closest relative, by about 100 genes, perhaps 50 of which are likely expressed in the brain.[7] Among those 50 will be the genes which contribute to cognitive capacities (abstract thought, complex linguistic construction, sophisticated future planning etc.) which distinguish us from chimpanzees. Ten such candidate genes which seem to modulate such functions as cortical growth, neuron number, neurotransmitter level, and linguistic ability have already been described. It is certainly possible that in future we may be able to augment human intelligence by altering the transcription and translation of such genes, one of the projects of the posthumanist perspective.

In perhaps thirty years the information processing capacity of computers may far outstrip the human mind. In fact, once the mind "program" is understood, there is no reason to think that it could not run on arbitrary hardware configurations. The virtual realities portrayed in Egan's *Permutation City* and *Diaspora* and in Pohl's Heechee saga are realizable. In Stross's *Accelerando*, viewpoint characters are augmented by wearable computers but, for the most part, they retain their biological identity as humans. However, society as a whole is approaching a Singularity in which the exponential increase in computing power will finally yield a posthuman society which will be unintelligible to non-augmented humans. Stross does a remarkably good job in describing a phase change in human nature which at heart must remain incomprehensible.

Thus the Singularity (or the Spike) has become a major trope in hard science fiction. Stross, in *Accelerando*, calls this trope the Rapture of the Nerds. This predicted technologically mediated transcendence indeed shares emotional commonality with the mysteries of the *Book of Revelation* and Fundamentalist End Times visions. Instead of emanating from Holy Scripture, these visions are extrapolated from rates of progress in computer science (for example, Moore's law states memory chip density doubles every two years), neuroscience, and nanotechnology. Such visions nonetheless offer a potential escape from the tribulations of a flawed, wild type humanity, forever perched on the precipice of nuclear, biological or chemical self-annihilation. And so we come round again to a techno-optimism about the uses of neuroscience and neuroengineering in improving human nature that harkens back to Arthur C. Clarke's *Against the Fall of Night*.

notes

1. Perrier, Anselme L., Vivane Tabar, and Tiziano Barberi et al. "Derivation of Dopamine Neurons from Human Embryonic Stem Cells." *Proceedings of the National Academy of Sciences* 101 (2004): 12543–12548.
2. But in television human evolution almost always results in paranormal abilities, as in the series *Heroes*.
3. Weiland, James. D. and Mark S. Humayun. "Intraocular Retinal Prosthesis. Big Steps to Sight Restoration." *IEEE Engineering Medicine Biological Magazine*. 25 (2006): 60–66.
4. Hochberg, Leigh R., Mijail D. Serruya, and Gerhard M. Friehs et al. "Neuronal Ensemble Control of Prosthetic Devices by a Human with Tetraplegia." *Nature* 442 (2006): 164–171.
5. The underlying idea is that the perceived "seat of consciousness" might be movable. Ehrsson, H. Henrik. "The Experimental Induction of Out-of-Body Experiences." *Science* 317 (2007): 1048.
6. Blockading the enzyme protein kinase C mzeta can eliminate a month of prior memory. Pastalkova, Eva, Peter Serrano, and Deanna Pinkhasova et al. "Storage of Spatial Information by the Maintenance Mechanism of LTP." *Science* 313 (2006): 1141–1144.
7. Actually this is probably underestimated because the same gene can occur in slightly different forms (polymorphisms) each of which can produce very different phenotypes. Also, some of these genes are likely to be transcriptional activators or inhibitors, master genes which can control the expression of scores of "downstream" genes. Non-coding regions of the genome often encode gene regulatory sequences which may differ greatly between humans and chimpanzees. Finally, the same gene on average may code three different proteins, depending on the distribution of start and stop codons. Thus, genetic differences between these species may be much greater than expected on the basis of simple counting rules. Pennisi, Elizabeth. "Mining the Molecules that Made Our Mind." *Science* 313 (1996): 1908–1911.

suggestions for further reading

Aldiss, Brian. "Shards." *Magazine of Fantasy and Science Fiction* 22 (1962): 49–56.

Disch, Thomas. *Camp Concentration*. New York: Doubleday, 1969.

Egan, Greg. "Reasons to be Cheerful." In Gardner Dozois (ed.) *The Year's Best Science Fiction: Fifteenth Annual Collection*. New York: St. Martin's Press, 1998.

Rucker, Rudy. *Software*. New York: Ace, 1982. 69–94.

Smith, Cordwainer. *Norstrilia*. New York: Ballantine, 1975.

Stross, Charles. *Accelerando*. New York: Ace, 2005.

17
physics through science fiction
gregory benford

Mustering the fantastic in the cause of the real, or the reverse, can be useful teaching strategies. Illuminating physical law through science fictional thought experiments can awaken students' inventive, playful side. Physics constrains action in ways that call up further study of the underlying physical laws.

David Theison (University of Maryland) and Gibor Basri (University of California, Berkeley) and I have focused physics/astronomy seminars on science examined through SF. The reverse works just as well. I have found the best approach is to begin by trying to talk about physics as a *life*. Alas, it's hard to find images of the scientist in fiction that hold up. "Conventional" fiction has C. P. Snow's novel *The Search,* and in SF, Fred Hoyle's novel *The Black Cloud* is heavily laced with science and also gives a picture of the way scientists think and work—the way it's really done, as opposed to the lab-smock image of commercial television. You can even use non-SF to make this point, as with *The Double Helix* by James Watson, with his solve-it-at-whatever-cost approach. That kind of bath of cold water right at the beginning is very useful to show students that science is not a monolith as it's lived, or as it's often described. You may have to justify such approaches, or indeed the scientific world-view, and curiosity itself. Sir Arthur Conan Doyle, in a Sherlock Holmes tale, touched on this. Dr. Watson is astonished to learn that his friend Holmes, who can infer so much from cat hairs or heel prints, does not know that the Earth moves around the sun. Holmes is ignorant of "the entire Copernican theory of the solar system." Holmes counters that while cat hairs, heel prints, and so on, affect his present life and liveli-hood, it makes absolutely no difference to him at all whether the Earth moves around the sun or the sun moves around the Earth. Therefore, he does not have to know such facts, and what's more, even though Dr. Watson has informed him of the truth of the matter, he intends to forget it as quickly as he can. This is utterly opposite from the hard SF culture. Perhaps those not shocked by Holmes should not be in a physics class, or an SF one.

My own principal teaching difficulty lies in finding the right approach. A motley class—people who think it's a gut course, engineers who want to argue about Larry Niven, humanities majors who want to find out what Le Guin really meant, and so on—require special effort. Stories that focus on problems that sharpen intuition work best.

the wrong stuff

Jean Piaget's ideas are useful here. Learn by doing, since people absorb much faster and better if they can *manipulate*, physically or mentally.

To approach scientific habits of mind, Tom Godwin's "The Cold Equations," uses a set-piece problem story but with no solution. Instead, it displays society's institutionalized delusions, set against the overwhelmingly, absolutely neutral point of the view of the universe. Scientists often assume this view unconsciously. Students should begin with their natural impulse to propose answers, until the point dawns.

The next stage might be that of literary analysis, to see what makes the stories work. Engineering students particularly like discussing an author's tricks and ingenuity and factual errors, and in a good discussion of this sort one part of the class can educate the other. Some notice that Larry Niven's *Ringworld*, for example, is actually unstable, and will not work the way it's described. That can kick off a discussion involving the basics of mechanics and of literary credibility. The same can be done with Poul Anderson stories about low-gravity planets; how does biology change? This shows how solved problems in a fictional matrix motivate students to learn physics a lot better than taking the canonical introductory textbook course. Integrating physics with biology stimulates the intuition. In Heinlein's "The Menace from Earth," people can fly in domes on the moon at ordinary atmospheric pressures, a startling application of straightforward mechanics.

Reading Poul Anderson's *Tau Zero*, reveals some clear cheats. Notably, if you run a spaceship into a star you cannot simply transform to another reference frame, à la Einstein, and show that it's the star that gets gobbled up instead of the spaceship. Mass seems to increase as a body approaches the speed of light; Anderson knew this, but finessed it by supposing that the star's rest frame is the right one to see the problem, and the starship's mass trumps the star's. Not so; consider the viewpoint of the ship, and the star is even more (relativistically) massive. Students can use this to understand that a relativistic reference frame does not mean that you can wipe out real physical effects.

It also leads to a discussion of the important general aesthetic question of how much you can cheat on the facts in fiction. There are few cheat-free stories, including my own, and playing the game of finding the error in a story seems to motivate a lot of students to engage in physics, who otherwise sit there and stare. Some students take malicious glee by nailing big-name writers on details like this. It's an introduction to criticism, and to physics, too. I highly recommend this and the other methods I've mentioned as ways of enabling students to respond with the proper spirit to physics, and to science in general. SF story creation, bending things a little bit to make your story hold together, is the same way scientists create a new theory. The act of enabling creating a new axiom in science, says Jacob Bronowski (the mathematician who hosted the BBC documentary series *The Ascent of Man*), is the same as creating a poem or a novel or a painting. The product may be different, but the act of creation is the same. (It even feels the same, to me.) SF can be used to get across this idea, which is startling to most literature students, and to most science students, too.

As commonplace as tides are, for example, few understand them. They become deadly when considering flight near a compact mass, the key idea in Larry Niven's "Neutron Star." Such stars pack a stellar mass into ten kilometers, and Niven's entrepreneur hero zooms by within a few hundred kilometers. The steeper gravitational potential well of a compact star means that tidal stresses can be large over distances of meters. The hapless human must then understand nature in a new way to survive. The stress is proportional to the different distances the human's head and feet are from the star. This may be the only case in fiction where the right answer to a plot problem is to curl up into the fetal position, lessening the tug at head and feet. Niven knew this and finessed his ending. When I taught this story (at the University of California, Irvine), I checked his work and found the fetus effect was not big enough; the character gets shredded anyway. But the ideas animate the story and can educate. And some students may make the same calculation, giving them a sense of participation in a story quite unusual in the classroom.

Generating a plot problem through applying physics takes the reader out of a human-centered narrative and into the realm of imagination, where nature provides a worthy opponent—maybe the only one worth our time, as Hal Clement once remarked. (Indeed, in most of our species' history nature was the obstacle, a view SF can recapture.) Such strategies can both teach science and reflect on the nature of narrative itself. Science fiction abounds in such examples, one of its charms.

The science does not have to be right to be useful. In Jerome Bixby's "The Holes Around Mars" (1954), explorers keep hearing odd whizzing noises and notice that the mountains have holes in them. Then a near-disaster reveals the awful truth—Mars has several moons at very low altitude, so they keep plowing through mountains. This is so implausible even the most benighted humanities major will begin to have doubts. What happens to the moon's kinetic energy, after all? How come it keeps boring holes and never crashes into the planet? Asking questions like these leads to some highly motivated learning of physics. Any student who cannot see the hole in this thrilling idea has not learned to think with a hint of a scientific attitude.

Similarly, in "The Big Bounce" by Walter Tevis, a ball rises higher on each bounce, a clear violation of the second law of thermodynamics. Such stories encourage students to use common sense first, then to see that careful scientific argument can illuminate the underlying logic, and to learn something about science's style and content as well.

A far better classic story, with a more subtle, illuminating scientific error, is "The Light Of Other Days" by Bob Shaw. Suppose the speed of light through different media could be made very slow, leading to windows made of "slow glass." This 1966 short story explores the human implications of a seemingly minor physical fact. A special glass slows light so much that it takes months to move a centimeter, that is, reducing its speed by at least seventeen orders of magnitude. Then a viewer outside a house can see his wife and child, inside the house, happy in the days before they died. The story skillfully builds to an emotional conclusion, using this implication of the physics.

But slow glass would also be a very dangerous explosive. Sunlight deposits about a kilowatt of power per square meter at high noon. So light slowed down in glass would carry that power, accumulated over months or years and stacked into a thin pane. Simple calculations a student can do (energy stored equals sunlight power multiplied by time duration) show that a window has far more energy stored in it than is in a hand grenade. Drop the windowpane, or break it with a rock…. Bob Shaw had not thought of this. (I asked him.) But for me his image of a captured past, with its artfully played implication, trumps such technical cards—a good example of the play between scientific fact and literary utility.

looking large

Beyond small-scale science lie grand visions the genre uniquely makes possible. Hal Clement's landmark *Mission of Gravity* began this SF trait with its detailed descriptions of a high-gravity planet and its insect-like natives, meticulous and well argued. Rich in physics and chemistry, containing an essay by Clement ("Whirligig World") about how he built up his ideas, this novel may mark the true beginning of hard SF as a recognized subgenre, though the term itself does not seem to have come into use until the middle 1960s, perhaps in reaction to the New Wave literary movement. (Though the New Wave was important in opening the field to wider influences, its greatest effect may have been to make hard SF into a recognized opposite.) Clement's bizarre but scientifically plausible world is a raw setting in which the protagonists struggle upward against great weight, a reflection of the sometimes grim but usually hopeful tone of hard SF.

Much of the charm of Frank Herbert's hugely successful *Dune*, written a dozen years after *Mission of Gravity*, lies in its approach to the implications of life on a desert planet. Herbert used massive research to buttress his imagination, and the book compels us because the consequences of the rigorous environment, as the plot unveils them, seem logical and *right*. His world has no obvious source of the oxygen his characters breathe (most of Earth's comes from sea plankton), but this does not damage the story.

Except for some super-strong materials to wire it all together, Larry Niven's *Ringworld* mostly conforms to physics as we know it now. It follows a band of explorers who trek across an immense ring which circles a star, spinning to create centrifugal "gravity." The ring is so immense it can harbor life across a surface many times larger than the area of the Earth. Making this all work is great fun, with ideas unveiled by plot turns at a smooth pace. The sheer size of everything overwhelms the reader, but the game is played straight and true, no cards up the sleeve. Frederik Pohl's *Gateway*, for example—a New Wave-influenced novel with futuristic psychotherapy and *angst* as a frame—uses stellar astronomy, scrupulously rendered.

Getting the voice right is essential. Pohl's "Day Million" is a frustrated rant, expressing the author's despair at ever conveying to his reader how wondrously different the far future will be—yet it tries anyway, with compact expository lumps like grumpy professorial lectures. This is one of the voices of hard SF itself, trying to punch through humanist complacency about the supposed centrality of human perspectives and comforts. Tom Godwin's "The Cold Equations" also hammers relentlessly and melodramatically, invoking the constraints of gravity, orbital mechanics, and fuel levels—the conservation laws of physics. These two stories talk across the rapid social evolution between Godwin's era (1954) and Pohl's (1966). Godwin uses the indifference of the universe to frame a morality tale in which a woman dies because her innocence does not matter to an indifferent universe. Pohl, though, does not personify human insularity in a woman, but in the reader—and ends by directly addressing that reader, assumed to be a callow young man (first published in *Rogue*). Perhaps the best SF short story ever written, it is a virtuoso performance, a story set in a future so distant and different that we can only glimpse it in mysterious reflections and intriguing images. It's also an exercise in the application of an unconventional style to the solution of a science fiction problem. What's so hard about it? The attitude is right, giving it the texture and feel of hard SF.

Both Arthur C. Clarke's "Transit of Earth" and Tom Godwin's "The Cold Equations" profit from not attempting a pleasant finish, remorselessly sticking with the assumptions of the story. The impersonality of the universe ultimately stands for its authority. Then match the Godwin against James Patrick Kelly's 1996 Hugo winner, "Think Like A Dinosaur."

smart speculation

Students enjoy stretching their intellectual muscles, especially with speculations. Some ideas open wide windows.

The Singularity envisioned by Vernor Vinge can be a useful classroom device to fuel discussion and reading. Many recent stories deal with various human augmentations, from the angelic to the horrible. The Singularity describes the black hole in history, created when human intelligence can be digitized and integrated with technologies, taking some of us beyond the comprehensible envelope of current concepts. It challenges the very idea of progress this way, a *how much can you take?* dare. When the speed and scope of our cognition gets wedded to the price-performance curve of microprocessors, our progress will double every eighteen months, and then every twelve months, and then every ten, and eventually, every five seconds.

No wonder that the Singularity occupies so much of the SF narrative now. Use of Vinge's novels can well illustrate this. Whether students respond best to science or to spirituality, you could hardly ask for a subject better tailored to technological speculation and drama.

Centering science raises questions about conventional literary methods, as well. Of course, more literary SF works have plenty of space for pretty sentences and deep character, especially since they do not engage in much thinking about anything else. Science-centered SF has to contend with many demands in the same story. There's a larger reason to foreground science: our culture has uplifted much of humanity with technology, but needs to think about the ever-faster pace of change. One of SF's aims is to bring along into the culture those who may well react against change, even if it proves beneficial though unsettling. Genomics, climate change, biotechs that bring techno-augmented bodies and electronically assisted brains, and so on—all need realistic treatment in *what-if?* scenarios. Just depicting today's science will not do that. Thinking forward is far tougher, compared with realistic present day stories.

suggestions for further reading

Benford, Gregory. *Beyond the Fall of Night*. New York: Berkley, 1991.

Benford, Gregory. *Timescape*. New York: Simon and Schuster, 1980.

Freedman, Roger A. and W. A. Little. "Teaching Modern Physics Through Science Fiction." *American Journal of Physics*. 48 (1980): 548–551.

Lambourne, Robert, Michael Shallis, and Michael Shortland. *Close Encounters? Science and Science Fiction*. Bristol, UK: Adam Hilger, 1990.

Schmidt, Stanley. "Science Fiction Courses: An Example and Some Alternatives." *American Journal of Physics*. 41 (1973): 1052–1056.

18
science fiction and biology
pamela sargent

The science of evolution is as central to science fiction as biology has become to our own twenty-first century, while the fear and animosity this theory has spawned are still with us today. H. G. Wells, the writer most often claimed as the father of modern science fiction, in fact studied biology under T. H. Huxley, the scientist known as "Darwin's bulldog" for the tenacity with which he would defend Charles Darwin's theory of evolution. Without such a scientific view, much of Wells's science fiction, including the classics *The War of the Worlds* (1898) and *The Time Machine* (1895), with their speculations about evolution among human-kind on Earth and alien lifeforms on Mars, which laid the groundwork for later science fiction, could not have been written. His novel *The Island of Dr. Moreau* (1896), took a somewhat different route; this tale of a scientist who surgically reshapes animals into human form more closely resembles a horror story, although Moreau's chimeras in this novel, had it been written today, might instead have been the products of genetic engineering.

If Wells is the genre's father, Mary Shelley has been claimed as science fiction's mother by, among others, Brian W. Aldiss in his influential history of science fiction, *Billion Year Spree* (1973; later revised and updated as *Trillion Year Spree*, 1986). He cites her novel *Frankenstein* (1814) as the first true novel of science fiction because in "combining social criticism with new scientific ideas, while conveying a picture of her own day, [she] anticipates the methods of H. G. Wells when writing his own scientific romances and of some of the authors who followed him." (Aldiss, *Billion Year Spree*: 26) Fanciful as her novel may seem by today's standards, it had a biological theme and was rooted in the science of its own time. To read much of science fiction since *Frankenstein* is to read about biology and its divisions.

So it is ironic that science fiction, in the minds of many, is more strongly associated with technological or engineering achievements and in particular with space travel, a venture whose greatest accomplishments so far lie in the past (at least for now), while there are news items to be read nearly every day about developments in cloning, organ transplants, stem cell research, reproductive technologies, viruses, possible epidemics, and the like, all of them centered around developments that would not so long ago have been considered science fiction. But perhaps part of the reason for embracing technological science fiction, as opposed to stories with biological themes, is that biological change, as J. B. S. Haldane put it, can seem like a "perversion," even blasphemous to some. In spite of medical advances, certain biological facts, until recently, were regarded as constants: human beings of two distinct genders would mature, reproduce in the usual fashion, age, and die. Even now, in an age of cloned livestock, the Human Genome Project, advances in microbiology, retroviruses and plagues, surrogate mothers, and other biological developments, there are those who still view a number of possible advances as blasphemous.

Wells and Shelley set the pattern for much of the biological science fiction that would follow. *The Time Machine* offers a sense of undirected evolutionary change taking place over a vast span of time and that eventually produces two strains of humanity in the Eloi and the Morlocks. Both *The Island of Dr. Moreau* and *Frankenstein*, in their different ways, follow the story template of a lone scientist producing an extreme change that, whatever its consequences in the story, does not change the world as a whole; indeed, one of the reasons the term "science fiction" usually evokes images of engineering feats rather than biological changes may be that horror writers and the authors of thrillers have largely taken over this sort of story. *The War of the Worlds*, in addition to being the progenitor of a number of tales about alien invasions, is also the ancestor of stories of biological warfare and microbiological threats; one of the better-known such stories, Michael Crichton's *The Andromeda Strain* (1969), can be seen as a kind of inverse direct descendant of Wells's novel.

Although authors of horror and suspense, among them such bestselling writers as Stephen King and Dean Koontz, have made inroads into science-fictional biological territory, science fiction of a more complex sort still offers a more useful forum for asking many of the questions these other literary forms often tend to avoid, such as: How does genetics shape and reshape us, and how might we reshape ourselves?

What other kinds of reproductive strategies might we or other species employ, or might be forced to employ? How will advances in biology affect our most deeply held values? Will such developments improve our lives, or only magnify the flaws and faults that so often divide us? At this point, what we may or will do about ourselves is less important than the fact that we can, and that we may soon have the means to remake ourselves. In *Brave New World* (1932), Aldous Huxley sets an example for later works dealing with such questions by depicting a society in which the breeding of specialized types of human beings is combined with artificial gestation; in spite of his satirical jabs, someone reading this novel now might wonder if the culture shown here is an improvement over our own.

The treatment of biological change in science fiction follows a line of development that moves from individual cases or accidents to a view of a future in which biological change is normal and creative. This suggests the analogy of evolution, in which mutations appear and most fail (as does Frankenstein's monster or the superman depicted in Olaf Stapledon's 1935 novel *Odd John*) but viable organisms survive. But what makes biological science fiction much more than a purely intellectual exercise are current developments in the biological sciences. Because human beings can do something does not mean that we will, but once we have the capacity to, for example, do stem cell research using discarded embryos in the hope of discovering new therapies, a number of ethical issues will have to be considered no matter what we do. To undertake such research, in the eyes of those who consider an embryo as the equivalent of an infant, is to devalue human life; to ban stem cell research or limit it could mean that people with certain diseases or injuries will suffer unnecessarily when they might have been treated or even cured. Prospective parents capable of having a fetus scanned for certain genes or medical conditions are in a different situation from parents who lack such a capability; one group must do whatever they think best in circumstances over which they have had no control, while the others must weigh the costs to themselves, their children, and others no matter what they decide to do. Such ethical dilemmas cannot be circumvented by simply cutting off certain kinds of research, or by deciding, as have the characters in earlier tales of biology gone awry, that there are "things man was not meant to know." As Brian Stableford put it in *The Encyclopedia of Science Fiction* (1993): "[T]he particular anxiety which attends speculation about experiments in human biology is entirely appropriate, but a too-ready acceptance of the horrified conviction that all biological experimentation is a sin against God or Gaia which will inevitably be punished by dire misfortune is a kind of intellectual cowardice" (Stableford: 124).

So to use the well-known writer Michael Crichton as an example, there is a fairly clear line of development from a novel like *The Andromeda Strain* (an unknown virus from space threatens humankind) to 1990s *Jurassic Park* (using genetic engineering to recreate dinosaurs results in mayhem). However entertaining such novels (and the movies made from them) are, they have more in common with the "man was not meant to know" tale than with the more complex questions raised in such novels as Bruce Sterling's *Schismatrix* (1985), Nancy Kress's *Beggars in Spain* (1993), and Greg Bear's *Darwin's Radio* (1999), to name only three examples. In *Schismatrix*, humankind's descendants are the Shapers, who are genetic engineers, and the Mechanists, who use computer-based technologies; eventually these offshoots of humanity become a number of subspecies. *Beggars in Spain* depicts genetically modified human beings and the social divisions that might result from such modifications, while *Darwin's Radio* deals with a mysterious retro-virus that threatens to become an epidemic. These writers, like others using biological themes, see their central ideas as part of a system, not simply as a notion to be explored in isolation or in a straightforward extrapolation, as Larry Niven does in his story of organ transplants and criminals trading in them, "The Jigsaw Man" (1967).

Treating innovative biological ideas as part of a system is central to the work of Joan Slonczewski, a molecular biologist who has also written some excellent science fiction. Along with such writers as Ursula K. Le Guin, Vonda N. McIntyre, and Joanna Russ, Slonczewski has explored sexual reproduction and gender roles, two past "constants" of human life that seem increasingly mutable. In *A Door Into Ocean* (1986), she depicts the Sharers, inhabitants of an ocean world, who are all female and who reproduce by the fusion of ova, a process that requires inter-vention by those Sharers known as "lifeshapers." Using these biological notions, Slonczewski shapes a rich and sophisticated story of non-violent political resistance; her Sharers, although they are an offshoot of humankind, cannot imagine using force against others, even when they are threatened by invaders. Octavia E. Butler, in her novel *Dawn* (1987), invents an alien species, the Oankali, genetic engineers who have been so successful with their own kind that they lack diversity and must interbreed with another species, human beings. As fanciful as such an idea might seem, recent research in genetics has revealed that humankind is much more closely related to other species than was once thought, and interbreeding of distinct species is now a possibility. From her premise, Butler constructs a story that seems exotic and alien but that also evokes humankind's own past experiences with slavery and conquest.

Immortality is yet another classic theme illuminated by science fiction rooted in biology, although it's more accurate to describe such stories as tales of life extension. Here again, two constants of past human existence, a relatively brief life span (as compared to geological time) and the certainty of aging, come into question. In *Holy Fire* (1996), Bruce Sterling's central character Mia, an old woman who decides to prolong her life, lives in a post-plague Earth controlled by an entrenched but relatively benevolent gerontocracy. This is a stable culture, in which only those who take reasonably good care of themselves into old age are granted an upgrade to extended life, but where the young are powerless and increasingly discontented with their powerlessness. *Holy Fire* is refreshing in that it does not treat extended life as something likely to lead only to boredom, stagnation, and ennui; there is a convincing depiction of both the old looking forward to indefinite life spans and the young longing to disrupt such stability, with the prospect of a transhuman (or post-human) world seeming almost inevitable. But Sterling also acknowledges that the inheritors of extended life are likely to be those with wealth and power.

Extended life and relief from disease may either exacerbate economic conflicts or quiet them. If the well-off have access to advances in medicine and genetic engineering that poorer people lack, the divisions between the rich and poor will only grow wider, and it's hard to believe that those on the bottom would endure such developments passively. The resistance and hostility directed toward controversial biological research appears to be rooted not only in the prejudices and convictions of those holding "traditional" beliefs, but also in the well-founded fear that such developments might threaten our present-day power structures. If those in power cannot control biological advances for their own benefit, some of them might prefer to use the fears and ignorance of others to slow down or stop any potentially destabilizing progress in biological research.

We are living through the beginnings of what may be the greatest historical transition in our history up to now. If the various crises we face do not overwhelm us and our biosphere completely, our technologies, and biological advances in particular, will continue to develop, to the point where humankind may be able to control its own future evolution. Science fiction offers us a way to look forward to what we might become, and back at what we were, from the perspectives of imagined future observers who might find their distant human ancestors unrecognizable.

Science fiction is replete with works reflecting such possibilities, among them the following biologically centered science fiction novels that students might enjoy reading.

Greg Bear's *Blood Music* (1985), to mention yet another work by an author who often deals with biological themes, describes a biology experiment which produces sentient human cells that can take over human bodies. Disease also figures in Michael Crichton's *The Andromeda Strain* (1969), mentioned earlier in this essay. This novel concerns the crash of an American satellite which releases an organism that kills almost everyone in the small town where it has landed. Even as scientists are studying the mysterious alien organism, it mutates into an even more deadly form before, in the end, becoming harmless.

Speculation about the future of medicine is at the center of James Gunn's *The Immortals* (1962), in which a young doctor discovers that a drifter who gave him a pint of blood to use in a transfusion may be an immortal. Gunn foresaw that an increasingly aging population could lead to a steep increase in medical expenses and that treating medical care as a commodity subject to market forces would create social instability. A TV movie and series loosely based on the novel were televised in 1969–1971.

Other specialized professionals appear in biological science fiction: detectives, drug designers, and superheroes to mention only a few. Harry Harrison's *Make Room! Make Room!* (1966) is a richly detailed futuristic detective novel set in a greatly overpopulated world rapidly outgrowing available resources. The well-known film *Soylent Green* (1973) was based on this novel. Paul McAuley's *Fairyland* (1996), an inventive novel of future biotechnology with a complicated plot featuring a future drug designer, features slavish 'dolls' created through genetic engineering and uploaded minds. John Wainwright, the protagonist of Olaf Stapledon's *Odd John* (1935), a man with superhuman abilities, must come to terms with his powers and is soon searching for others like himself. *Odd John* is a picaresque, contemplative novel about a human mutant by one of philosophical science fiction's pioneers.

Jack Williamson's *Dragon's Island* (1951), published just before the structure of DNA was revealed, is an absorbing novel that hovers at the edges of an era of vast biological change. The term "genetic engineering" was coined by Williamson and first used in this book. Nancy Kress's *Beggars in Spain* (1993), mentioned earlier, explores the possibilities insomnia might offer. In Kress's novel, the first in a trilogy about human beings genetically engineered to go without sleep, it soon appears that the "Sleepless" may also have superior intelligence and a much longer life span than do the "Sleepers." In James Blish's *The Seedling Stars* (1957), human beings colonize other worlds by biologically altering themselves to survive in alien environments. A classic novel that pioneered this concept (called "pantropy"), *The Seedling Stars* greatly influenced later science fiction. In the overcrowded future Earth John Brunner depicts in *Stand on Zanzibar* (1968), having children is a luxury reserved only for those with clean genotypes. Brunner imagines that discovering how to give everyone the ability to have perfect children might threaten an already precarious demographic balance.

Some biological transformations involve tampering with our definition of humanity itself. In *Where Late the Sweet Birds Sang* (1976) by Kate Wilhelm, after plagues cause civilization to collapse, a small community attempts to survive by reproducing through cloning. Octavia E. Butler's Lilith, the protagonist of the *Xenogenesis Trilogy* (1987–1989), which includes her novel *Dawn*, decides with great ambivalence to bear half-human children for the alien Oankali. A new species, the product of crossbreeding, must struggle for acceptance among both Oankali and humankind. With this depiction of a kind of slavery, Butler's inventive biological science fiction echoes the African-American experience. Bruce Sterling, in *Schismatrix* (1985), also imagines a humanity that has become a number of different species.

Animals are among the different species readers encounter in biological science fiction. Michael Crichton's *Jurassic Park* (1990) describes how dinosaurs cloned from ancient DNA preserved by mosquitoes embedded in amber manage to escape when the security systems of the park that contains them fail. H. G. Wells imagines changing animals on an isolated island. In his *The Island of Dr. Moreau* (1896), a scientist tries to make animals more "human" by somatically altering them through surgery. This atmospheric early story of biotechnology inspired three motion pictures: *Island of Lost Souls* (1933); *The Island of Dr. Moreau* (1977), and a third feature film with the same title (1996).

Biological science fiction comments upon the world we know through utopian visions and satirical criticism. Joan Slonczewski's *A Door Into Ocean* (1986) is a feminist utopia set on an ocean world that was intended by its author as a contrast to Frank Herbert's desert planet in *Dune* (1965). *Galapagos* (1985), by Kurt Vonnegut, satirically focuses on all the mistakes human beings have made; the novel describes what humankind has become a million years in the future. Vonnegut's point resembles one made by the late zoologist Stephen Jay Gould: survival for a species has more to do with luck or chance than with any move toward an imagined "progress."

The entire history of biological science fiction, from the horrors or blasphemies of *Frankenstein* and *The Island of Dr. Moreau*, leads through the warnings of *The Time Machine* (with the world itself as a time machine), through the struggles of medicine to repair and preserve a human physiology made by natural selection, to the goal of a creative control of ourselves, from a knowledge of where we come from to what we are, and to what we may wish to become. Science fiction has paralleled this progress, with hope and with warnings along the way. Social constraints have modified us, but these also reflect our biology. Knowledge as a power of change is also a social instruction, a new right hand to a dreaming left. Reading biological science fiction is an opportunity to explore the issues more freely, and to try on critical stances.

suggestions for further reading

Broderick, Damien. *The Last Mortal Generation*. London: New Holland Publishers, 1999.

Dyson, Freeman. *A Many-Colored Glass: Reflections on the Place of Life in the Universe*. Charlottesville, VA: University of Virginia Press, 2007.

Rose, Michael R. *The Long Tomorrow*. New York: Oxford University Press, 2005.

Sargent, Pamela. (ed.) *Bio-Futures*. New York: Vintage Press, 1976.

Westfall, Gary and George Slusser. *No Cure for the Future: Disease and Medicine in Science Fiction*. Westport, CT: Greenwood Press, 2002.

19
science fiction and philosophy
james gunn

Science fiction is popularly supposed to be related to science—exploring the human implications of scientific discoveries or technological developments. I suggest that science fiction may be better described as a laboratory for philosophy. Plato had his dialogues and science fiction has its stories. I'm not claiming that Plato wrote science fiction—although August Derleth considered "Critias," with its Atlantis story, a progenitor—but that may be because in Plato's time the novel and the short story had not yet been invented.

Perhaps I am persuaded by my own predilections. I wrote *The Joy Makers* about a world that has developed a science of happiness, after reading an essay in the *Encyclopedia Britannica* on "Feeling," which turned into a discussion of how people feel happy and ended with the provocative sentence "But the true science of applied hedonics is not yet born." But looking back upon my other stories and novels, I notice the same inclination to take a philosophic question and ask what would happen if it were explored in a realistic scenario. *The Immortals*, for instance, was developed around the question of whether immortality would be a blessing or a curse, and how one should behave if one were the only immortal person and one's blood could rejuvenate others; *The Dreamers* dealt with the question of what would happen to human existence if memories could be transmitted; *The Listeners* considered how a human enterprise could be built to last a century and the impact of the discovery of extra-terrestrial intelligence. Even my very first published story, "Paradox," arose from a speculation about telepathic aliens meeting humans whose minds can hold several contradictory beliefs simultaneously.

I am not alone. Isaac Asimov, at John Campbell's suggestion, took Ralph Waldo Emerson's statement—"If the stars should appear one night in a thousand years, how would men believe and adore, and preserve for many generations the city of God"—and wrote a novelette, "Nightfall," about a world on which the stars appeared every two thousand years and everybody went mad. His robot stories were far more concerned with philosophy than with mechanical creatures. The stories are all built around conflicts among the three laws of robotics: in "Liar!" a robot has a conflict between the first law, not to injure a human being, and the second law, to obey an order given by a human; in "Reason," a robot questions the logic of inferior creatures assembling him and works its way through a philosophy of superior beings and in the process evokes the way in which humanity create supernatural belief systems.

Solipsism fascinated Robert A. Heinlein, who wrote "By His Bootstraps" about a time-traveling experimenter who interacts with himself at different periods in his existence and followed it with a more ideal scenario, "All You Zombies," in which a time-traveling agent becomes his own father and mother, so that he knows where he came from but "what about all you zombies?" In "The Nine Billion Names of God," Arthur C. Clarke considered the impact of computerizing the counting of the names of God by Tibetan monks, and more soberly, in "The Star," confronted a Jesuit priest with the knowledge that a great alien civilization was destroyed to create the star that shone over Bethlehem. The problem of religious dogma when it seems to conflict with the natural world is a frequent contemplation, as in James Blish's "A Case of Conscience," in which another Jesuit priest must cope with the discovery of aliens who live in a state of grace without ever knowing Christ; and in Harry Harrison's "The Streets of Ashkelon," which forces innocent aliens, who don't know what a lie is, to deal with a missionary who insists upon the literal truth of the Bible.

Clarke often considered philosophical questions. In *The City and the Stars*, he compared the bliss of stasis with the need for humanity to keep moving forward. This consideration of the essential nature of the human enterprise seems basic to science fiction, which I have sometimes defined as the literature of the human species. Traditional utopian fiction, which also occupies a significant place in science fiction literary history, imagines a static state of near perfection, made so by wise laws and proper political organization. This, too, got its start with Plato, in "The Republic." In more contemporary fiction, the static state is usually a dystopia, as in George Orwell's *Nineteen Eighty-Four*, although Edward Bellamy's nineteenth century *Looking Backward* could still be static and benign. Science fiction prefers change; in fact, science fiction, to quote another definition, is the literature of change. A particularly effective statement of that position emerged from Henry Kuttner and

C. L. Moore's novel *Fury* (incidentally William Burroughs's favorite SF novel), in which humans who are contented in their impervium domes under the shallow seas of Venus (which makes it a kind of alternate history in the light of contemporary scientific knowledge) are forced out upon a surface made deadly by ravening creatures in order to continue humanity's march to the stars.

Thomas More followed Plato's speculation about a stable political state with "Utopia," and Francis Bacon wrote "The New Atlantis." By the early days of the twentieth century, H. G. Wells was speculating about the nature of citizenship and his "New Samurai" in *A Modern Utopia,* and Heinlein, who was influenced by Wells, dealt with the same issue in *Starship Troopers*, whose message about restricting the vote to those who had served got overshadowed by the more dramatic battles with the alien Bugs. Some decades later Orson Scott Card, in his *Ender's Game* novels, considered the ethical questions of the brutal training of children to become defenders against alien invaders, followed by questions of alien understanding and species genocide.

The spaceship became the icon of science fiction because it symbolizes movement, exploration, expansion. When H. G. Wells's film "Things to Come" was released in 1936, science fiction readers acclaimed it the only good science fiction movie ever made. That was not so much for its anti-war message as for its final segment, when two young people living in a spotless white utopia are fired off into space from a giant electric cannon, and Raymond Massey tells his friend, who wonders if there will never be any peace for humanity, that there will be peace enough in the grave and that the role of humanity is to keep searching for answers: "and when he has conquered all the deeps of space and all the mysteries of time, still he will be beginning."

John W. Campbell, Golden Age editor of *Astounding Science Fiction* (now *Analog*), described the defining quality of humanity as curiosity, and his time traveler, in "Twilight," upon discovering that humanity a couple of millions years in the future has lost its curiosity, sets a machine to the task of creating a curious machine. In contrast, mainstream author E. M. Forster's 1909 "The Machine Stops," considers corruptibility the defining quality of humanity. He also defines the machine as something that creates dependence and then breaks; Campbell, on the other hand, believed that a machine, in theory, should last forever. In Jack Williamson's "With Folded Hands" and *The Humanoids*, it is not the imperfect machine but the perfect one that is perfectly destructive.

As a literature of the human species, science fiction bases its ethics on what is good for the species rather than what is unjust or tragic for the individual. Thus, the science fiction reader would understand the ending of "Twilight" as a triumph for the human spirit, while the mainstream reader might well feel that the end of humanity was not redeemed by machines picking up the human burden of seeking answers to the Great Questions of existence. In Clarke's *Childhood's End*, on the other hand, the triumph of the human children joining the Overmind is offset by their callousness in destroying Earth and the rest of humanity to provide the energy necessary for their transcendence. I've always felt more empathy for the Overlords, condemned to do the bidding of the Overmind but not allowed to join it: "They would serve the Overmind because they had no choice, but even in that service they would not lose their souls."

Aliens offer the opportunity for science fiction authors to consider "the other"—in one sense someone who is different from you and me, because of class, race, origin, intelligence, culture, education, belief, gender, sexual orientation, or any other characteristic that departs from those of the culture judging it. Or the alien can represent anyone other than me.

Aliens once were used by science fiction writers to deal with issues of race, from Fredric Brown's "Dark Interlude" to John Wyndham's "The Living Lies," Frederik Pohl's "The Day the Martians Came," and almost all of Octavia Butler's body of work. Wells introduced them even earlier, in *War of the Worlds* as the ultimate not-us evil that wants to conquer and/or eat us. Wells's squid-like menaces evolved into the fairy god-mothers of human evolution in Arthur C. Clarke's (and Stanley Kubrick's film) *2001: A Space Odyssey*, into curious observers in Stephen Spielberg's "Close Encounters of the Third Kind," and back into ultimate menaces again in George Zebrowski and Charles Pellegrino's *The Killing Star* and Greg Bear's *The Forge of God*. Terry Carr described the ultimate failure of understanding in dealing with aliens in "The Dance of the Changer and the Three."

Beginning in the 1960s authors began to shift their use of aliens toward gender and its influence on behavior. Theodore Sturgeon, who always was pushing the boundaries of acceptability, created a stir at the beginning of the decade with *Venus Plus X*, in which it takes three to tango, and at the end of the decade, with "If All Men Were Brothers, Would You Let One Marry Your Sister" among others. The feminist utopia became popular during the 1970s, most of them using more-or-less ingenious methods for disposing of men, beginning with Joanna Russ's *The Female Man* and continuing through Suzy McKee Charnas's *Motherline*, Pamela Sargent's *The Shore of Women*, Joan Slonczewski's *The*

Door into Ocean, and Marge Piercy's *Woman on the Edge of Time*. Ursula K. Le Guin's *The Left Hand of Darkness* dealt with the sociological implications of humans who could become either sex, and Alice Sheldon, writing as James Tiptree, Jr., began exploring feminist issues beginning in the early 1970s.

More fundamental than the issues of race or gender are the issues of humanity. What does it mean to be human? How did we get to be human? What is humanity's role in the universe? Where do we go from here? And, finally, how do we know who is human?

Darwin's theory of evolution influenced the evolution of science fiction almost immediately. H. G. Wells was a student of Thomas H. Huxley, and the body of Wells's work, as Jack Williamson pointed out, is devoted to testing theories of evolution, from *The Time Machine* to *The War of the Worlds* and *The Island of Dr. Moreau*. The basic principle of science fiction philosophy became Darwinian—that is, the belief that humans are adaptable as opposed to the mainstream belief in the fallen state of man. Change the circumstances, science fiction says, and humanity will change.

A substantial body of science fiction is devoted to pre-historic evolution: Stanley Waterloo's *The Story of Ab*, Jack London's *Before Adam*, Wells's "A Story of the Stone Age," and others up to and including Jean Auel's novels of a Cro-Magnon girl among Neanderthals beginning with *Clan of the Cave Bear*. Contemporary or near-future stories show humanity adapting to new conditions, as in Asimov's *The Caves of Steel*, in which people have become so accustomed to living in roofed-over cities that they are afraid to go outside and must be re-conditioned to become space travelers. More recently, novels such as Charles Stross's *Accelerando* show people adapting to their new existence in a sea of information, called by Vernor Vinge "the Singularity," in which expanding technology finally exceeds human control or even understanding.

Beyond the issue of what we are is what we might become, and a large category of stories are dedicated to the proposition that evolution is not at an end. In *The Time Machine* Wells showed humanity, under the pressure of the class system, devolving into the Morlocks and the Eloi, but many other stories deal with humanity evolving into superhumans. A. E. van Vogt, whose stories dealt with godlike human abilities capable of being unleashed by knowledge or discipline or science, culminated in *The World of Null-A*, which begins with a future humanity liberated by non-Aristotelian thinking along with the biological development of men with two brains; it made Korzybski's *Science and Sanity* into a bestseller. Other superhumans, beginning with Olaf Stapledon's *Odd John*, develop increased intelligence by mutation and the issue turns to how they will be able to co-exist or even survive among normal humans who fear and hate them. In *More Than Human*, Theodore Sturgeon suggested that superhumans would be gestalt groups of social outcasts gifted with special abilities. Cordwainer Smith imagined humans evolving into godlike creatures capable of controlling the energy of entire suns while animals are evolved into humanlike form

In our current information-dense computer culture, the question becomes: what is human? Descartes's formulation "I think therefore I am" becomes problematic if machines also become capable of "thought," and Asimov pointed this out in "Reason," when QT-1 makes the point that his one sure assumption is: "I, myself, exist because I think." Increasingly we acquire our knowledge without discernible human intervention and sometimes have difficulty knowing whether we are dealing with people or machines. The Turing test suggests that if we can't tell whether the responses are human or machine then the distinction may be meaningless. Many SF stories have been developed around the concept of computers acquiring free will, usually ending in disaster for humanity, as in D. F. Jones's (and Joseph Sargent's film) *Colossus, The Forbin Project*, and Harlan Ellison's "I Have No Mouth and I Must Scream." In Frederik Pohl's *Gateway*, a computer psychiatrist replies to the tormented plaint of the protagonist's "Do you call this living?" with "Yes...and I envy it very much."

The creation of robots and humanlike creatures, and their inevitable confusion with humans, began with Mary Shelley's *Frankenstein*, in which the monster blames his murderous acts on his creator's failure to treat him like a human being. The same kind of issue is addressed nearly three centuries later in the film *Blade Runner*, in which human-like (android) "replicants" have short life-spans, sometimes rebel, and have to be "retired." In the film, based on Philip K. Dick's *Do Android Dream of Electric Sheep*, at least one of the presumed humans turns out to be a replicant and, according to the director, the replicant hunter as well. How does anyone know the difference? If false memories are implanted, only external clues or a shortened life span may be the sole determinants—and even then the replicants' claim on humanity may be as legitimate as that of the "blade runners" who kill them. John W. Campbell, in "Who Goes There?" (filmed twice, inadequately, as *The Thing*), considered the problem of determining humanness when confronting a shape-changing alien that can imitate a human down to cells and memories. "The Invasion of the Body Snatchers" (the frequently filmed adaptation of Jack Finney's *The Body* Snatchers) explores a similar quandary in people being replaced by pod creatures, interpreted by some critics as dealing with Communist infiltration and others as more general intrusions into American lives. In Asimov's robot stories, the issue of who is human is critical to the second law of robotics, which requires a robot to obey a human instruction unless it conflicts with the first law, which is that a robot must not harm a human or, by inaction, allow a human to come to harm. In Asimov's "The Bicentennial Man" (filmed under that title as well), the more customary concern of a human discovering himself an android (or "replicant") is reversed when a creative and humane robot wants to be human and finally discovers that he can be so only by accepting death.

Dick was concerned not only with what is human but what is real and how can we know it. Memories are no assurance, as Dick demonstrated in "We Can Remember It for You Wholesale" (filmed as *Total Recall*), nor is solipsism as in *Ubik*, nor even history, as in *The Man in the High Castle*. Dick wrote in his journal, "I am a fictionalizing philosopher, not a novelist." The question of whether what we perceive is real also goes back to Plato and his metaphor of the shadows on the cave wall. Science fiction's questions about reality began early, as in Heinlein's "They," the ultimate paranoia story in which a patient in a mental hospital has figured out that reality has been constructed to keep him confused about his true identity. Sturgeon suggested, in "The Ultimate Egoist," that reality exists only because one person believes in it, and David Gerrold, in "With a Finger in My I," that reality is a consensus and when the consensus begins to break up reality will follow. The film *Dark City*, in which a man keeps reliving the same events, reveals that reality is a capsule metropolis controlled by aliens. In the film *The Truman Show*, Jim Carrey discovers that his life is a television program, and in *The Matrix* series what appears to be real is happening inside a computer simulation. Some authors, such as Australian Greg Egan, in *Permutation City* and other novels, have explored the possibilities of humans downloading themselves into computers, and John Varley has dealt with questions of downloading memories into clones, sometimes of different sexes, as a kind of immortality and blurring of gender issues.

I have not attempted to deal with speculative fiction written in other languages, but it should be understood that international writers are far more likely to deal in philosophical issues than those who write in English. I offer as examples the Polish savant Stanislaw Lem, the Russian writers Boris and Arkady Strugatsky, the Italian writers Dino Buzzati and Italo Calvino, and the Latin American writers Jorge Luis Borges, Gabriel Garcia Marquez, and Carlos Fuentes. Nor have I dealt with mainstream or near-mainstream writers such as Kurt Vonnegut, whose *The Sirens of Titan*, among others, considers the question of existence in a universe without meaning.

I am not suggesting that all science fiction is philosophy tested in human scenarios. A good deal of science fiction is adventure fiction, and some is extrapolatory, if-this-goes-on fiction, whose philosophical concerns may be marginal. But the speculative, what-if stories tend toward those questions that philosophy has addressed over the centuries: how one should live, what sorts of things exist and what are their essential natures, what counts as genuine knowledge, and what are the correct principles of reasoning. I am not suggesting, either, that science fiction writers have contributed any original philosophical observations (with the possible exception of W. Olaf Stapledon and his *First and Last Men* and *Star Maker*, but Stapledon was a professional philosopher), only that they have dramatized philosophical issues and tested them out in human (and alien) scenarios.

The word philosophy comes from Greek roots that mean lover of wisdom. Science fiction has been called knowledge fiction. The union of the two may be no accident.

suggestions for further reading

Asimov, Isaac. *Foundation*. Garden City, NY: Doubleday, 1951.
Asimov, Isaac. *Foundation and Empire*. New York: Gnome, 1952.
Asimov, Isaac. *Second Foundation*. New York: Gnome, 1953.
Herbert, Frank. *Children of Dune*. New York: Berkley, 1996.
Herbert, Frank. *Dune*. New York: Ace, 1965.

20
science fiction and the internet
bruce sterling

The Internet was invented by computer scientists who knew that they were doing something otherworldly.

The first, high-concept description of the Internet was J. C. R. Licklider's extremely visionary, well-nigh hallucinatory, 1960 technical article, "Man-Computer Symbiosis." Licklider's article soberly proposed a cognitive union between "Artificial Intelligence" and "Mechanically Extended Man." Neither of these speculative entities existed in 1960, but, from behind his dual desks in academia and the defense establishment, Licklider figured they were bound to emerge, and, furthermore, merge.

As Licklider wrote: "The hope is that, in not too many years, human brains and computing machines will be coupled together very tightly, and that the resulting partnership will think as no human brain has ever thought and process data in a way not approached by the information-handling machines we know today."

Nothing remotely like this vision has in fact occurred, so the Internet's primeval concept remains intensely science-fictional. However, being an electrical engineer from MIT, Licklider followed his vision with a demonstration: a plan to link computers into a symbiotic network. These experimental machines of the early 1960s had no common language. Licklider explicitly framed this challenge in science-fictional terms: it was a "First Contact" situation, the classic SF thought-experiment of alien races struggling to find a lingua franca.

Licklider soon become the first head of the computer research program at the Pentagon's "Advanced Research Projects Agency." He then had the means, motive, and opportunity to put his self-titled "Intergalactic Computer Network" into play.

Licklider's many colleagues and disciples—such legendary worthies as Leonard Kleinrock, Ivan Sutherland, Bob Taylor, and Lawrence Roberts—set to work to make computers speak together—an obvious and pragmatic first step toward the eventual grand goal of a world-girdling Hard-AI transhuman cyborgism.

The year 1965 saw a TX-2 computer in Massachusetts connected via telephone to a Q-32 in California. This almost forgotten experiment with long-defunct machines was the Internet's intergalactic spore.

Following this working proof of concept, the pioneer visionaries proposed the creation of an "ARPAnet" to their Pentagon sponsor. ARPA, which prided itself on financing projects that no other bureaucracy would dare to consider, was nothing loath. The prospect of real-life funding and hardware contracts quickly attracted attention from military theorists RAND and military contractors Bolt Beranek and Newman.

After a blizzard of computer-science white-papers and a dense collegial tangle of conference-hopping, the world's first ARPAnet node was physically constructed at Los Angeles in September 1969. In a very Lickliderian fashion, the second node of the infant Net was Douglas Englebart's "Augmentation of Human Intellect" studio, located in Stanford.

Two more comp-sci studios followed suit at the University of California, Santa Barbara and the University of Utah. ARPAnet, the protoplasmic ancestor of today's Internet, became a real-world machine. At first, no one knew quite what to do with it. The next logical step should have been in the direction of Artificial Intelligence, but to this day, that goal remains as elusive as time travel.

Instead, much like ham radio, the original ARPAnet was used mostly to work on the ARPAnet. An imaginary network is a gorgeous thought experiment, but an actual network has real-world social consequences. The original ARPAnet was the electronic manifestation of a pre-existing social network of computer scientists and their institutional sponsors: Licklider, Sutherland, Taylor, Roberts, Merrill, Davies, Cantlebury, Baran, Heart, Frank, Elizabeth Feinler, and their overheated cloud of colleagues, co-workers, contractors and graduate students. They had not built a vast Artificial Intelligence, but a scholar-connecting machine: one whose mode of operation, radically decentralized packet switching, was entirely new in the world.

Computers were intensely rare and precious at the time, so much so that "computer science" is the only branch of science ever named after its hardware. The ownership of computing resources was the basic ticket to the ARPAnet. If you had that treasure and stood ready to pitch it in, there was no further need for discussion. Until 1972, users of the future Internet were on a first name basis.

In 1972, email was invented. For the first time, the ARPAnet was blatantly used to hook readers together instead of connecting machinery. Humanity's reaction was naturally much more enthusiastic. Years later, in 1993, after the invention of a simple, user-friendly graphic interface (the "World Wide Web"), the scale of enthusiasm hit a manic pitch unknown in the history of technological development. Business models have failed the Internet—repeatedly—but popular enthusiasm has never balked.

The Internet grew quite rapidly, but the Internet-cum-web has had its own stages of growth:

1993–1997: Explosive, 850% per year.
1998–2001: Rapid, 150% per year.
2002–2006: So-called Maturing growth, a mere 25% a year.

Today's "mature" growth is still enough to transform the planet's current 100 million websites into double that number by the end of the decade. A billion people are using this technology.

These are not dry and abstract statistics; these are the sound of previous forms of media being crushed. Those are vinyl records dying, VHS tapes dying, Sony Walkmans disappearing, hand-written letters joining the coelacanth. It is an irruption from the ivory basements of MIT and some of California's kookiest longhairs, kicking the world as we knew it to the curb.

And the Internet is by no means restricted to the "computer-literate," or to Anglophones, or to "the developed world," or to any other of the imaginary barriers of a so-called digital divide.

Computers were fated to become bizarrely common and fantastically cheap, cheap enough to tuck under one's arm and casually abandon in dumpsters. No one had any idea how quickly that would happen, or how completely the global Internet would differ from its visionary underpinnings.

As Licklider postulated in 1960: "It seems reasonable to envision, for a time 10 or 15 years hence, a 'thinking center' that will incorporate the functions of present day libraries together with anticipated advances in information storage and retrieval and the symbiotic functions suggested earlier in this paper. The picture readily enlarges itself into a network of such centers, connected to one another by wide-band communication lines and to individual users by leased-wire services. In such a system, the speed of the computers would be balanced, and the cost of the gigantic memories and the sophisticated programs would be divided by the number of users."

That was a very apt prediction, entirely reasonable, but reasoning is not what most people do with their time. The Internet had nothing to do with intelligence and everything to do with a logarithmic, institution-smashing tidal wave of mobile packets.

Licklider himself ruefully pointed out that most of his visionary work consisted of giving orders and hustling paper rather than contemplation. The paperless office is at hand: at last, it really is, and I know, because I have one and I'm using it now.

Digital modernity is an extremely hardware-centric occupation. The planet has been colonized by packet-shuffling hardware. So much so that the loss of one of Licklider's "extensions"—a broken cellphone, a stolen laptop—can be instantly mutilating.

People have shown a consistent inability to understand the Internet's ability to add new abilities. Every time the Internet adds bandwidth and shuffles its packets faster, it eats some pre-digital mode of communication. And it has no respect for the previous media order.

Licklider predicted that the existence of a Net would lead to an explosion of books. He loved books and considered himself a humanist. "The first thing to face is that we shall not store all the technical and scientific papers in computer memory. We may store the parts that can be summarized most succinctly—the quantitative parts and the reference citations—but not the whole. Books are among the most beautifully engineered, and human-engineered, components in existence, and they will continue to be functionally important within the context of man-computer symbiosis. (Hopefully, the computer will expedite the finding, delivering, and returning of books.)"

A tremendous feat of futuristic insight there, in anticipating the domination of Amazon. Still, his concept that books would feature as the hard-copy backup for his scholarly network proved absurd. The capacity of memory marched along on the same Moore's Law period-doubling route to chaos that integrated chips did. It led, leap by dizzy leap, to the current bizarre situation where college library book stacks are well-nigh empty of people and every nook and cranny of academia is crammed with workstations.

No computer engineer, no engineer of any kind, could survive as a professional today with nothing more than those "beautifully engineered and human-engineered components." The reign of books at the peak of intellectual effort is over.

And books are surviving the packet revolution with relative ease.

For the pre-Internet generation, there was a natural and unquestioned hierarchy of media, based on the analog costs of production and distribution. "Science fiction" was a product of that media milieu—mostly, the very bottom of it. Hugo Gernsback sold radio components from pulp catalogs. "First Fandom" was a network built around his pulp-fiction magazines.

Typed manuscripts. Homemade fanzines. Comic books. Pulp "mags." Glossy magazines. The big national slicks. The small press. The major publishing houses. Radio. Television. Movies at the top of media commerce: not only were these a hierarchy of analog media, they created a hierarchy of science fiction writers. These media, somewhat reluctantly, supported science fiction as a subculture: a group of keenly committed enthusiasts who networked through Gestetner duplicates and gelatin pads, always aching to find a one decent, big-budget SF movie that wasn't vaguely demeaning.

Computer networks, and computers themselves, were commonly first seen as maidservants of this natural and unalterable media order. They were and are profoundly corrosive of it. Packets of one and zeros, spread worldwide at extremely low cost, are a kind of universal solvent of analog media.

Packets are not "electronic text" or "electronic images" any more than a car is a "horseless carriage." Electronic text is packets displayed as text, while electronic images are packets displayed as images. The display is what an interface is programmed to show the human user: the actual packets themselves are practically impossible to see.

A recent back-of-the-envelope calculation of all the packets transiting the Internet suggests that the whole shebang weighs about three ounces.

Of course, that doesn't count the vast tonnage of digital hardware, routers and storage media: but those too obsolesce so rapidly that they're remarkably ephemeral. The Internet is a river in which you cannot step twice. No two human beings have ever used the Internet in precisely the same way.

A publishing house is an institution whose reason for being is to search-out and publish: it would never publish everything it receives. Its main value-addition for society is to keep you, the purchaser of books, from buying awful junk.

The Internet, in stark contrast, is a publish-and-search engine. It's entirely full of junk, and survives through potent junk-weeding machinery. Over 90 percent of the email sent today is sent by unmanned computers commandeered by malefactors ("bot-nets") and it consists of email directly intended to harm the reader: spam and phishing. This vast flow of mechanized fraud has been characteristic of the Internet ever since its global spread first exceeded regional legal jurisdictions. It's not a bug, but a feature.

It follows that the Internet has torn into every aspect of the previous media order, very commonly illegally. Holographic manuscripts have vanished headlong, replaced, if they are replaced at all, by the printout. Fanzines were on their way out as soon as the ARPAnet produced one of the world's first and most popular email lists, "SF-LOVERS." Magazines about the Internet naturally boomed—but nobody any longer imagines that a website is like an electronic magazine. Both newspapers and magazines are in serious trouble as their ad revenue migrates online.

For-pay content, hidden behind firewalls, will not be found by Internet search engines. So it will not be found by people. For creators of "content," the only thing worse than not being paid is being ignored entirely.

For decades, there has been an expectation that some political solution would be found that restores the revenue streams of the previous order: a mass of literary artisans, weeded out by mass media, their works read by mass consumers. Common sense held that "literature" would become, say, "electronic books": a sensible line of reasoning, but akin to thinking that when the invention of gunpowder smashes the castle, new castles will be built from the cannons.

The logic of packets is not to reproduce analog literature, seen in a book, into packetized literature, seen on a screen. The logic is to reproduce all forms of media to a radically distributed mélange of packets, an insidious liquid flow of pervasive micromediation, percolating through a billion screens.

"Digital Rights Management" systems are dikes and bulwarks against this logic.

Unfortunately, these rights are not associated with the analog forms of media, but with computing platforms that handle packets. Intellectual property rights are still perceived as a keystone of global law and order—the creator ought to be rewarded, that surely seems good and proper—but in a system as diffuse and extra-legal as the Net, "law and order" is always perceived as a tiresome burden best born by some other user.

Users presented with free content will vote with their mice. The upshot is not a good and proper and legal system, but a ninety-percent "ungood" and improper system that is fast, cheap, and out of control.

To mechanically control the packet platform is very hard, but a relatively simple matter. To get the public to pay for such a complex scheme is quite difficult. To get the entire global public to cordially obey such abstract strictures—when the planet is seething with narcoterror—seems merely silly. How can a society police flows of packets when it can't police flows of heroin and oil?

This is by no means a merely literary difficulty. It extends through the entire structure of analog media, one in which text suffers rather mildly. Broadcast radio has a limited bandwidth and a few local languages. Internet "radio" has endless bandwidth and a global reach. Television is still entertaining people, but it's no longer entertaining enough to make up for its numbing lack of interaction. Both broadcast television and cable television lose viewership wherever the Internet spreads. The day of the massively financed ultra-glossy hit TV show is fading fast, replaced by cheap reality TV and game shows, niches whose core demographic is the poor and the poorly educated.

Local bookstores have friendly local clerks who can sell small-press books of regional interest. Amazon has a vast global machinery that will sell you anything from toothpaste to lawnmowers. This purported "bookseller" will even enable owners of secondhand books to sell used books to each other. A digitized, globalized book market is a phenomenon violently divorced from the quieter, localized, analog book market. It's got about as much to do with the previous means of literary production as a credit card does to a sack-full of pieces-of-eight.

The old arguments that one "can't read off a screen" are evaporating day by day. One can't read paper books from a screen, and one can't sell chunks of packets as if they were paper books, but even physical books are no longer sold, produced or consumed in the context they once were.

People read like crazy on the Internet—but they're not reading sixty thousand narratively coherent words in a row. On the contrary, young people growing up on today's Internet are having an increasingly difficult time making distinctions between earlier forms of media. They live within a flow of mediated microparticles: pirated MP3s, video snippets, butchered bits of "Main Stream Media" articles debunked or adorned with blogger commentary.

And there are new forms of media arising, unknown before the Internet: search engine interfaces, social network sites. And, most crucial for science fiction: the interactive fantasy worlds of massive, multiplayer, online role-playing games. Networked role-playing games are fandom as an almost literal way of life. Games are almost unique among Internet phenomena in having workable firewalls and predictable revenue streams. People venture into Internet games not just to get away from the mundane world, but to get away from the Internet.

Furthermore, they go into game worlds to enjoy the intensely science-fictional experience of an imaginative elite socially gathered in a permanent costume convention. Gaming is not a literary experience—but it's probably the most science-fictional cultural experience that the world has yet invented. Far more so than fanzines, magazines, television, movies—the works.

Games are a fandom apotheosis, and to a somewhat lesser extent, so is the Internet. The Internet is especially like fandom in its clannish, grabby, chatty, never mind the money, we're all-in-this together methods of cultural production.

The Internet is certainly much more like science fiction fandom than it has ever been like a cyberspace. William Gibson's description of "cyberspace," though intensely literary, was very much in the visionary Licklider tradition. Gibsonian cyberspace, as depicted in his novels, was intensely class-based and exclusive: a gated military/corporate construction of immersive, neural, consensus hallucination. Today's Internet is almost precisely the opposite: sprawling, promiscuous, louche, quotidian and seething with "console cowboys."

Gibson's 1980s vision now seems almost as romantically distant as Licklider's comp-sci futurism of the 1960s. The plot of *Neuromancer* is about its titular character, an Artificial Intelligence, moving people as pawns. That never came to pass, for the Internet has no master intelligences. It has no centrality; it has no single purpose. It's just very, very big, and scarily popular. Even Al Qaeda loves to use the Internet. Even Red China decided to embrace and extend it. There is no society anywhere so poor and backward that its children will not take to the Internet like ducks to water. The day is likely not far off when household pets will have an Internet presence.

The basic role of science fiction writers was to serve as a cultural interface between science and the readers of fiction. That was a worthwhile role, and it has by no means been fulfilled. The gulf between the general population and the scientific enterprise is yawning scarily wider. But even Creationists and fundamentalists dote on the Internet; it is their sword of divine justice against "Main Stream Media."

If you want to learn of goings-on within the lab and the ivory tower, a magazine is limited to its page count. The Internet will feed you as much science as you can swallow—it will feed you as much of ANYTHING as you can swallow, and then some, by orders of magnitude.

Science fiction was a period expression of a technological, scientific, industrial society. It appeared and flourished only when pre-industrial societies were conclusively hitting the skids. Today's post-industrial society may lack the stability for that role to be reprised in a coherent subcultural form. It is not that science fiction vanishes. It is that it is subsumed.

To wax riskily Lickliderian at my essay's end, it would appear that distinctions between the "virtual" Internet and "physical" reality are disappearing. Today's visionary term "Internet-of-Things" is highly unsatisfactory, though it's likely the best shorthand we have for tomorrow's symbiosis. That is not a symbiosis of human thought and machine processing, but a commercial symbiosis between machine processing and formerly physical objects.

Tomorrow's Internet protocol, Internet Protocol Version Six, has enough address space within it to give a machine identity to every object we care about; in a fine Intergalactic Computer Network fashion, IPv6 could number every pebble in the known universe.

Licklider's manifesto was written fifty-seven years ago; fifty-seven years from now, to make a distinction between "science fiction" and the "Internet" may seem almost as arcane. It's not that those terms didn't matter, in their day. It's just: there won't be anything left of those two categories that isn't already somehow both.

suggestions for further reading

Techmeme http://www.techmeme.com/
Popurls http://popurls.com/
Worldchanging http://www.worldchanging.com
Everything is Miscellaneous http://everythingismiscellaneous.com/
Great Principles of Computing http://cs.gmu.edu/cne/pjd/GP/gp_overview.html

the *reading science fiction* blog

What follows is the world's first blog that has ever appeared in a textbook. We hope it functions as a segué to the *Reading Science Fiction* website that will follow the volume's publication, a bridge between the textbook you hold in your hands and the website blog we invite *you* to read and to write. The website can be found at www.aboutsf.com/readingsf.

launching the *reading science fiction* blog: episode 1, the reader response force is with you

marleen s. barr

Hi students! Do you usually define textbook co-editors as stuffy removed from the world something Other than human entities who function solely as the source of your homework assignments? Luckily, although we live in a science fiction world, technology has not yet replaced human textbook creators. Yes, your professor has assigned specific pages in "Gunn, Barr, and Candelaria." Theodore Sturgeon wrote *More Than Human; Reading Science Fiction* emphasizes that we are three very human more than mere co-editors. This is at it should be. Enough already with all the distancing which separates textbook readers from textbook writers. The existing electronic technology which was once science fiction can bring us together. Simply stated, we can blog.

* * *

blog entry: childhood's end

How to fill this "textbookesque" *My Space*? I would like to take a different approach to reader response criticism (the reading practice which, as I explain below, permeates my scholarly writing as a result of my graduate school experience studying with Norman N. Holland). Reader response critics usually explain how their life influences the meanings they find in texts they do not generate. I want to discuss how my early life motivated me to author theoretical discourse about science fiction. I will focus upon my experiences relating to childhood (students have already been there and done that), graduate school, and being a young professional (the future in relation to undergraduate students). I will touch upon how these experiences relate to my present work. Without further ado, back to the past. Back to how the once upon a time Marleen chronicles yields the present I, feminist science fiction scholar.

One second thought, there is a little further ado: Joanna Russ wrote a brilliant essay called "What Can A Heroine Do Or Why Women Can't Write." Positioning myself as a heroine in my own beginnings, I try to assuage the unfortunately still alive and well penchant for turning women writers into so many science fiction invisible women. I am, in other words, devoting my space in the *Reading Science Fiction* blog to position an usual form of reader response criticism as an alternative to the conditions Russ describes in *How to Suppress Women's Writing*.

As I plunge into the biographical "way back machine" characterizing this blog entry, I emphasize that I was born into initial post World War II Forest Hills, Queens. Getting to know my world involved progressing from exploring the interior of my father's closet to investigating my apartment building at large. I discovered aliens in the elevator. (I am not speaking in the language of science fiction. Like my French Canadian husband, these aliens are immigrants.) The aliens, who spoke English with strange accents, were called "refugees."

"What are refugees?" I asked my mother because I was intrigued by the strange sounding word.

"People from the other side," she answered matter of factly.

If "people from the other side" does not echo the language of science fiction, I don't know what does. My mother's word choice was quite reality-centered, though. She meant the other side of the Atlantic Ocean, what today's United States denizens flippantly refer to as "across the pond." I quote her because she said "people from the other side" *period*. I cannot blame her. How do you tell a child whose neighbors had been Auschwitz prisoners that Auschwitz is not science fiction? The worst science fiction villain ever imagined is not scarier than Hitler. Some of my childhood friends' parents had been *Musselmanner*, Auschwitz slang used to describe people near death from starvation. My refugee neighbors were protagonists of the science fiction stories Hitler made real.

These stories were never told to me; I was at once surrounded by Holocaust survivors and total silence about the Holocaust. (Perhaps when Forest Hills residents Paul Simon and Art Garfunkel referred to the scientifically impossible—and, hence, science fictional—"sounds of silence," they alluded to survivors' unarticulated stories which spoke volumes.) I first learned about the Holocaust during my initial forays within the Forest Hills branch of the Queensboro Public Library. I loved what I found in the section which contained Isaac Asimov's and Robert Heinlein's work. There was so much library and so little time, though. So, after neatly placing Madeleine L'Engle's *A Wrinkle In Time* and Eleanor Cameron's *The Wonderful Flight to the Mushroom Planet* back in their appointed places, I investigated a different shelf. Turning my attention to books about history, I found words that were even stranger than "refugee": "Babi Yar." My fledgling reader brain thought that "Babi Yar" was a misprint and somehow akin to Jean and Laurent de Brunhoff's Babar the Elephant series. I lost my childhood innocence when I learned that the Ukranian Babi Yar Massacre involved a killing field for thousands of Jews. I lost my innocence when I realized that reading about Babi Yar had nothing to do with reading science fiction and everything to do with why my Jewish neighbors became refugees. It is difficult to be a child who, since she is surrounded by alien refugee Holocaust survivors, must face the full implications of the alternative reality story the Nazis turned real. Maybe I turned to reading science fiction, especially *Superman* comic books, to escape from reality. It occurs to me that Marvel Comics chairman Stan Lee lived in Forest Hills and Lee's character Peter Parker (a.k.a. Spiderman) lives there too. (The legendary science fiction editor Hugo Gernsback also resided in Forest Hills.)

Lee, a Jewish World War II veteran, had to encounter refugees in Forest Hills; perhaps he too is involved with science fiction due to his experience there. Perhaps Lee created Spiderman as an alternative to the Nazi's Aryan master race mythology which equated Jews with vermin. He might have derived satisfaction from imbuing American popular culture with super heroes who spring from the New York Jewish imagination. I can unequivocally state that I read Lee's science fiction super hero comic books because they spoke directly to my need for power fantasies.

But enough already about Hitler.

Some of my best friends are Austrians and Germans. Really. Growing up with refugees impacted upon me to the extent that, in order to find out exactly what characterized the world on "the other side," I spent three years teaching in Austria and Germany. I love the people I met there. Jeanne Cortiel is one of them. Her contribution to this volume, the wonderful essay on Joanna Russ I invited her to write, would not exist if, according to some alternative reality, my childhood based desire to teach in Germany did not occur. I will have the pleasure of interacting with Jeanne again when I begin my spring 2008 Fulbright to Germany.

comment: jeanne cortiel

I will respond with the story of how I came to science fiction, which is almost completely the obverse of yours, Marleen. I grew up "on the other side" more than 20 years after the war's end in a shabby, lower class neighborhood in a city that's not supposed to have such neighborhoods—Salzburg, Austria. It was also a city of many silences, but there was nothing grand or heroic about them. They were the banal, lingering silences that trail after great evil. My childhood, though full of fantastic schemes on my part, was devoid of science fictional potential. I came to science fiction late in life, as a student in my early twenties in a scholarly landscape that had already been shaped by your work, Marleen—your presence on this side both as a writer and as a teacher. It was in a wonderfully inspiring class on feminist utopian texts taught by Elizabeth Kraus in Graz that my first conscious encounter with science fiction was Joanna Russ's *The Female Man*, and I still believe that's the best introduction anyone could wish for. So I utterly lack the desire to imagine a world in which you did not come to teach on this side of the Atlantic. It would be a bleak and empty universe indeed. Come back often. :-)

blog entry: marleen barr and the fantastic graduate school mentors

I entered graduate school secure in the knowledge that I wanted to devote my life to being a science fiction critic—to reading science fiction. Upon arrival, I found (wonder of wonder and miracle of miracles) a literature professor who was a science fiction critic! (Science fiction critics, after all, do not grow on trees in the manner of, say, garden variety accountants and lawyers.) While at the University of Michigan, twenty-one year old me marched into twenty-eight year old Professor Eric S. Rabkin's office. Soon after ensconcing myself on the window sill in the space between the window pane and the file cabinet, I issued a proclamation: "When I grow up, I want to be a science fiction critic just like you."

Currently, in the present which constitutes the future in relation to my good old days at Michigan, Rabkin and I are ever so much older than our twenties. I state the obvious because reading science fiction involves finding life-long friends. (This means *you* too: never fear if your life has been devoid of science fiction critics. As I emphasize above, you now are acquainted with me and Jim and Matt—and you can better get to know us and all of our contributors when we all blog together.)

My graduate education also enabled me to engage with a maverick colossus who bestrode the twentieth century American literary critical arena in the manner of Einstein and physics. The late Leslie Fiedler was my teacher while I pursued a Ph.D. at the State University of New York at Buffalo. I watched Leslie (as he was known to his students) puff upon his trademark cigar while I told him that science fiction is kosher literature. I read science fiction because Leslie read science fiction. (Leslie famously emphasized his Jewishness, especially his childhood roots in Jewish Newark, New Jersey.) When, circa 1978, I announced to a skeptical SUNY Buffalo English department community that Ursula K. Le Guin was a great American writer, Leslie affirmed that I was right on target.

comment: eric s. rabkin

Marleen, no matter how old you—we—get, I'll always remember that perch of yours on the window sill. To your right, a window on the world; to your left, a cabinet full of academic papers; in between, a smart, irrepressible bundle of iconoclastic energy looking right at me eager to make connections that matter whether the world—the ordinary, realistic world—supported that or not. Some might have thought you were squashed in, sitting there. I think you were pupal. Of course I supported you. Who could resist? And the future proved us both right.

comment: james gunn

I met Eric Rabkin at a Science Fiction Research Association meeting and got to know him even better at an International Association for the Fantastic in the Arts Conference and Norman Holland when he came to give a talk on reader response criticism here at the University of Kansas. In fact, we shared a commuter flight from the Kansas City airport to the Lawrence airport when those were still available and I was coming back from a meeting—in Akron, I think.

I met Leslie Fiedler at the second meeting of the Science Fiction Research Association (SFRA) in Toronto, at the Spaced-Out Library. It was the first SFRA meeting for both of us. He was a newcomer to science fiction, and he told me he had started reading it because his children told him he should. Later he edited an anthology of SF, *In Dreams Awake*, and wrote a novel, *The Messengers Will Come No More*. Like Robert Scholes, whom I met at a subsequent SFRA meeting, Fiedler often liked

SF for reasons different from many of us—in Fiedler's case because it was outside traditional scholarship, like pornography. In fact Fiedler reserved his highest praise for works that combined the two genres. It helps to come to SF early ("the golden age of SF is twelve") even though one's critical approach may mature.

blog entry: 1984

When I became an assistant professor, I started to devote my professional life to convincing my colleagues and students to read science fiction—one person at a time. Toward this end, in 1984, I went so far as to publish the late eminent feminist theorist Carolyn Heilbrun's essay "Why I Don't Read Science Fiction" in the special feminist science fiction journal issue I named "Oh well, Orwell, Big Sister Is Watching Herself." I was aware that Heilbrun's title fell short of affirming science fiction. But, in 1984, even feminist critics wielded a big boot to stomp on those who read and wrote nonrealistic literature. I was anxious to publish a major feminist critic who addressed science fiction. At least, despite its title, Heilbrun's essay lauded Joanna Russ and Ursula Le Guin.

I modeled my novel *Oy Pioneer!* after Heilbrun's mystery novel series. She wrote mysteries featuring a woman professor. I am following suit in terms of a science fiction premise. I will soon start another novel about my feminist science fiction theorist protagonist.

blog entry: "you, u. k. le guin" and *you*

My initial scholarly professional act was to publish *Future Females: A Critical Anthology* (1981), the first scholarly essay collection about women and science fiction. The book included a result of my continuing efforts to convince stellar literary scholars to address themselves to reading science fiction. I made a space for a late twentieth century literary criticism eminence to write about science fiction: my dissertation director Norman N. Holland contributed "You, U. K. Le Guin" to *Future Females*.

Norm had a tremendous impact upon my thinking. His *5 Readers Reading*, a description of how reader response criticism locates meaning in the individual reader, informs my belief that the personal should be a part of literary studies. What I learned from Norm is directly responsible for the existence of the *Reading Science Fiction* blog. It is, then, appropriate for me to end this entry with the exact words Norm used to conclude "You, U. K. Le Guin": "That is my feeling throughout the novel [*The Left Hand of Darkness*]—a constant reaching out for completion... I think that is why ... I keep thinking about you [Le Guin] ... I reach out to *you*, U. K. Le Guin, to join my hand to yours to re-create *The Left Hand of Darkness*."

Jim, Matt and I—and all of our contributors—reach out to *you*, our student readers. Join hands with us; blog with us; re-create the text which is *Reading Science Fiction* via your feeling about reading it in particular and reading science fiction in general.

I have kept thinking about those words Norm used. It means something very special to me to include them here... Oh no. I interrupt this blog entry to bring you the news that something supernatural is at this very moment transpiring in my apartment. There is a big smoke cloud in the middle of my living room. An immortal vampire science fiction critic wearing a cape and carrying a monocle is emerging from the cloud and walking toward me with his hand extended. As a feminist science fiction reader response scholar, I of course know what this means: Ilya Lugosi, a protagonist in *Oy Pioneer!*, wants to re-create that text in my blog.

"Ilya, what are you doing in here? Who ever heard of a vampire science fiction critic showing up in a blog?"

"Calm down, Marleen. Not to worry. After all, who ever heard of a blog appearing in a textbook?"

"True. You have a point. I guess I have read too much science fiction and too much reader response theory. Why are you here?"

"I want to tell you to be prepared. A voice from the future is soon going to take over your text."

comment: norman n. holland

Marleen, you are indefatigable as always. And a good reader response critic. Sometimes we profs get an idea across, and you've taken it and run with it in your writings. That gives me a good feeling, as it evidently does you. It seems to me that a blog like this really continues the reader response idea. That is, the meaning of what we say here lies not on our screens but in the spaces between what we say to one another. I reach out my hand to you, Marleen, and to your fellow bloggers.

comment: marleen s. barr

I love the image of you reaching out to me and my fellow *Reading Science Fiction* bloggers. For twenty-six years, I remembered how you ended the "You U. K. Le Guin" essay with the hand reaching comment. Now it has a current version. I'm ecstatic.

comment: ilya lugosi

I'm very jealous. You quoted Norman Holland, Marleen. What about me? I've been writing science fiction criticism for thousands of years. Surely you could have found something of mine to quote.

comment: marleen s. barr

Even science fiction critics have to cite real mortals, not supernatural protagonists. Please stop popping into my blog. And don't under any circumstance materialize in the classrooms of my colleagues who are assigning *Reading Science Fiction*. Being a feminist science fiction scholar is hard enough. I can't have my fantastic protagonists running rampant. Silly vampire, *Reading Science Fiction* is meant for real kids.

comment: ilya lugosi

Okay, I see that one vampire reader reading is not welcome. But American political reality seems pretty akin to science fiction to me. I asked your Marxist critic contributor Carl Freedman to say a thing or two about your current political landscape. His comment underscores that the sex scandals are certainly more beyond beyond than anything I ever pulled off in *Oy Pioneer!*.

comment: carl freedman

One cannot take as much delight as one would wish to take in the recent wave of sex crimes by various Republicans and conservatives because of the simple fact that in a free society their shenanigans would not be indictable crimes at all. Senator Larry "Widestance" Craig, for instance, was minding his own business in an airport restroom. Perhaps he was offering to mind someone else's business too, but it was, at worst, just an offer. So much for free speech. Then there is the prophet of God, and leader of the Fundamentalist Church of Jesus Christ of Latter-Day Saints, Warren Jeffs. It certainly was not very nice to convince a 14-year-old girl to marry her brutish 19-year-old cousin, especially since Jeffs invoked the divine authority that he seems to abuse almost as regularly as the Pope. But accessory to rape? Anyone who cannot tell the difference between being persuaded to make a totally stupid marriage and being raped should spend time with some actual rape victims. And let us not forget Senator David "Whoremaster" Vitter. He has not been indicted for his patronage of the hard-working ladies of the New Orleans night, but there is talk he may yet be. What about the right of free contract between buyer and seller?

blog entry: from a future female, star date april 1, 3008

I just like jacked the reader unit into my brain information access portal because I from time to time enjoy reading the ancient text *Reading Science Fiction*. My clone-line originator Marleen S. Barr co-edited it. Even though I am a college student at Mattapoisett University, one of the best universities in the entire solar system, I just don't get everything she mentions in her life's work about how reading feminist science fiction can change the patriarchal world. Like, what's a patriarchy? Like, women and men have been equal for thousands of years and I can't get my head around dystopian concepts. Well, enough already with reading about what was science fiction. I see a cute boy. Like, I could care less if he's from Mars and I'm from Venus. Oy, all ten of my clone mothers incessantly tell me to get married. I hope I don't look fat.

Luv, msb225—Jennifer

suggestions for further reading

Barr, Marleen S. "Being Marleen S. Barr, Writing *Oy Pioneer!*: How To Succeed In Creating Jewish Humorous Feminist Science Fiction Without Really Trying to Be Influenced by 'Tradition, Tradition.'" *Extrapolation* 48 (March 2007), 168–169.

Barr, Marleen S. *Oy Pioneer!: A Novel*. Madison, WI: University of Wisconsin Press, 2003.

Heilbrun, Carolyn. "Why I Don't Read Science Fiction." in Marleen S. Barr (ed.) *Women's Studies International Forum* 7 (1984): 117–119.

Holland, Norman N. "You, U. K. Le Guin." in Marleen S. Barr (ed.) *Future Females: A Critical Anthology*. Bowling Green, OH: Bowling Green State University Popular Press, 1981, 125–137.

Smith, C. Jason and Ximena Gallardo. "Oy Science Fiction: On Genre, Criticism, and Alien Love: An Interview with Marleen S. Barr." *Reconstruction: An Interdisciplinary Cultural Studies Community*. 5.4 (Fall 2005). *www.reconstruction*.ws.

bibliography

Aldiss, Brian. *Billion Year Spree: The True History of SF*. Garden City, NY: Doubleday, 1973.

——. "Shards." *Magazine of Fantasy and Science Fiction* 22 (1962): 49–56.

——. and David Wingrove. *Trillion Year Spree*. London: House of Stratus, 2001.

Alkon, Paul. *Origins of Futuristic Fiction*. Athens: University of Georgia Press, 1987.

——. *Science Fiction Before 1900: Imagination Discovers Technology*. New York: Routledge, 2002.

Altman, Rick. *Film/Genre*. London: BFI, 1999.

Anderson, Poul. *Brain Wave*. New York: Ballantine, 1954.

——. "Plot in Science Fiction." *Literature of Science Fiction film series*. 1968

Arnason, Eleanor. *A Woman of the Iron People*. New York: William Morrow, 1991.

Ashcroft, Bill, Gareth Griffiths, and Helen Tiffin. *The Empire Writes Back: Theory and Practice in Post-Colonial Literatures*. London: Routledge, 1989.

——. *Post-Colonial Studies: The Key Concepts*. London: Routledge, 2000.

Asimov, Isaac. *The Fantastic Voyage*. Boston: Houghton Mifflin, 1966.

——. *I, Robot*. New York: Signet, 1956.

Attebery, Brian. *Decoding Gender in Science Fiction*. New York: Routledge, 2002.

Atwood, Margaret. *The Handmaid's Tale*. 1985; rpt. New York: Fawcett, 1987.

Barnes, Barry. *Interests and the Growth of Knowledge*. Boston: Routledge and Kagan Paul, 1977.

Barr, Marleen S. *Alien to Femininity: Speculative Fiction and Feminist Theory*. Westport, CT: Greenwood, Press, 1987.

——. *Feminist Fabulation: Space/Postmodern Fiction*. Iowa City, IA: University of Iowa Press, 1992.

Bazerman, Charles. *Shaping Written Knowledge: The Genre and Activity of the Experimental Article in Science*. Madison, WI: University of Wisconsin Press, 1988.

Bear, Greg. *Darwin's Radio*. New York: Del Rey, 1999.

——. *Eon*. New York: Bluejay, 1985.

Beley, Gene. Lincoln, NE: iUniverse 2006. POD volume, http://www.iuniverse.com/bookstore/qsearchresults.asp?choice=title&inputstr=Search, accessed on June 12, 2008.

Bell, Andrea L. and Yolanda Molina-Gavilán. *Cosmos Latinos: An Anthology of Science Fiction from Latin America and Spain*. Middleton CT: Wesleyan University Press, 2003.

Benford, Gregory. *Timescape*. New York: Simon and Schuster, 1980.

Bhabha, Homi. *The Location of Culture*. London: Routledge, 1994.

Bloor, David. *Knowledge and Social Imagery.* 1976. Chicago: University of Chicago Press, 1991.

Board on Life Sciences, National Research Council and Health Sciences Policy Board, Institute of Medicine. National Academy of Sciences. *Guidelines for Human Embryonic Stem Cell Research.* Washington, DC: National Academies Press, 2005.

Boehmer, Elleke. *Colonial and Postcolonial Literature: Migrant Metaphors.* New York: Oxford University Press, 1995.

Bradley, Marion Zimmer. *The Ruins of Isis.* New York: imon and Schuster, 1978.

Brin, David. "Metaphorical Drive-Or Why We're Such Good Liars." in George. E. Slusser and Eric S. Rabkin (eds) *Mindscapes: The Geographies of Imagined Worlds.* Carbondale, IL: Southern Illinois University Press, 1989. 60–77.

Bujold, Lois McMaster. *Shards of Honor.* New York: Baen Books, 1986.

Bull, Emma. *Bone Dance.* New York: Ace Books, 1991.

Butler, Judith. *Gender Trouble: Feminism and the Subversion of Identity.* New York: Routledge, 1990.

Butler, Octavia. "Bloodchild" 1984. in Donald A. Wollheim (ed.) *The 1985 Annual World's Best SF.* New York: DAW, 1985. 193–212.

——. *Dawn* 1987. *Xenogenesis: Dawn, Adulthood Rites, Imago.* New York: Warner Books, 1989.

Candelaria, Matthew. "The Overlords' Burden: The Source of Sorrow in Arthur C. Clarke's *Childhood's End." ARIEL* 33 (2002): 37–62.

Capek, Karel. *R.U.R.* New York: Doubleday, 1923.

Chapman, Edgar. *The Road to Castle Mount: The Science Fiction of Robert Silverberg.* Westport, CT: Greenwood Press, 1999.

Chayefsky, Paddy. *Altered States.* New York: Harper & Row, 1978.

Clarke, Arthur C. *Against the Fall of Night.* New York: Pyramid, 1953.

Clute, John and John Grant. *The Encyclopedia of Fantasy.* London: Orbit, 1997.

——. and Peter Nicholls. *The Encyclopedia of Science Fiction.* New York: St. Martin's Press, 1993.

Collins, Harry. *Changing Order: Replication and Induction in Scientific Practice.* Beverly Hills, CA: Sage, 1985.

Cortiel, Jeanne. *Demand My Writing: Joanna Russ/Feminism/Science Fiction.* Science Fiction Texts and Studies. Liverpool, UK: Liverpool University Press, 1999.

——. "Determinate Politics of Indeterminacy: Reading Joanna Russ's Recent Work in Light of Her Early Short Fiction." in Marleen S. Barr (ed.) *Future Females, the Next Generation: New Voices and Velocities in Feminist Science Fiction Criticism.* Lanham, MD: Rowman and Littlefield, 2000. 219–236.

——. "Joanna Russ: *The Female Man.*" A Companion to Science Fiction. in David Seed (ed.) *Blackwell Companions to Literature and Culture: 34.* Malden, MA: Blackwell, 2005. 500–511.

Crichton, Michael. *The Terminal Man.* New York: Knopf, 1972.

Delany, Samuel R. "Joanna Russ and D. W. Griffith." *PMLA* 119 (2004): 500.

——. "Orders of Chaos: The Science Fiction of Joanna Russ." in Jane B. Weedman (ed.) *Women Worldwalkers: New Dimensions of Science Fiction and Fantasy.* Lubbock, TX: Texas Tech Press, 1985. 95–123.

——. "Science Fiction and 'Literature'—or, The Conscience of the King." in James Gunn and Matthew Candelaria (eds) *Speculations on Speculation: Theories of Science Fiction.* Lanham, MD: Scarecrow Press, 2005. 95–118.

Disch, Thomas. *Camp Concentration.* New York: Doubleday, 1969.

Donawerth, Jane. *Frankenstein's Daughters: Women Writing Science Fiction*. Syracuse, NY: Syracuse University Press, 1997.

——. and Carol Kolmerten. *Utopian and Science Fiction by Women: Worlds of Difference*. Syracuse, NY: Syracuse University Press, 1994.

Donovan's Brain. 1953. United Artists. Directed by Felix E. Feist.

Dorsey, Candas Jane. "(Learning About) Machine Sex." in Ursula K. Le Guin and Brian Attebery (eds) *The Norton Book of Science Fiction*. New York: W. W. Norton, 1993. 746–761.

Duncan, Andy. "Think Like a Humanist: James Patrick Kelly's 'Think Like a Dinosaur' as a Satiric Rebuttal to Tom Godwin's '*The Cold Equations*.'" *The New York Review of Science Fiction* 94 (1996): 8–11.

Easterbrook, Neil. "State, Heterotopia: The Political Imagination in Heinlein, Le Guin, and Delany." in Donald Hassler and Clyde Wilcox (eds) *Political Science Fiction*. Columbia, SC: University of South Carolina Press, 1997. 43–75.

Edwards, Paul. *The Closed World: Computers and the Politics of Discourse in Cold War America*. Cambridge, MA:MIT Press, 1996.

Egan, Greg. *Diaspora*. New York: Eos, 1999.

——. *Permutation City*. New York: Eos, 1995.

——. "Reasons to be Cheerful." in Gardner Dozois (ed.) *The Year's Best Science Fiction: Fifteenth Annual Collection*. New York: St. Martin's Press, 1998.

Ehrsson, H. Henrik. "The Experimental Induction of Out-of-body Experiences." *Science* 317 (2007): 1048.

Einstein, Albert. *Out of My Later Years*. New York: Philosophical Library, 1950.

Elgin, Suzette Haden. *Native Tongue*. New York: DAW Books, 1984.

Elkins, Charles, Martin Greenberg, and Thomas Clareson (eds) *Robert Silverberg's Many Trapdoors: Critical Essays on His Science Fiction*. Westport, CT: Greenwood Press, 1992.

Farmer, Philip Jose. "Sail On! Sail On!" in James Gunn (ed.) *The Road to Science Fiction #3: From Heinlein to Here*. Lanham, MD: Scarecrow Press, 2002. 167–175.

Finch, Sheila. "Dispatches from the Trenches: Science Fiction in the Classroom." *Extrapolation* (Spring 2000): 28–35.

Firestone, Shulamith. *The Dialectic of Sex; The Case for Feminist Revolution*. New York: Morrow, 1970.

Forman, Paul. "Behind Quantum Electronics: National Security as Basis for Physical Research in the United States, 1940–1960." *Historical Studies in the Physical and Biological Sciences* 18 (1987): 149–229.

Foucault, Michel. "Orders of Discourse: Inaugural Lecture Delivered at the Collège de France." *Social Science Information* 10 (1971): 7–30.

Freedman, Carl. *Critical Theory and SF*. Middletown, CT: Wesleyan University Press, 2000.

Gardiner, Judith Kegan. "Empathic Ways of Reading: Narcissism, Cultural Politics, and Russ's 'Female Man'." *Feminist Studies* 20 (1994): 87–112.

Gattaca. 1997. Columbia/TriStar Directed by Andrew Niccol. With Ethan Hawke and Uma Thurman.

Geiger, Roger L. *Research and Relevant Knowledge: American Research Universities Since World War II*. New York: Oxford University Press, 1993.

Gerlach, Neil and Sheryl N. Hamilton. "A History of Social SF." *Science Fiction Studies* 30 (July 2003): 161–173.

Gernsback, Hugo. "Scientifiction." *Amazing Stories*. 1929.

Gerrold, David. *When Harlie Was One.* New York: Ballantine, 1972.

Gibson, William. *Count Zero.* New York: Arbor House, 1986.

——. *Neuromancer.* New York: Ace, 1984.

Ginway, M. Elizabeth. *Brazilian Science Fiction: Cultural Myths and Nationhood in the Land of the Future.* Lewisburg, PA: Bucknell University Press, 2004.

——. "A Working Model for Analyzing Third World Science Fiction: The Case of Brazil." *Science Fiction Studies* (November 2005).

Godwin, Tom. "The Cold Equations." in James Gunn (ed.) *The Road to Science Fiction Volume Three: From Heinlein to Here.* Lanham, MD: Scarecrow Press, 2002. 216–237.

Gordon, Joan. "Incite/On-Site/Insight: Implications of the Other in Eleanor Arnason's Science Fiction." in Marleen S. Barr (ed.) *Future Females, The Next Generation: New Voices and Velocities in Feminist Science Fiction Criticism.* Lanham, MA: Rowman and Littlefield, 2000. 247–260.

——. "Utopia, Genocide, and the Other." in Veronica Hollinger and Joan Gordon (eds) *Edging into the Future.* Philadelphia, PA: University of Pennsylvania Press, 2002. 204–216.

Greenberg, Martin Harry and Patricia S. Warrick. *Political SF: An Introductory Reader.* Englewoods Cliffs, NJ: Prentice-Hall, 1974.

Gunn, Eileen. "Stable Strategies for Middle Management." 1988. in Ursula K. Le Guin and Brian Attebery (eds) *The Norton Book of Science Fiction.* New York: W. W. Norton, 1993. 705–715.

Gunn, James. "A Touch of Stone." in James Gunn (ed.) *The Road to Science Fiction Volume Three: From Heinlein to Here.* Lanham, MD: Scarecrow Press, 2002. 213–215.

Gusterson, Hugh. *Nuclear Rites: A Weapons Laboratory at the End of the Cold War.* Los Angeles, CA: University of California Press, 1996.

Hacking, Ian. *Representing and Intervening.* New York: Cambridge University Press, 1983.

Haraway, Donna. "A Manifesto for Cyborgs: Science, Technology, and Socialist Feminism in the 1980s." *Socialist Review* 15 (March–April 1985): 65–107.

——. *Primate Visions: Gender, Race, and Nature in the World of Modern Science.* New York: Routledge, 1989.

Harding, Sandra. *The Science Question in Feminism.* Ithaca, NY: Cornell University Press, 1986.

Hawley, John. "*The War of the Worlds,* Wells, and the Fallacy of Empire." in David Ketterer (ed.) *Flashes of the Fantastic: Selected Essays from The War of the Worlds Centennial: Nineteenth International Conference on the Fantastic in the Arts.* Westport, CT: Praeger, 1998. 43–52.

Hayles, N. Katherine. *Chaos Bound: Orderly Disorder in Contemporary Literature and Science.* Ithaca, NY: Cornell University Press, 1990.

Heinlein, Robert A. "Gulf." *Astounding Science Fiction* 44 (1949).

——. *I Will Fear No Evil.* New York: Berkeley, 1971.

——. *The Moon is a Harsh Mistress.* New York: Putnam, 1966.

——. *The Puppet Masters.* New York: Doubleday, 1951.

——. *Stranger in a Strange Land.* New York: Putnam,1961.

Herbert, Frank. *Dune.* Philadelphia, PA: Chilton, 1965.

Hicks, Heather J. "Automating Feminism: The Case of Joanna Russ's *The Female Man.*" *Postmodern Culture: An Electronic Journal of Interdisciplinary Criticism* 9.3 (1999). http://www.iath.virginia.edu/pmc/text-only/issue.599/9.3contents.html.

Hillegas, Mark. "SF in the English Department." in Jack Williamson (ed.) *Teaching SF: Education for Tomorrow.* Philadelphia, PA: Owlswick Press, 1980. 97–101.

Hochberg, Leigh R., Mijail D. Serruya, Gerhard M. Friehs, Jon A. Mukand, Maryam Saleh, Abraham H. Caplan, Almut Branner, David Chen, Richard D. Penn and John P. Donoghue. "Neuronal Ensemble Control of Prosthetic Devices by a Human with Tetraplegia." *Nature* 442 (2006): 164–171.

Hollinger, Veronica. "Contemporary Trends in Science Fiction Criticism, 1980–1999." *Science Fiction Studies* 26 (1999): 232–262.

——. "Feminisms, Criticisms, Science Fictions." Unpublished Paper.

——. "(Re)Reading Queerly: Science Fiction, Feminism, and the Defamiliarization of Gender." in Marleen S. Barr (ed.) *Future Females, the Next Generation: New Voices and Velocities in Feminist Science Fiction Criticism.* Lanham, MD: Rowman and Littlefield, 2000. 197–215.

Hughes, Thomas P. *American Genesis: A Century of Invention and Technological Enthusiasm.* New York: Penguin Books, 1989.

Huntington, John. *Rationalizing Genius: Ideological Strategies in the Classic American Science Fiction Short Story.* New Brunswick, NJ: Rutgers University Press, 1989.

"Independent Television." *Wikipedia.* January 3, 2007. http://en.wikipedia.org.

Irvine, Alexander. "*The War of the Worlds* and the Disease of Imperialism." in David Ketterer (ed.) *Flashes of the Fantastic: Selected Essays from The War of the Worlds Centennial: Nineteenth International Conference on the Fantastic in the Arts.* Westport, CT: Praeger, 1998. 33–42.

Jacobis v. Ohio. No. 374. Supreme Court of the US. 22 June 1964.

James, Edward. "Yellow, Black, Metal, and Tentacled: The Race Question in American Science Fiction." in Philip John Davies (ed.) *Science Fiction, Social Conflict, and War.* Manchester, UK: Manchester University Press, 1990, 26–49.

Jameson, Frederic. "Acceptance of the 2006 Pilgrim Award." *SFRA Review* 276 (2006): 15.

Jeter, Kevin. Wayne. *Dark Seeker.* New York: Tom Doherty, 1987.

Jones, Gwyneth. "Metempsychosis of the Machine." *Science Fiction Studies* 24 (1997): 1–10.

Kalish, Alan, Michael Faith, Chris Ehrman, John Gant, and Richard D. Ehrlich. "'For Our Balls Were Sheathed in Inertron': Textual Variants in the Seminal Novel for *Buck Rogers.*" *Extrapolation* (1988): 303–318.

Kay, Lily. *Who Wrote the Book of Life? A History of the Genetic Code.* Stanford, CA: Stanford University Press, 2000.

——. *Secrets of Life, Secrets of Death: Essays on Language, Gender, and Science.* New York: Routledge, 1992.

Kelso, Sylvia. "'These are not the Aliens You're Looking For': Reflections on Race, Writing, and Theory in Contemporary Science Fiction." in David Ketterer (ed.) *Flashes of the Fantastic: Selected Essays from The War of the Worlds Centennial: Nineteenth International Conference on the Fantastic in the Arts.* Westport, CT: Praeger, 1998. 65–76.

Ketterer, David. *Flashes of the Fantastic: Selected Essays from The War of the Worlds Centennial: Nineteenth International Conference on the Fantastic in the Arts.* Westport, CT: Praeger, 1998.

Kevles, Daniel J. *The Physicists: The History of a Scientific Community in Modern America.* New York: Knopf, 1977.

Keyes, Daniel. "Flowers for Algernon." in Isaac Asimov (ed.) *The Hugo Winners, Volume 1.* New York: Doubleday, 1962.

Kipling, Rudyard. "The White Man's Burden." in Irving Howe (ed.) *The Portable Kipling.* New York: Penguin, 1982. 602–603.

Knorr-Cetina, Karin D. *The Manufacture of Knowledge: An Essay on the Constructivist and Contextual Nature of Science.* New York: Pergamon Press, 1981.

Kress, Nancy. "Beggars in Spain." *Asimov's Science Fiction* April 1991.

Landon, Brooks. "Synthespians, Virtual Humans, and Hypermedia-Emerging Contours of Post-SF-Film." in Veronica Hollinger and Joan Gordon (eds) *Edging into the Future: Science Fiction and Contemporary Cultural Transformation.* Philadelphia, PA: University of Pennsylvania Press, 2002. 57–72.

Larbalestier, Justine. *The Battle of the Sexes in Science Fiction.* Middleton, CT: Wesleyan University Press, 2002.

Latour, Bruno. *The Pasteurization of France.* Cambridge, MA: Harvard University Press, 1988.

——. *Science in Action: How to Follow Scientists and Engineers Through Society.* Cambridge, MA: Harvard University Press, 1987.

——. and Steve Woolgar. *Laboratory Life: The Social Construction of Scientific Facts.* Beverly Hills, CA: Sage Publications, 1979.

Lee, Tanith. *Drinking Sapphire Wine.* New York: DAW, 1977.

Lefanu, Sarah. *Feminism and Science Fiction.* Bloomington, IN: Indiana University Press, 1988.

Le Guin, Ursula K. "American SF and the Other." in Susan Wood (ed.) *The Language of the Night.* New York: G. P. Putnam's Sons, 1979. 97–100.

——. "The Carrier Bag Theory of Fiction." in *Dancing at the Edge of the World.* New York: Harper & Row, 1989. 165–170.

——. *Eye of the Heron.* New York: HarperCollins, 1978.

——. *The Left Hand of Darkness.* 1969. New York: Ace Books, 1975.

——. "On Teaching SF." in Jack Williamson (ed.) *Teaching SF: Education for Tomorrow.* Philadelphia, PA: Owlswick Press, 1980. 21–25.

Letson, Russell. "'Falling through Many Trapdoors': Robert Silverberg." *Extrapolation* 20 (1979): 109–117.

Leslie, Stuart W. *The Cold War and American Science: The Military-Industrial-Academic Complex at MIT and Stanford.* New York: Columbia University Press, 1993.

Levins, Richard and Richard Lewontin. *The Dialectical Biologist.* Cambridge, MA: Harvard University Press, 1985.

Licklider, J. C. R. "Man-Computer Symbiosis." *IRE Transactions on Human Factors in Electronics.* Volume HFE-1. March 1960, 4–11. http://groups.csail.mit.edu/medg/people/psz/Licklider.html, October 2007.

Lorraine, Lilith. "Into the 28th Century." *Science Wonder Quarterly* 1 (Winter 1930): 250–267, 276.

Martin, Emily. *The Woman in the Body: A Cultural Analysis of Reproduction.* Boston: Beacon Press, 1992.

Marx, Karl. *Capital.* Volume One. Trans. Ben Fowkes. London: Penguin, 1976.

——. *A Contribution to the Critique of Political Economy.* Trans. S. W. Ryazanskaya. Moscow: Progress Publishers, 1977.

Max Headroom. 1987. ABC. Written by Howard Brookner, David G. B. Brown et al. Produced by Brian E. Frankish. Directed by Todd Holland, Francis Delia et al.

Miller, Fred Dycus, and Nicholas D. Smith (eds) *Thought Probes: Philosophy Through Science Fiction Literature*. Englewood Cliffs, NJ: Prentice Hall, 1981.

Miller, Joseph D. "Neuroscience Fiction: The Roman à Synaptic Cleft." in George E. Slusser and Eric S. Rabkin (eds) *Mindscapes: The Geographies of Imagined Worlds*. Carbondale, IL: Southern Illinois University Press, 1989. 195–210.

Mintz, Catherine. "Letter." *The New York Review of Science Fiction* 60 (1993): 22.

Mohr, Dunja. *Worlds Apart: Dualism and Transgression in Contemporary Female Dystopias*. Jefferson, NC: McFarland, 2005.

Moore, C. L. "No Woman Born." in Lester Del Rey (ed.) *The Best of C. L. Moore*. New York: Ballantine Books, 1975. 236–288.

Moylan, Tom. *Demand the Impossible: Science Fiction and the Utopian Imagination*. London: Methuen, 1986.

——. *Scraps of the Untainted Sky: Science Fiction, Utopia, Dystopia*. Boulder, CO and Oxford, UK: Westview Press, 2000.

Nicholson, Linda. "Interpreting Gender." *Signs* 20 (Autumn 1994): 79–105.

Niven, Larry. "The Organleggers." *Galaxy* January 1969.

Noble, David F. *America By Design: Science, Technology, and the Rise of Corporate Capitalism*. New York: Oxford University Press, 1977.

Parrinder, Patrick. *Science Fiction: Its Criticism and Teaching*. New York: Methuen, 1980.

Pastalkova, Eva, Peter Serrano, Deana Pinkhasova, Emma Wallace, André Antonio Fenton, and Todd Charlton Sacktor. "Storage of Spatial Information by the Maintenance Mechanism of LTP." *Science* 313 (2006): 1141–1144.

Pennisi, Elizabeth. "Mining the Molecules that Made Our Mind." *Science* 313 (1996): 1908–1911.

Perrier, Anselme L., Viviane Tabar, Tiziano Barberi Maria E. Rubio, Juan Bruses, Norbert Topf, Neil L. Harrison, and Lorenz Studer. "Derivation of Midbrain Dopamine Neurons from Human Embryonic Stem Cells." *Proceedings of the National Academy of Sciences* 101 (2004): 12543–12548.

Philips, Michael (ed.) *Philosophy and Science Fiction*. Buffalo, NY: Prometheus, 1984.

Philmus, Robert. "Murder Most Fowl: Butler's Edition of Francis Godwin." *Science Fiction Studies* 23 (1996): 260–269.

Pickering, Andrew. *Constructing Quarks: A Sociological History of Particle Physics*. Chicago: University of Chicago Press, 1984.

Piercy, Marge. *Woman on the Edge of Time*. Greenwich, CT: Fawcett Books, 1976.

Pohl, Frederik. *Heechee Rendezvous*. New York: Ballantine, 1984.

——. *The Way the Future Was*. New York: Ballantine, 1978.

——. and C. M. Kornbluth. *The Space Merchants*, New York: Ballantine, 1953.

Pordzik, Ralph. *The Quest for Postcolonial Utopia: A Comparative Introduction to the Utopian Novel in the New English Literatures*. New York: Peter Lang, 2001.

The President's Analyst.1967. Paramount. Directed by Theodore J. Flicker.

Trudeau, Gary B. *In Search of Reagan's Brain*. New York: Henry Holt, 1981.

Rabkin, Eric S. *The Fantastic in Literature*. Princeton, NJ: Princeton University Press, 1976.

Reanimator. 1985. Empire Pictures. Directed by Stuart Gordon.

Roberts, Robin. *A New Species: Gender and Science in Science Fiction*. Urbana, IL: University of Illinois Press, 1993.

Rosinsky, Natalie M. *Feminist Futures: Contemporary Women's Speculative Fiction*. Ann Arbor, MI: UMI Research Press, 1984.

Ross, Andrew. *Strange Weather: Culture, Science and Technology in the Age of Limits.* New York: Verso, 1991.

Rucker, Rudy. *Software.* New York: Ace, 1982.

Russ, Joanna. *Alyx.* Boston: Gregg Press, 1976.

——. *And Chaos Died.* New York: Ace, 1970.

——. *The Country You Have Never Seen: Essays and Reviews.* Liverpool, UK: Liverpool University Press, 2007.

——. *Extra(Ordinary) People.* New York: St. Martin's Press, 1984.

——. *The Female Man.* 1975. London: The Women's Press, 1985.

——. *How to Suppress Women's Writing.* Austin, TX: University of Texas Press, 1983.

——. *On Strike Against God.* New York: Out and Out Books, 1980.

——. "Sword Blades and Poppy Seed With Homage to (Who Else) Amy Lowell." in Jessica Amanda Salmonson (ed.) *Heroic Visions.* New York: Ace, 1983. 157–162.

——. *To Write Like a Woman: Essays in Feminism and Science Fiction.* Bloomington, IN: Indiana University Press, 1995.

——. *The Two of Them.* 1978. Middletown, CT: Wesleyan University Press, 2005.

——. *We Who Are About To....* 1977. Middletown, CT: Wesleyan University Press, 2005.

——. *What Are We Fighting For?: Sex, Race, Class, and the Future of Feminism.* New York: St. Martin's Press, 1998.

——. "What Can a Heroine Do? or Why Women Can't Write." in Susan Koppelman Cornillon (ed.) *Images of Women in Fiction.* Bowling Green, OH: Bowling Green University Popular Press, 1972. 3–21.

——. "When it Changed." 1972. in James Gunn (ed.) *The Road to Science Fiction. Volume 3: From Heinlein to Here.* Lanham, MD: Scarecrow Press, 2002. 526–533.

Said, Edward. *Culture and Imperialism.* New York: Vintage Press, 1994.

Sargent, Pamela. *The Shore of Women.* 1986. New York: Bantam, 1987.

Scholes, Robert. "Editor's Foreword." *Isaac Asimov: The Foundations of Science Fiction.* New York: Oxford University Press, 1982. vii.

Schow, David. *The Outer Limits: The Official Companion.* New York: Ace, 1986.

Schweitzer, Darrell. "Letter." *The New York Review of Science Fiction* 99 (1996): 23.

Scott, Melissa. *The Kindly Ones.* New York: Baen Books, 1987.

——. *Shadow Man.* New York: Tom Doherty, 1995.

Shapin, Steven and Simon Schaffer. *Leviathan and the Air-Pump: Hobbes, Boyle, and the Experimental Life.* Princeton, NJ: Princeton University Press, 1985.

Shelley, Mary. *Frankenstein; or, The Modern Prometheus.* London: Lackington Hughes, 1818.

Slonczewski, Joan. *A Door Into Ocean.* New York: Arbor House, 1986.

Smith, Cordwainer. *Norstrilia.* New York: Ballantine, 1975.

Smith, Erin A. *Hard-Boiled: Working Class Readers and Pulp Magazines.* Philadelphia, PA: Temple University Press, 2000.

Smith, Jeffrey D. and Jeanne Gomoll (eds) *Khatru.* 1975. Madison, WI: The Obsessive Press, 1993.

Smith, Nicholas D. (ed.) *Philosophers Look at Science Fiction.* Chicago: Nelson-Hall, 1982.

Spencer, Kathleen L. "Rescuing the Female Child: The Fiction of Joanna Russ." *Science Fiction Studies* 17 (1990): 167–187.

Stableford, Brian. "Biology." in John Clute and Peter Nicholls (eds) *The Encyclopedia of Science Fiction*. New York: St. Martin's Press, 1995. 122–124.

Sterling, Bruce. *Islands in the Net*. New York: Arbor House, 1988.

——. *Schismatrix*. New York: Arbor House, 1985.

Stross, Charles. *Accelerando*. New York: Ace, 2005.

Sturgeon, Theodore. *More Than Human*. New York: Ballantine, 1953.

Suvin, Darko. *Metamorphoses of Science Fiction: On the Poetics and History of a Literary Genre*. New Haven, CT: Yale University Press, 1979.

——. and Charles Elkins. "Preliminary Reflections on Teaching SF." *Science Fiction Studies* 6 (1979): 263–270.

Tiptree, James Jr. "Beam Us Home." *Ten Thousand Light Years From Home*. New York: Ace, 1973.

——. "The Girl Who Was Plugged In." *Warm Worlds and Otherwise*. New York: Ballantine Books, 1975. 79–121.

Traweek, Sharon. *Beamtimes and Lifetimes: The World of High Energy Physicists*. Cambridge, MA: Harvard University Press, 1988.

Trudeau, Gary B. "Ron Headrest." *Recycled Doonesbury*. New York: Andrews McMeel, 1990.

Tucker, Robert. *The Marx-Engels Reader*. New York: W. W. Norton, 1972.

Tucker, Robert, Ed. *The Marx-Engels Reader*. Second Edition. New York: Norton, 1978.

Van Vogt, A. E. *Null A Three*. New York: DAW, l985.

——. *The Players of Null-A*. New York: Berkeley, 1974.

——. *The World of Null-A*. New York: Ace, 1953.

Vinge, Vernor. *Rainbows End*. New York: Tor, 2006.

Wagner-Lawlor, Jennifer A. "The Play of Irony: Theatricality and Utopian Transformation in Contemporary Women's Speculative Fiction." *Utopian Studies* 13 (2002).

Weiland, James. D. and Mark S. Humayun. "Intraocular Retinal Prosthesis: Big Steps to Sight Restoration." *IEEE Engineering Medicine Biological Magazine* 25 (2006): 60–66.

Wells, H. G. *The Island of Dr. Moreau*. 1896. New York: Bantam, 1994.

Westfahl, Gary. *Science Fiction Quotations*. New Haven, CT: Yale University Press, 2005.

——. *Space and Beyond: The Frontier Theme in Science Fiction*. Westport, CT: Greenwood Press, 2000.

Williams, Patrick and Laura Chrisman. *Colonial Discourse and Post-Colonial Theory: A Reader*. New York: Columbia University Press, 1994.

Williams, Raymond. *Keywords: A Vocabulary of Culture and Society*. New York: Oxford University Press, 1985.

Williams, Walter Jon. *Hard Wired*. New York: Tom Doherty, 1987.

Winner, Langdon. *The Whale and the Reactor: A Search for Limits in an Age of High Technology*. Chicago: University of Chicago Press, 1986.

Wolansky, Taras. "Letter." *The New York Review of Science Fiction* 66 (1994): 18–19.

Wolfe, Gary K. "Evaporating Genre: Strategies of Dissolution in the Postmodern Fantastic." in Veronica Hollinger and Joan Gordon (eds) *Edging into the Future:*

Science Fiction and Contemporary Cultural Transformation. Philadelphia, PA: University of Pennsylvania Press, 2002. 11–29.

——. "Malebolge, Or the Ordinance of Genre." *Conjunctions 39: The New Wave FABULISTS.* Fall (2002): 405–419.

Wolmark, Jenny. *Aliens and Others: Science Fiction, Feminism and Postmodernism.* Iowa City, IA: University of Iowa Press, 1994.

Woodcock, John. "Teaching SF: Unique Challenges (Proceedings of the MLA Special Session, New York, December 1978)." *Science Fiction Studies* 6 (1979): 249–262.

World Almanac and Book of Facts. New York: World Almanac Books, 2006.

Young Frankenstein. 1974. Twentieth Century Fox. Directed by Mel Brooks.

Zelazny, Roger. "Home Is the Hangman." in Isaac Asimov (ed.) *The Hugo Winners, Volume 4.* New York: Doubleday, 1985.

Zicree, Scott. *The Twilight Zone Companion.* New York: Bantam, 1989.

Zink, David Stewart. " Letter." *The New York Review of Science Fiction* 66 (1994): 19–21.

index